Tabloid Britain

From Tony Blair and his cabinet, to celebrity chefs and footballers, the British tabloids provide sensational coverage of the private and public lives of political figures and celebrities alike, shaping the nation's perceptions of people and events. These often derided newspapers are important and influential factors in the mediation of everyday life in the UK.

Tabloid Britain examines four popular tabloid newspapers and uncovers the variety of linguistic strategies they employ to depict contemporary Britain. These strategies are shown to construct, in a circular fashion, an impersonation of the language of the community of readers which the newspapers seek to attract.

Including examples taken from a month-long study, Martin Conboy considers how this imaginary community of the British nation is drawn through themes such as 'outsiders', 'insiders', women, celebrity, history and politics. Conboy also demonstrates how the tabloids constitute a successful modern variation of journalism which has spread its influence beyond the boundaries of print and triggered much debate about the related phenomenon of 'tabloidization'.

This critical study of the newspapers' version of popular rhetoric will be of interest to students and researchers of English, Media and Communication, and Journalism.

Martin Conboy is a Reader in Journalism Studies at the University of Sheffield. He is the author of *The Press and Popular Culture* (2002), *Journalism: A Critical History* (2004) as well as being the co-editor of a series of books on Journalism Studies.

Tabloid Britain
Constructing a community through language

Martin Conboy

Routledge
Taylor & Francis Group

LONDON AND NEW YORK

First published 2006
by Routledge
2 Park Square, Milton Park, Abingdon, Oxon OX14 4RN

Simultaneously published in the USA and Canada
by Routledge
270 Madison Ave, New York, NY 10016

Routledge is an imprint of the Taylor & Francis Group

© 2006 Martin Conboy

Typeset in Bembo by Taylor & Francis Books
Printed and bound in Great Britain
by The Cromwell Press, Trowbridge, Wiltshire

British Library Cataloguing in Publication Data
A catalogue record for this book is available from the British Library

Library of Congress Cataloging in Publication Data
A catalog record for this book has been requested

ISBN10: 0-415–35552-4   ISBN13: 978-0-415-35552-0 (hbk)
ISBN10: 0-415–35553-2   ISBN13: 978-0-415-35553-7 (pbk)

Taylor & Francis Group is the Academic Division of T&F Informa plc.

This book is dedicated to Jane Taylor and all the staff and students on the Journalism degree at Farnham 1995–2005

Contents

Preface

The material for this book was gathered during a relatively short period of time between late April 2004 and early June of that same year. It was hoped that this would provide a topical and characteristic slice of the representation of Britain from the perspective of a range of British papers. This approach, as any approach, has its weaknesses, chiefly that thematic issues which could be more extensively developed by tracking their coverage over a longer period are too briefly alluded to. Nevertheless, the coverage does amount to an analysis of a 'month in the country' which I believe compensates for whatever thematic deficiencies there may be with an intensive study of the language over these few weeks, as it echoes and criss-crosses around the issues of the moment in a way which demonstrates how this language may work in constructing a readership. This approach, I hope, enhances the overall linguistic emphasis of the study.

I am very much aware of the narrowing divide between the once-broadsheet press and the tabloids, as well as the volatility in editorial approaches within the 'red-tops' and other traditional tabloid format newspapers. This has led to a certain terminological flexibility within the book. In writing of the tabloids in Britain, I did not want to restrict myself to the 'red tops', which do not by themselves include the second best-selling newspaper in the British market which provides an interesting and commercially astute variation of the tabloid format. Nor did I want to include newspapers which have shifted, in one case during the writing of the book, from a broadsheet to a tabloid format. Although this process is linked to overall questions of 'tabloidization', the inclusion of these newspapers would have distracted from the concentration on a very specific set of popular rhetorical strategies which continue to be identified more with traditional tabloids. To keep a clarity in these matters I have chosen to refer to these traditional tabloids as 'popular tabloids' where appropriate and to the broadsheet press as the 'elite press'.

Despite these methodological shortcomings, I hope to have provided a thorough linguistic exploration of the language which plays such an important part in the construction of a contemporary national community: tabloid Britain.

Acknowledgements

The writing of this book has been assisted enormously by the generous contributions of time and effort by a variety of people. I hope that the result goes some way towards repaying them. Some might be surprised to learn how significant they were to the overall momentum of the project.

Close to home, the support and encouragement of Jim Beaman and Dr Andy Darley and their provision of coffee, cakes and company at key moments are not to be underestimated. Mick Conboy, risking reputation at his local newsagent's, supplied the Scottish tabloids which I had found hard to come by. Paul Nathanson provided robust and definitive advice in the later stages of the book. Steve Usher was an invaluable source of insights into the world of tabloid journalism and Emma Britton provided important guidance with regard to contacts.

Thanks to the Daily Mail, the Sun, the Daily Mirror and the Daily Star for permission to reproduce material from the popular tabloids for critical commentary. I am particular grateful to Lisa Rayman at Mirrorpix and Neil Hudd at News International for their genuine interest and assistance.

At Routledge, the initial enthusiasm of Christy Kirkpatrick was decisive in ensuring that this book could see the light of day. She appreciated the importance of exploring the content of the British tabloid press from a specifically linguistic perspective. Later, Louisa Semlyen was helpful in discussion at key moments in the development and tone of the book. Lucie Ewin and the rest of the production team have moved the draft to publication with a minimum of fuss and high levels of efficiency.

My thanks are also due to Professor Bob Franklin for reorienting my professional compass during the writing of the book. Finally, thanks to Simone and Lara for providing the perfect complement to my working life through their energy, love and their irrepressible talent for generating an excitement in living.

1 When did the populars become tabloid?

Matthew Engel writes that American visitors to Britain are shocked by the riot of competing libertine tabloids (Engel, 1996a: 31), but he could have added any number of other nationalities as well as many of the indigenous population themselves. A major part of the appeal of these newspapers is their national and linguistic specificity. They belong to, and for better or for worse, represent contemporary Britain to a carefully targeted popular audience. They have developed over time the language they use to weave their version of the fabric of national life. Much of the power of the tabloids has been accrued by the evolution of this language and its relationship to the broader patterns of popular print culture which have developed over centuries. Tabloid newspapers are merely the latest and most marketable permutation of the language of the people in periodical form.

The link between print media and the language of the ordinary people is as old as print itself. Printers soon realized that there was money to be made by distributing popular printed material which could reach the widest possible readership in order to maximize profits. The best way to appeal to that audience was to build upon accepted patterns of popular culture (Burke, 1978) and to frame printed material as much as possible in a language with which the audience would be familiar. Even while literacy rates were low, there were still markets for printed matter which could be read, often out loud, or sung and which appealed to a community of readers and listeners by means of the language which they employed. Much of this early popular print culture in the sixteenth and seventeenth centuries deliberately followed the rhythms and patterns of the spoken language of the ordinary people (Ong, 1982). In addition, it used illustration to draw the illiterate (Watt, 1991) into the new print culture. Early printed ballads, broadsheets and ephemeral productions such as the almanacs, which sold straight to the streets and markets of the Early Modern period, were the typographic and stylistic precursors of popular and later tabloid journalism in their appeal to a popular and specifically national audience in a highly stylized version of the common language (Shepard, 1973: 24).

Early print culture and national community

Print culture had widened the audience for a written vernacular which distinguished each European nation from the Latin landscape of the mediaeval period. The development of local languages enhanced the feeling that each linguistic community had its own specific attributes and political interests, which were directly linked to the communicative power of these languages to draw in a wider community of speakers and listeners as active participants in the nation. Anderson (1987: 15) emphasizes the linguistic basis of the evolution of nationalism and demonstrates how it was given textual coherence by the emergence of novels and most importantly, for our purposes, newspapers. The latter enabled an 'imagined political community' to be able to picture itself as moving through history as one body with common interests and a common language, reflecting on that process on a regular basis. Barker (1998) has also pointed out how this community of readers began to broaden out and perceive itself as a national public, articulating its own set of identifiable opinions. Although both of these evolutionary processes had more to do with the emerging bourgeois class than the working people, they certainly established a template for the development of a nation in print through the use of a widely accepted set of linguistic patterns, in a vernacular which was to move from bourgeois to proletariat as markets for the lower classes emerged. When Anderson writes about the language of novels providing an 'hypnotic confirmation' (1987: 33) of nationhood this can be applied also to newspapers, particularly with their wider and more regular distribution, and reaffirms that in matters of national identity it is style not substance which is the ultimate guarantor of success. Language has been the medium for the broadening of a popular sense of community. In terms of credibility, as conduits for overtly nationalistic perspectives the tabloids have at the very least a lot of style!

The evolution of the popular newspaper in Britain

For many years however, regular periodical print publication was restricted to the wealthier classes and the poor had to make do with more ephemeral literature. Popular newspapers, of a particular sort, commercial and orientated as much towards advertisers as readers, became an established part of print culture in Britain only from the middle of the nineteenth century. The lifting of taxes and duties on the press from the 1830s onwards made newspaper and magazine production a much more profitable activity and one which was over time increasingly targeted at lower socio-economic groups for its readers. To maximize their appeal, these new publications built upon the language of those readers, represented in a stylized communal idiom. Inevitably, there were political implications in the sort of popular journalism which emerged after the market liberalization of the press of the mid-Victorian period. Incorporating the ordinary people into a commercialized press which had a stake in economic prosperity and capital growth, the popular press became an institution of political control (Berridge, 1978).

Before this incorporation, there had been highly successful attempts at addressing the common people in popular periodical publications, representing them and their concerns in a direct vernacular aimed at constructing a tangible, effective and radical political community. At the start of the nineteenth century Wooler, Cobbett and Carlile used their unstamped and illegal papers to develop a sense of the rights of working people and adopted a tone and style of address to appeal to them. This strategy helped establish the convention of articulating an idiom to match an audience which was outside the traditional bourgeois readership targeted by the mainstream press of the time. Previously, newspapers and magazines had assumed that their readership was a relatively homogeneous upper middle class with interests and opinions which, although varied, were nevertheless characteristic of the range of bourgeois opinion of the time and this had been manifested in their language.

Having established an authentic tone of language for the targeted readership represented as a community with common aspirations and values, the popular press developed through the 1830s into a new generation of radical popular political papers, the most successful and long-lived of which was the Chartist *Northern Star*. This paper created a textual community which incorporated petitions, fund-raising and political polemic within a rhetoric which claimed to speak on behalf of the working-class reader. Nevertheless, it was eased out of the growing market for popular readers by a brand of weekly newspaper which exploited that same vernacular but employed it in a commercially astute and depoliticized form. Language had become the site where radical political alternatives were addressed or suppressed. The language of these new popular commercial newspapers enabled a relationship to evolve between the readers and the businessmen running the papers which reflected much of the idealized voice of the working people. It was a popular language and needed to give an authentic account of itself to its readers if it was to continue to be successful. From this point on, the major task of any popular newspaper was to successfully capture a market-orientated idiom and direct it at its readers. The history of the development of the popular newspaper into the tabloid newspaper in Britain is the story of the evolution of that idiom across shifting economic and historical circumstances. Its language was to become the articulation of a particular, proletarian version of Britain.

With further liberalization of the market for popular publications from the 1850s, a more commercialized form of this appeal to the working classes came in *Reynolds' Weekly News*, *Lloyd's Illustrated London Newspaper* and the *News of the World*, and would have its first mass popular blossoming in the miscellanies of Newnes' *Tit-Bits* from 1881 and the *Star* of T.P. O'Connor later that decade. Up until the late Victorian developments in popular newspapers, the general public had been excluded from regular daily newspapers by their content, price and distribution patterns. However, from the 1880s onwards there was an accelerating trend towards the production of newspapers and magazines which sought ever more lucrative, mass markets by appealing to wider and lower social readerships. The beginnings were in the New

Journalism which combined in a daily paper accessible layout with 'a shift away from Parliamentary and political news to sport, gossip, crime and sex' (Wiener, 1988: 54). When Engel comments that 'The New Journalism, in a sense, had always been there; it was now merely breaking out of its bounds' (1996a: 46) it is to the increased regularity of this journalism on a daily basis that he is referring. It developed a style of journalism which was stridently self-promotional in its crusades, entertainment values and sensationalism – 'the phenomenon existed by calling attention to itself' (Koss, 1981: 343).

Yet, beyond all technical and economic details, the fact remains that the New Journalism was a linguistic phenomenon in the way that it appealed explicitly to working people and their lifestyles. T.P. O'Connor began his *Star* in January 1888 on his return from America, where he had observed at first hand the rush to popular forms of journalism. From his radical perspective, he understood that it was in the language as well as the layout where the interests of the people could be articulated in a way which could distinguish his paper in the market:

> We live in an age of hurry and of multitudinous newspapers. ... To get your ideas across through the hurried eyes into the whirling brains that are employed in the reading of a newspaper there must be no mistake about your meaning: to use a somewhat familiar phrase, you must strike your reader right between the eyes.
>
> (O'Connor, 1889: 434)

From 1896 the *Daily Mail* provided a lively format for its wide range of news reports, yet it was a profoundly respectable and unsensational paper aimed very much at an aspirational upwardly mobile lower middle class. Although it was to become the first million selling newspaper in Britain, it would not be until the 1930s that the full potential of the combination of circulation and popular address would be appreciated in a way which was to shift the onus in the daily press towards what we recognize as tabloid culture today.

American influences on the form and content of the British popular press

At the same time as experiments in the articulation of a popular voice in print were being pursued in Britain, developments in the market for mass readerships in the United States of America were to draw the attention of British newspaper owners. It is often claimed that American influences led the push towards popular mass newspapers in Britain (Wiener, 1994). Technically this is true but the route to the modern British tabloid has been a more complex and socially inflected affair which demonstrates the national specificity of cultural developments as opposed to the simple importation of transatlantic practice into a receptive vacuum.

Horace Day's *Sun* from 1833 was the first mass newspaper to address its urban readership in a tone 'based on the language of the common man'

(Whitby, 1982: 25), and Michael Schudson argues that two models of journalism could be identified from this point onwards; a journalism of analysis and a journalism of entertainment (1978: 89). This latter variety quickly began to establish formal and stylistic characteristics. It was during the Mexican war of 1846 that, for example, headlines in multiple deck headlines were introduced and the gold rush in 1848–9 made them a common feature in both the *Sun* and the *Herald*. These headlines grew in size and quantity depending on the scope of the story, and the identifiable tabloid tendency to omit verbs emerged (Mott, 1961: 292). Editorials in some of the cheaper papers concentrated on short sentences for easy reading. They often included a large degree of scepticism about the motives of politicians which consciously tapped into a populist reflex. Interviews and stories which exposed the interest of prurient readers in the affairs of their social superiors were first explored by Gordon Bennett in his reports in the *Herald*, illustrated by some of the first interviews in 1836, on the background to the trial of the socialite, Robinson, accused of murdering a prostitute named Jewett. There was also a good deal of early sensational reporting of gunfights, spiritualism and boxing. In this period, from a stylistic perspective, there was a good deal of what has been called 'editorial billingsgate' (Mott, 1961: 310) designed to echo the rough and tumble of popular name-calling.

Later, under the influence of Pulitzer's *World* from 1883, there was an increase in the prominence of crusades which were designed to promote the newspaper at the same time as chiming with the concerns of readers, human interest stories with a great emphasis on sensationalist gossip and scandal, crime and disaster reporting and a great deal of illustration. A liberal use of colourful adjectives in all stories facilitated a preference for hyperbole in these papers. Pulitzer also concentrated on a style and content of explicit appeal to a popular female readership. He was widely acknowledged as returning to the sensationalism which had first become widespread in the mainstream popular penny press of the 1830s. This tendency, in keeping with the ethos of the mass-selling popular press, was combined with the anti-authoritarian instincts of the readership which culminated in the muck-raking journalism of magazines such as *McClure's* from 1893.

Once Pulitzer discovered that in Hearst's *Journal*, he had a rival who was willing to attempt to outperform him in all aspects of his populist ambition, 'yellow journalism' was born. It included a further intensification of the language of popular journalism. It turned, in an interesting formulation, 'the high drama of life into a cheap melodrama' (Emery and Emery, 1992: 191) although as Gripsrud (1992) has demonstrated with regard to tabloids in general, melodrama is not an insignificant social phenomenon, especially when included in the fabric of popular newspapers. The yellow journalism of the period of competition between Pulitzer and Hearst brought about a significant set of shifts in typographical layout which enabled the papers to be more easily and quickly digested. Scare-heads in either red or black made even the most trivial story scream with attention-grabbing force. It also developed an explicitly textual appeal to its readers in a version of their own colloquial speech patterns in its reported speech. Their campaigns against abuses suffered by the common people displayed an 'ostentatious sympathy with the "underdog"' (Mott, 1961: 539) and were very much in keeping with the populist rhetoric of older forms of folk culture, identifying with the people against the powerful. The typographical features also had an impact on the style of language used, making it more precise, simple, snappy, condensed, lively and more consistently populist in tone. In this they attempted to recreate the urban vernacular of mass-readership America.

The early twentieth century consolidation

As American popular journalism entered the twentieth century, it began to consolidate the language and the layout of that language in ways which would come to inform the first truly tabloid newspapers. It was a language that was first and foremost directed at building up a palatable sense of connection with readers through an accumulation of devices which had been part of certain weekly magazines for many decades before, but found themselves now imported into a commercialized idiom, accompanied by pictures and advertising, all combining to cement the idea of the daily newspaper as a worker's entertainment.

The first American tabloid in spirit as well as format encapsulated the extreme of the process of visualization within popular journalism. The *Illustrated Daily News* from 1919 was composed almost completely of pictures apart from a large banner headline and a small number of captions accompanying the pictures. It established the content and style of the early tabloid and Bessie stresses the way in which populist editorial ambitions could be enhanced by an astute use of language:

> Each day play up one story, preferably related to crime, sex or heroic achievement. ... Stand vigorously upon an editorial platform which is broad enough to permit policy to be liberal, conservative, patriotic or moral as the occasion seems to demand but never forget that the tabloid's causes must be popular causes, at least in name. Practice a limited, colourful vocabulary. In sum, produce a picture newspaper which is a compendium of extraordinary happenings and simple comment, exciting, entertaining, reassuring and couched in the living language of the day.
>
> (Bessie, 1938: 131)

To many, coming at them from an elitist cultural perspective, the tabloids are the lowest form of media life, a profane besmirching of the traditions and heritage of a free press. To others, from an economic perspective, they are simply evidence of what happens at the end point of the marketization of popular news. Bird, from a more integrated, almost anthropological perspective, sees the contemporary tabloid as unimaginable outside other historical and cultural phenomena: 'They complement the star system, the other popular media, the class system, and the gender system. They exist because of television, newspapers, movies, and a vast range of folk narratives and values' (Bird, 1992: 1–2). She pays particular attention to their ability to exploit the 'highly stereotyped prose' (1992: 8) so typical of the language of folk narrative as an illustration of how they owe their success in great measure to their ability to map themselves onto older cultural traditions.

Tabloids UK – a brief history of a very British format

Despite the fact that it was the Americans who first produced what we would recognize as the first daily newspaper embodying modern tabloid values, the pioneer in format and regularity was British. On 1 January 1901 Alfred Harmsworth ran an experimental one day half-size newspaper for Pulitzer, borrowing his New York *World* for the stunt and calling it a 'tabloid newspaper', prophetically announcing that it would be 'the newspaper of the twentieth century'. The *Daily Mirror* from 1903 was the first attempt to produce a regular popular newspaper in this format, targeting a female readership with a heavy emphasis on illustration. In broader terms of connecting in its language to a popular reader and aiming at the lower end of the social spectrum, this was not however a precursor of the tabloid in anything other than size; neither was it a commercial success.

Fierce circulation wars in the 1930s between various British daily newspapers, all aimed variously in their language and layout at differing versions of the working classes, led to developments which aimed at a clearer, more succinct, more populist and more commercially successful format for a mass readership. The *Daily Herald*, with a solid working class pedigree, launched originally as a strike sheet in 1911, learnt how to co-opt the voice of the worker and the interests of the Labour Party in a commercially acceptable idiom, but retained its broadsheet format. Its circulation peaked at two million in 1933 at the height of the popular press wars in Britain. A revitalized *Daily Mirror* which, building on the revolutionary changes in layout introduced by Christiansen on the *Daily Express* in 1933, exploited its own version of the tabloid to take the popular newspaper in a totally new direction. From 1935 the *Daily Mirror* had larger, darker type, shorter stories and less items on a page compared to the *Daily Express*, and began to articulate a more stridently proletarian voice than any other newspaper. In addition, it was able to do this in a form which advertisers found appealed to the new sense of solidarity among the working classes as the war drew to an end. It was a format which meshed with the language and the aspirations of its idealized readers, as Smith has commented: 'a paper that will conveniently stuff into the pocket of overalls, and that can be read in brief intervals between manual work' (Smith, 1975: 233). The *Daily Mirror* came to symbolize the emergence of a truly British version of the tabloid newspaper from its relaunch in the 1930s, at which point it began a process which was to enable it to claim to be the defining popular organ of the day. It was a position which it maintained until the *Sun* emerged to redefine the contemporary tabloid in Britain in the 1970s. The *Sun* from 16 November 1969 became a belated vehicle of the Zeitgeist of the 1960s as it began to change both the face of journalism and the face of Britain. Emblematic of this shift on 17 November 1969 was its first 'Page 3 Girl'. Murdoch claimed it was 'a statement of youthfulness' (Taylor, 1992: 50) and it provided a further development of the tabloid as something quite distinctive within British culture.

The *Sun's* rapid rise saw it power past the *Daily Mirror* reaching a daily sale of over 1.5 million within four months of its relaunch. By 1978 it boasted a daily sale of over four million. It appealed in a complex way to women (Holland, 1983) and presented itself as a fun product in tune with the liberated sexual mores of the period and the growing affluence of its consumerist-orientated readers. Its popular cultural credentials were established from the start by its astute exploitation of television advertising to reinforce itself as a brand in the public mind and by its increasing synchronicity with the agenda of popular television programmes and stars in its own content. It was a brash, vulgar and entertaining new variety of tabloid journalism but still based its appeal on an identification in language with its working class readers and their interests. Even when the *Sun* became increasingly associated with a right wing populism, particularly with Kelvin Mackenzie as editor, it maintained this populist momentum, following the hegemonic shifts of the Thatcher and then the Major years in its claims to represent the views and interests of the British working people. Even its fiercest critics were adroitly drawn in to provide evidence that they were enemies of the fun-loving readers of the *Sun* and thus Clare Short was dubbed 'the absolute enemy of the working man' for opposing the Page 3 Girl (Taylor, 1992: 54).

Engel comments (1996a: 17) that each generation of successful, popular newspapers has been undercut by a new wave which has been able to capture the readership of a lower social grouping and integrate that readership within the widest range of appropriate other media such as advertising, cinema and television. The *Daily Star* certainly attempted to outperform the *Sun* in this respect in the basement of tabloid taste. It was aimed at the lowest end of the market in terms of sensation and dubious journalism ethics, sexualization of popular culture with appeal to an even younger market than the *Sun's*. From 1978 the *Daily Star* was described as having, 'a circus layout that fairly burst from the pages ... the paper used more taping, more italics, more reverses, and more graphics in conjunction with sensational heads and stories to give a sense of excitement and power' (Taylor, 1992: 45). Taylor goes on to point out that in addition to this carnivalesque display of visual identity the editor was prudent enough to provide 'a distinctive new voice supporting the interests of the working class'; for instance, in populist campaigns for an increase in pensions for war widows and pay rises for ambulance drivers (Taylor, 1992: 360). However, Snoddy (1992) claims that the *Daily Star* had found the lowest limits that the newspaper buying public and the journalism establishment were willing to tolerate by the end of the 1980s and it was subsequently forced to retreat to safer territory. Recently it has produced something of a comeback in terms of sales through an astute targeting of a young audience eager for news with a distinct television and popular culture agenda and a focus on celebrity.

Nation and language

The language and structure of contemporary tabloid newspapers provide both a banal and a vigorous daily flagging of nationalism in Billig's terms (1995). Tabloids provide an explicit sense of place, a textual locus for a popular national community. This national community is located within a range of other areas of popular culture and popular media, from sport to television soap operas. As such it is, as in all national narratives, a two-dimensional narrative of common sense assumptions of national identity, teaching anew certain core ideas and reinforcing a pantheon of national heroes and heroic acts. The tabloids police the borders of national identity, for these are the parameters of their survival strategy in a highly competitive area of globalized culture. It is therefore no surprise that they depend on a vigorous form of popular nationalist vernacular to promote their distinctiveness and maintain their market share within a fragmenting news media environment. Nationalism and a populist vision of contemporary Britain are embedded in the language of these papers on a daily basis.

The tabloid press performs a significant role as a social educator (Smith, 1975: 11). An important part of this process is the normalization of certain modes of social belonging. Those connected to national identity are particularly prevalent in their pages. The production and reading of the tabloids involve a constant process of interpretation akin to the 'daily plebiscite' which Renan (1990) claims nationalism must conduct. In terms of the language community of tabloid Britain this plebiscite is continuing through negotiation with overtly nationalistic and socially located discourses. This study concentrates on one strand of a complex flow of institutional, economic and journalistic processes, namely the language used to create and maintain a readership which is predicated on a sound grasp of a British national identity and a propensity to sense and exploit issues likely to stir nationalist feelings within the readership (Rhoufari, 2000: 173–4). A cultural approach to this language must emphasize the historical as well as the social parameters of its effectiveness. Both social class and nationalism are combined in the tabloids in a highly successful, contemporary, commercialized product, and they can best be explored through the approach of critical language study. Critical language studies (Fairclough, 1989; Fowler, 1991; Van Dijk, 1991) will be used to demonstrate how tabloid Britain is constructed through an identifiable range of textual strategies. Though they are in decline in terms of readership, the tabloids retain an influence and a place within the British national landscape which is difficult to avoid and they are involved in exporting many characteristics to other parts of the media environment in the process referred to as 'tabloidiza-tion'. The mainstream news media can be seen as becoming more involved in the stylistic and narrative language patterns of the tabloids. Even their critics acknowledge the ability of the tabloids to determine agendas at a national–popular level such as when Rooney bemoans the fact of their 'eleva-tion of the mere trivial to matters of national discourse' (Rooney, 2000: 106). The agenda of the tabloids is therefore, even at a seemingly trivial level, firmly rooted in discourses of a national–popular and this has important political consequences. The idiom/style which the tabloids embody can be defined as a popular–hegemonic approach to national audience building.

The tabloid sphere

As a popular style of journalism, the tabloids departed from an emphasis on political coverage and a predominant engagement with broadly public issues of the day a long time ago. Indeed, Rooney claims that these non-serious newspapers have 'abandoned the public sphere' (Rooney, 2000: 101). The movement from radical unstamped, through the *Daily Mirror* of the post-war years to the *Sun* of today, for instance, has been one characterized not by an absolute neglect of politics but by an increasingly eclectic dialogue with ordi-nary people on major political issues. The tabloids are very selective in their inclusion of political or wider public information and include it only when it fits in with the wider patterns of their coverage or when it concerns major issues which can be covered in sensational fashion. Politically, they might describe the contours of a journalistic lowest common denominator. However, the campaigns which they do pursue serve to maintain a relation-ship with a particular readership articulated within the accepted public idiom of the tabloids. We might then see the rest of their coverage as a social conversation which at best borders political reality in the country. It is often claimed that they provide a melodramatic, not a rational public sphere, which means it is one in which display, spectatorship and 'anarchic existentialism' (Langer, 1998) replace any idea that readers could be involved in changing the political realities of their lives. Rooney has proposed an explanation for this retreat which shifts responsibility from the newspapers themselves to the political institutions: 'Their readers probably do not have any interest in the workings of the establishment or establishment organizations and do not wish to monitor them. This is probably because they feel they have no way of enforcing change' (2000: 107). Although targeted at a mass audience, the tabloids nevertheless in their idiom have a consistent appeal couched within a close textual display of intimacy with idealized individual readers – they seem to say, not 'We know where you live!' so much as, 'We know who you are and what makes you tick!' This shared idealization of community is actually a version of the citizen-ideal of the public sphere, albeit one without the anal-ysis of central social issues other than when they are refracted through sensation, celebrity and a prism of everyday life. McGuigan has characterized the altered state of public participation in the following terms: 'the popular national daily empowers its audiences, not directly as actors in the public sphere but as consumers' (1993: 178). Trivia and sensation detract, some might say, from the responsibilities of mainstream journalism yet, in a capitalized news media environment, the tabloids are merely battling to maintain a market share by going for a guaranteed and profitable national readership.

However, commentators on the contemporary tabloid (Fairclough, 1995: 13–14; Bird, 2000: 215) stress that their conversational style need not rule out engagement with serious issues, especially if it allows such engagement to be conducted in the language of accessibility, which enables readers to make sense of complex social and political issues on their own terms. If this were possible more regularly then the familiarity of tone expressed characteristically in tabloid language might be able to recapture some of the authenticity of a democratic idiom and not rely exclusively on the ideological ventriloquism which characterizes so much of their contemporary output. Beyond the content of these newspapers, it is their style which creates a distinctive 'public idiom' (Hall, 1978) which links them to aspects of the everyday life of their readers. In exploiting this idiom commercially they form part of a broader social and technological shift in both news values and the popularization of public information.

Language and social class

The tabloids are a very distinctive version of what Halliday has called a 'social semiotic' (Halliday, 1978 :109). In using a range of distinctive and identifiable dialects, the tabloids enable the reader to use the newspaper as a textual bridge between their own experience of the culture in which they live, and their own attitudes and beliefs within a range of language which is a close approximation to what they imagine themselves to be using when they speak of these things themselves. In other words, the language of the tabloids talks their language. We can use language analysis to begin to understand what Rooney considers one of the imperatives of our times, to find 'new ways to explain their importance within working-class culture' (Rooney, 2000: 107). Tabloids combine dialect and register in their deployment of a language which draws on social sensitivities about who uses which forms of language. In appropriating the idiom of the ordinary people of the country – the non-elite – the tabloids have managed to produce a marketable combination of social class and language. Historically, Smith saw in this the final vestiges of an authentic bond between the language of the working class and the language of the popular newspaper embodied in the post-war version of the *Daily Mirror*. Yet he argues that this was quickly formulated into a parody of that language (Smith, 1975: 238).

In order to maintain its ideological control, the language of the contemporary tabloids needs to be immediate, contemporary, mythological in the sense that Barthes (1974) meant when he talked of myth as a device which extracted events from their historical and political contexts. The immediacy of tabloid

Britain has therefore a subversively political agenda of omission. In constructing a version of the British nation and a variety of popular idiom, it presents an ahistorical account of Britain constructed in terms of superficial and transitory political values, very much in keeping with much of the broader contemporary news media environment. The language of the tabloids is a commercially astute attempt to articulate what Bourdieu (1990) has called the *habitus* of its readership; a clever and profitable game of linguistic ventriloquism by the journalists and sub-editors with a clear appeal to the readers that it targets. It does this by presenting forms of group knowledge constructed through versions of 'social memory' within the lifestyle experiences of individual readers in ways described by the analytical work of Van Dijk (1991).

Tabloid features

The tabloids are now identified as drawing upon and amplifying all the following features of popular journalism down the years: sensationalism, emotive language, the bizarre, the lewd, sex, suppression fees, cheque book journalism, gossip, police news, marriage and divorce, royal news, celebrities, political bias and any form of prurience which can be included under the general heading of human interest. Sparks encapsulates the present condition of tabloid news succinctly when he writes, 'it devotes relatively little attention to politics, economics, and society and relatively much to the personal and private lives of people, both celebrities and ordinary people, and relatively little to political processes, economic developments, and social changes' (2000:10). In addition we might add that it comprises fewer international news stories and more pictures against less text.

Historically, the evolution of the tabloid and its distinctive use of popular idiom has been shaped upon older patterns of cultural identification. As early as the 1930s this had been identified in the following terms: 'just as in the old ballads there were accepted ways of expressing common facts and conceptions, so now in the tabloids there are certain generic epithets that have become so conventionalized that they too tell their tales' (Johnston, 1935: 119). Bird identifies the common features of oral narratives such as folk tales, which encourage standardized language and characters and standardized ways of interpreting the world, and points out that these strategies have much in common with contemporary celebrity stories in their formulaic and predictable attributes (1992: 170). There is a consensual 'ideological effect' (Hall, 1978) within such familiar narrative structures which makes it particularly easy for tabloid papers to operate as McGuigan describes:

> The *Sun* is, arguably, symptomatic of and contributory to a political culture in which popular pleasure is routinely articulated through oppressive ideologies that operate in fertile chauvinistic ground. It is populist in the worst possible sense.
>
> (1993: 184)

They maintain the status quo politically and culturally in their editorial stance towards their readership and in their nationally based idiom they continue to stabilize a strong sense of Britain. Tabloids demonstrate that there is a receptive audience for stories which demonstrate directly or indirectly a disrespect for those in certain positions of social authority, reinforcing the sense of distance between the powerful in society and those excluded from these circles. It is the roll call of those who receive such critical treatment from the British tabloids and the vehemence of the language used to attack them that draw an interesting and possibly disturbing picture of popular political attitudes in Britain today.

When Taylor writes, 'tabloid journalism is the direct application of capitalism to events and ideas. Profit, not ethics, is the prevailing motivation' (1992: 409), she articulates why the tabloids are such accurate barometers of the contemporary commercialized landscape which is Britain in 2004. The political economy which underpins their success makes them culturally such important products to study. It is their highly specific concentration on a popular variety of language which articulates a British national community that enables them to retain their market share. Their success may well be embodied in the language which enables a 'greater proximity to the lifeworld of the audience' (Tomlinson, 1997: 77). Yet this representation also recalls something of Baudrillard's simulacrum, an identical copy without an original. The idealized reader of the contemporary British tabloids displays all the signifiers of community – vernacular, shared tastes, shared habits of media consumption – but without a concrete social community. Newspaper readerships simulate such a community and particularly within the popular press that community is marketed through a rhetoric which attempts to capture a flavour of the speech and tastes of the readers. The tabloids in Britain are as much a refraction of contemporary obsessions and lifestyles as older patterns of folk stories. They may not constitute undiluted reality – what form of market-driven media product does? – but they are certainly of use in indicating the state of Britain today, warts and all, 'beating in tune with the common experiences of its readers' (Conboy, 2002: 183). If one were to consider leaving a realistic selection of cultural artefacts in an honest display of the realities of daily lived experience of the early twenty-first century for posterity or even for alien visitors to the planet, then it would be hard to argue against the inclusion of copies of the most prominent tabloids in such a time capsule. Perhaps they cannot be called newspapers, perhaps they are as Rooney puts it 'completely separate cultural artefacts' (2000: 102), but this does not rule out the need to explore what the language of the tabloids can tell us about the state of Britain in the twenty-first century.

2 The rhetorical patterns of tabloid language

The use of a range of language specific to a particular newspaper is an editorial strategy, among many others, which enables a readership to be targeted. The language of the popular tabloid press in Britain is as accurate a prediction of the assumed social class and income of its readership as the advertisements and news content. Bell has called the language of newspapers an exercise in audience design (1984: 145–204), and this is certainly born out by the tabloids which display a confident grasp of the identity of their ideal reader. Newspapers which use the tabloid size but do not use its language, such as the recent format shifts in Britain with the *Independent* and the *Times* or the longer tradition of a newspaper such as *Le Monde* in France, demonstrate that it is the language which is more important in the make-up of a tabloid than the format itself. *BILD Zeitung* in Germany remains a very large format paper although it shares all of the linguistic features and editorial agendas of the tabloid press in Britain. It has been argued that it is in the language of different types of newspapers, not in their layout, that the distinction lies; between the neutral language of those aiming to be considered as serious newspapers of record and the 'emotionally charged' language of the popular tabloids (Kitis and Milapedes, 1997: 562).

Language is employed across the tabloid paper in a systematic way to build a composite version of the vocabulary and style of their ideal average reader; a sort of vernacular ventriloquism (Conboy, 2002: 162). This is in evidence when the colloquial expression, 'nice one, son' is transferred onto a story about a child born twenty-one years after his father's sperm was frozen.

ICE ONE, SON

(*Daily Mirror*, 25 May)

Throughout this book, I refer to this systematic language use as rhetoric; not a high-flown, abstract style but a set of language devices used with the deliberate and consistent aim of confirming the existence of a national tabloid readership. It is a range of language deployed by the tabloids to effectively inscribe a readership within its pages through the use of metaphor, irony, alliteration, rhyme or parallelism (Van Dijk, 1991: 47). This rhetoric gains its coherence by being repeated across the various sections of the tabloid paper. This sees a narrowing of the approaches to sport and politics, celebrity and disaster as the language tends to be drawn more towards a common approach than in traditional serious newspapers. This is an important point to stress; it is not simply that the tabloids have an extreme version of traditional news values (Harcup and O'Neill, 2001: 277) but, more importantly, it is expressed in a language which manifests a great deal of continuity throughout the paper.

As well as being a marketing strategy which supports the matching of advertising to income level of readership, this identification of a common language, targeted at an idealized reader of lower socio-economic status, combines into serving a broader normative function. This style of language forms an essential part of an ideological pact with the readership. For the purposes of this study, it might be said that it is in the two-way process between language and reader that 'ideology is inscribed in social practice' (Hodge and Kress, 1993: 210). This ideological relationship makes sense of the world and reduces contradictory elements in a language which amplifies references to popular culture, television shows, populist politics and a world where the individual is at the mercy of the larger random forces of fate whether they be catastrophe, winning the lottery or the vindictiveness of traffic wardens. This language is rich in its own tradition of metaphor, word play, categorization and compression of narratives. These are features which embody a particular social relationship between a newspaper's readership and the contemporary world. Hall has pointed out that these 'epistemic choices' in the popular press have been established for relatively long periods of time (1975: 20). The tabloids do not merely serve up an inferior version of journalistic language; they provide their readers with a distinct linguistic compendium with its own, highly influential range of language use. The tabloids are profoundly rhetorical in their own right. This chapter will begin by looking at a selection of devices which contribute to this tabloid rhetoric.

News values and tabloid people

We may start by making a connection between the rhetoric of the tabloids and their broader news values. An essential part of tabloid news values is the exaggerated foregrounding of sensation and 'human interest'. These features have the effect of structuring the world in a way which rejects fundamental political issues and focuses instead on random events within a world of common sense (Curran *et al.* 1980). This concentration on sensation and human interest means that the tabloids tend to feature people at the extremes of human experience and behaviour. This applies to age, where we can read of 'grans' and 'OAPs' as well as 'tots' and 'toddlers':

GRAN, 82, IS KILLED FOR HER BUS PASS

(Daily Mirror, 3 May)

Tot scare at dentist

(Sun, 28 April)

It also applies to 'yobs' and 'loonies' at an extreme of social behaviour, while nearer to the consensual centre of its discourse, it categorizes people in terms of nationality as newsworthy, as in 'Britons'. Nairn (1977: 368) has pointed out that there are no Britons outside of the discourse of contemporary newspapers, and still today the only time the otherwise anachronistic term 'Britons' can be heard in contemporary Britain, apart from in the words of the ever-popular jingoistic dirge 'Rule Britannia', is in the pages of the tabloids:

The Briton who is about to become Internet billionaire

*(Daily Mail,*1 May)

At one end of a scale of moral acceptability we have 'internet tycoons' and at the other we have 'evil drug dealers'.

Multi-millionaire internet tycoon Martha Lane Fox was seriously ill last night after a road crash.

(Sun, 4 May)

EVIL drug dealers are swamping Britain with ever-rising supplies of cocaine

(Daily Star, 12 May)

This emphasis on language which emphasizes the extremes of human experience amplifies a polarization which is characteristic of the tabloids. It also fits well with the use of dramatization, exaggeration and hyperbole which have been described as the main rhetorical tricks of the popular press to make the news more exciting (Van Dijk, 1991: 219). Categorization into binary divisions of the world suits the tabloids' news values and fits in with the melodramatic/Manichaean representation of the world described by Gripsrud (1992). In the following example, we can see how the discourse of madness and its binary division of the world into readers and outsiders is able to structure the report of 'our' children behaving badly within the pattern implicit in the use of the possessive adjective. This is an important part of the linguistics of consensus, creating an illusion of similitude between readers and exploiting the fact that the possessive adjective, 'us', can encompass all other possessive adjectives in its communal reach (De Cillia, Reisigl and Wodak, 1999: 164). Further rhetorical features including the category of 'experts' and the tabloid tendency to create lists and to use illustrations are prominent here in both the *Daily Star* and the *Daily Mail*:

LOONY JUICE

Soft drink additives 'drive our kids mad'

CHEMICALS found in soft drinks could be driving our children crazy, experts warned yesterday.

(Daily Star, 11 May)

There follows lists of additives and '10 BEST SELLERS – AND WHAT'S IN THEM'

Children's drinks are a chemical cocktail

THE BEST-SELLING DRINKS ... AND THEIR COCKTAILS OF ADDITIVES

(Daily Mail, 11 May)

The binarism which is at the heart of tabloid representations of characters in the news can be extended beyond the trite and sensational to more serious political issues. This can have reductive ideological implications which while not being exclusive to tabloids (Hodge and Kress, 1993) do provide a framework for some of the rare foreign news in these newspapers which portray the division of the world into simplistic archetypes as in the tragic case of the foreign worker Nick Berg in Iraq, who was beheaded by militant supporters of Al-Zarqawi as a violent political gesture to the occupying coalition forces:

SATAN & THE SAINT

(Sun, 13 May)

In terms of categories of extreme behaviour, there is nothing like the category of the yob for the tabloids to involve themselves in a bout of class-baiting. This is paradoxical as the newspapers are written to appeal to the working classes but go to some lengths to castigate this particular character type as if to draw on the Victorian moral distinction between the deserving and the undeserving poor. Criticizing how poor people spend their undeserved wealth has always been one of the tabloids' favourite occupations. It would seem as if the papers patrol the acceptable parameters of the behaviour of society, both rich and poor. In the following examples from the *Sun* (14 May), drawing on the news that Michael Carroll who had won a fortune on the lottery has a mere half a million pounds left from his £9.7 million winnings after a year and a half of extravagant living, we see a whole range of popular/folk items drawn upon: song ('HEY PIG SPENDER'); tabloid insults ('LOTTO YOBBO', 'LOTTO lout', 'LOTTO THUG'); grotesque rudeness ('FILTHY rich yob'). Following this story there is a graphic breakdown of how the money has been spent with a typically tabloid picture list. These sorts of tabloid outburst tend to reinforce the parallel agendas of the particular papers, especially when it comes to the idle and undeserving who come from working class backgrounds. There is a strong moralistic narrative at play in such stories which complements the analysis of tabloid morality applied to wealthier celebrities (Connell, 1992). Yet categorization does not always lead to simple sets of values and preferences. The apparently simple category of 'cop' can be reversible as either untouchable hero (when dead) or idol with feet of clay when alive and fallible. This sort of narrative reveals a fault line in the values of the tabloid press with regard to law and order, where they are traditionally hard, but where they are equally quick to revel in allegations of abuse or incompetence concerning those in positions of power or responsibility.

HERO COP IN STAB DEATH SHOCK

A HEROIC policeman was killed by a machete-wielding man yesterday.

(*Daily Star*, 22 May)

Cops shoot naked, innocent man dead then THEY sue for compo

(*Sun*, 22 May)

Word play

Humour is never far from the top of the tabloids' list of priorities. Indeed, this is identified as one of their chief and problematic attractions by Fowler (1991: 45). Though far from being the sole preserve of the tabloids, they take word play into areas of irreverence and mockery inconceivable for the more serious-minded newspapers. Playing with words features strongly in their armoury and therefore puns are prominent among the rhetorical devices deployed. It is important to stress that puns call upon a very active involvement from their readers which is very much in keeping with the traditional irreverence of popular culture though the ages (Burke, 1978). They are never more at home than making news from an item which has little traditional appeal but which can be transformed through a witty catchphrase to provide an interesting hook for readers. The pun demonstrates the ever-present potential for humour in popular culture. The jokes elaborated are very narrow in their range, targeted towards a national readership, to such an extent that they would be almost completely indecipherable for a foreign readership, tourists in Britain or a strain on the powers of comprehension of non-native speaking residents, confirming that the tabloids are very much their own country.

The EU has really been a gift to pun-hungry headline writers able to weave it within the political agendas of their papers and to attach it to the demotic of popular outrage.

EU WHAT?

Brits haven't a clue about the 10 new states joining Europe
(*Daily Mirror*, 28 April)

It is a favourite gambit of the tabloids to tie in puns to the salacious agenda of exposing the sexual antics and the alleged hypocrisies of those caught in the media spotlight as with the actor in a controversial film, the 'filthiest ever', which had won praise at a film festival:

MARGO, THE PORN AGAIN CHRISTIAN
(*Daily Star*, 19 May)

Matching word play to the tradition of the individual tabloid newspaper is an important part of the agenda of the tabloids and seems to often precede the strict news agenda as if a good pun is as good if not better than a good storyline. There is nothing better therefore than the opportunity to trade on the humour implicit in a story such as the following. In these cases, the presentation of the story takes on a carnivalesque life of its own with word play the whole point of the piece and the understanding that it will appeal to its readers.

FRY ME KANGAROO BROWN, SPORT

Scoffing 'Skippy' can help beat cancer

by AND-ROO PARKER

HOPPY EATER

Starters:

Mar–soup–ial

Pouched eggs

Leap and potato soup

Main courses:

Hop pot

Roos–otto

Spring roll

Dessert:

Flan–garoo

(*Sun*, 28 May)

Letters and interaction with readers

The language of the letters' pages is one of the most explicit sites for the celebration of the assumed community of the tabloids, providing an ideological link between newspaper institution and readership. This language is centred on a nationally specific set of priorities. In the *Sun*, the letters' page is not only where readers air their opinions, it provides a forum which the paper claims, is a truly national one in explicit language – its own version of a blunt demotic. Each of the main tabloids has its own way of locating the identity of their ideal reader on their letters' page. They each portray a tone and a set of semiotic triggers which locate the attention of their own community of readers.

The *Sun* letters are presented as talking directly to the whole of the country:

THE PAGE WHERE YOU TELL BRITAIN WHAT YOU THINK

The *Daily Mirror* emphasizes the epistolary bridge between 'US' and 'YOU' as it calls on its readers: 'TELL US WHAT YOU THINK'. It regularly focuses on 'The great debate', with contributions from readers to editorially selected themes in letters and texts.

The *Daily Mail's* corresponding page is called 'Peterborough' and has a daily poem from its readers and also contains the signs of community in language it shares with the other tabloids. It is a less raucous place than the letters' pages of the lower end of the market tabloids:

Heartwarming, eccentric and funny … it's the column that belongs entirely to you, the reader

The *Daily Star* has a more proletarian version, the '*Daily Star* Forum', but also stresses that it is a part of the paper which is written by the readers and has a selection of features from letters and e-mails, Joke Bloke and Text maniacs to support the tone of this community:

FROM RANTS TO JOKES … IT'S THE PAGE YOU WRITE

The letters in all these papers are editorially themed around particular issues which act as a constructed dialogue between readers and newspaper, prioritizing the newspapers' agenda but in terms which appear to illustrate a seamless continuity between newspaper and readers as evinced by their letters (Wahl-Jorgensen, 2001). In this way highly controversial opinions, articulated in line with the ideological positioning of the newspaper, can be elicited from the mouths of the readers in an edited version of their own language to legitimate the newspapers' own positions in a circular train of identification and recognition. The following strapline, for example, accompanies and sets the tone for a range of readers' letters on the issue of ethnically designated housing:

Asians-only flat block will spark race hatred

(*Sun*, 4 May)

The letters' pages can be used to explicitly support the views and campaigns of their host tabloid on national issues as in the following examples.

On 12 May in the *Sun*, the letters' page is headlined, '**Well done to The Sun for backing Our Boys**' and provides an accumulation of phrases which generate a strong image of national consensus on the editorially selected theme of letters for that day:

> gratitude ... disgusted ... fighting sons and daughters ... getting behind ... staunchly ... stabbed in the back ... praising ... grit ... compassion ... bad apples ... old-fashioned British guts ... spirit of Trafalgar, Waterloo and the Falklands ... salute you ... dignity and professionalism ... New Labour ... penny pinching. ... Long may the Sun continue to be the favourite newspaper of the Armed Forces

On the same day the *Daily Mirror* clusters an oppositional nation's opinions around its own political projections:

We were utterly betrayed on Iraq

> betrayed ... protest ... wrong ... war crimes ... sanctimonious ... oil-grabbing ... imperialist ... Vietnam ... abuse ... shame

(*Daily Mirror*, 12 May)

Both of these letters' page specials provide semantic maps of the newspapers' own political positions on the Iraq conflict over the issue of the photos of alleged abuse.

The interactivity of the letters' page is echoed in other parts of the paper, where readers are constantly being reminded of their potential to play a part in contributing to the content of their paper in a variety of technological interactions.

When the *Sun* asks its readers to phone or e-mail the *Sun* News desk, it asks them to forward the following stories: 'showbiz gossip, political scandal or a heart-warming tale'. The brief list of issues in which the paper expresses an interest provides a microcosm of its news agenda. It is an interactive highway but one with editorial control still very much in the hands of the paper. The comuunication channels listed confirm the illusion of community as well as providing potentially limitless amounts of free news. It is, if nothing else, an extremely cheap form of news gathering masquerading as reader-led involvement. On the sports' pages in the *Sun* there is the colloquially borrowed and interactive: 'GIVE US A YELL'.

The *Daily Mail* also draws in populist support via its e-mail facility and its connection to its own website.

www.dailymail.co.uk

On your favourite family website today. ...

(Vote Blair to go? London for Olympics? Free Celebrity Gossip, Win Cruise, Property, Weather)

(*Daily Mail*, 18 May)

The interactivity here is one in which readers are invited to make points on a story made topical in the main by the popular press itself. It is a self-reflexive and self-generated world to a large extent. The interactivity is merely a rhetorical illusion. Yet the language is full of emphasis on the dialogue between 'YOU' and 'US'. The political economy of this dialogue is quite clearly far from a democratic exchange. The readers may provide the letters and to an extent the stories of a more trivial nature, but they are editorially selected to fit the demands of a pre-existent newspaper agenda.

Familiar names

Familiar names and nicknames are used in the tabloids as a bridge of famil-iarity, connecting readers to a world outside the confines of their lived experience. Yet in media terms they are familiar with these people because of their presence in the news and other media. Such language reinforces the linkage between the tabloid news agenda and broader aspects of popular culture including television, film and popular music. Such intertextuality is what assists in the broad 'cultural discourse' (Dahlgren, 1988: 51) of modern popular journalism. The framing of such characters in the language of famil-iarity helps to establish the 'naturalness' of the presence of these people and their affairs in the pages of the newspaper while at the same time helping the popular press justify how it sidelines more serious issues about the contempo-rary world in favour of what it claims its readers want.

CHILD-SEX RAP COPS GRAB JACKO UNDIES

(*Daily Star*, 3 May)

The familiarity of 'Jacko' serves, in conjunction with the sordid details of his seized underwear, to trivialize the allegations of child abuse. The reference to 'cops' also ensures that this investigation is squarely within the same parame-ters of sensationalized reporting and categorization as other celebrity news. This tends to obscure the wider-reaching problems implicit in the case. Tabloid features are never stand-alone, but always complex interactions between the political economy of the newspapers themselves and the culture in which they are bought and read. They are the linguistic element in a 'web of significance' (Geertz, 1973). This complexity is captured in the language of the papers and the ways in which it interacts dynamically with a fast evolving contemporary culture. First with the hard news? Maybe not, but the tabloids are often first with the identification in print of popular trends and expressions and leap enthusiastically onto them whenever they pass, and this includes to a large extent the breaking of celebrity news, gossip and scandal. When Michael Jackson's former employees are called upon to talk to police about their experience of his household and behaviour patterns, he is referred to by his full name in the article which follows but the headline use of familiar nickname and slang conveys the tone of familiarity which sociolinguists (Trudgill, 1995) have identified as indicative of a male tendency to bond with lower socio-cultural patterns of language. This certainly fits with the blue collar appeal of the newspaper in question as it seeks to match language with readership.

STAFF TOLD: GRASS UP WACKO OR GO TO JAIL
(*Daily Star*, 4 May)

Nicknames and familiarity of expression can also be used to apply to news of politicians – or in this case – their wives.

Cherie's pal takes on MoD

A barrister from Cherie Blair's chambers will try to win compensation for the families of Iraqis killed by British soldiers.
(*Daily Star*, 4 May)

This reduction of a 'barrister' from 'Cherie Blair's chamber's into a 'pal' of Cherie's, indicates the way in which such techniques of familiarization go beyond making the reader comfortable with the world presented to them on their terms and in their language and move into territory which is more subtly politicized. Bringing personalities into the familiar reach of the tabloids' vernacular moves them closer to the simplified and binary politics of much of their coverage. Familiarization may demystify but it can also be used to foment contempt for celebrities and politicians alike and erode any residual public confidence in the latter just as it reduces the humanity of the former.

The politics of slang

One of the more obvious ways in which the tabloids attempt to reinforce their relationship with their readership is by employing colloquial expressions and slang. This strategy appears to allow the newspapers to talk to a readership in its own, informal manner and further extends the explicit appeal of these papers to be on the side of the people, leading discussion in an editorial version of the language of the people. The implication of this language is that the tabloids are on the side of the people as readers and opposed to the interests of the power bloc (Fiske, 1994). It is a deliberate strategy to cement that ideological bond with a readership which sees itself as sceptical of the establishment and by implication its language. This variety of demotic language is not always associated with political matters but can often be woven throughout the papers as a regular feature. Slang can be used in the most tragic of circumstances, perhaps because of the editorial need to compress the language of the news to save space but also as part of the irreverence and familiarity which match other aspects of the tabloid agenda.

> Step-bro of Di dies in hostel
>
> (*Daily Mirror*, 28 May)

In the language of abbreviation and slang of the tabloids, where it is used to drive the story, protagonists are reduced to caricatures and coverage can be an insensitive intrusion into the lives of real people; people whose feelings must take second place to tabloid agendas and style. Furthermore, it fits into the melodramatic mode of representation discussed earlier. The same familiarity and trivialization can be used when the victim is not rich and famous but merely fits in with the style of reporting stories which are in line with a sensationalized agenda.

GIRL SEES BRUV, 12, DIE IN SCHOOL BUS CRASH

> (*Sun*, 25 May)

Over three tabloid reports we can see examples of how slang meshes with reporting style, in effect translating the news into a series of echoes of popular slang and television police drama. The foiled bullion raid at Heathrow airport provides:

> **Sweeney ...**
>
> (*Daily Mail*, 18 May)

and

> You're nicked
>
> (*Daily Mirror*, 18 May)

A third story uses the term 'DODGY MOTORS' (*Sun*, 6 May), which sounds like it comes out of a script of the classic television comedy series 'Minder', to describe cars which can be checked by new police camera technology.

A decision to scale down the amount of sick pay available to workers was highlighted in the tabloids in terms of language familiar to workers in all walks of life, the 'sickie'. This provides an interesting illustration of how, across the board, the tabloids merge popular speech into a populist storyline and indeed, in one case, select it as a story to be commented on interactively, indicating that it is something about which the paper has already selected an editorial preference, based on high populist expectations of touching a common experience of the phenomenon.

Store war on sickies

(Daily Star, 17 May)

The topic is drawn into the interactivity of one newspaper as it asks readers to e-mail their views on the phenomenon:

More bosses get tough with staff over the growing sickies epidemic

… Are bosses right to stamp down on sicknote culture? Tell us at [email address]

(Daily Mail, 20 May)

The following example provides a good illustration of how popular speech is looped from the tabloids back into popular speech. This means that people are reported speaking as the tabloids write; not only giving people what they want but making it sound like the people themselves have digested the idiom of the tabloids. 'Stunned' and 'unbelievable' echo the hyperbole and cliché of the language of the tabloids:

Horror as hearse is nicked

Heartless thieves left a family devastated when they stole a hearse with a grandmother's body in the back. …

Her son Andy, 40, said:

'We were stunned. It has not been the easiest of times and to have this as well was unbelievable.'

(Sun, 28 May)

Noun phrases and scripts

Noun phrases, because of their ability to compress information, are frequently used in newspapers. They have the added advantage of having a discrete ideological function as they can also be linked to provide simple references to certain categories which reinforce established preferences on particular newspapers.

Face of a tot grab suspect

(Daily Mirror, 28 April)

Truancy mum jailed

(*Daily Mirror*, 29 April)

Such noun phrase compression, as here with regard to issues around children, links in with the use of reductive 'scripts' (Hall, 1978) or 'media frames' (Gitlin, 1980: 7; Entman, 1993) in the tabloids. These scripts provide short semantic or visual signals to readers which are drawn from an archive of preferred meanings which consciously or unconsciously predispose the reader to a particular range of interpretations of the information before them. They provide semantic and syntactic short cuts to the accumulated views of the newspaper on certain issues. They provide the nudge and the wink of abbreviated opinion or ideological pact in that they assume that we share the same view of the world as them.

Celebrity can be crammed into a noun phrase to give an already sensational story a further attraction within the tabloid agenda. The noun phrase compression can be further reduced by the use of a colloquial abbreviation:

TONY ADAMS' EX HAD DEAD WOMAN IN CAR

(*Sun*, 28 May)

The 'fresh cronyism row' in the following refers to a particular script which has haunted aspects of the Labour administration's decisions on appointments to high office and runs as a counterpoint to the criticisms of the previous Conservative government's 'sleaze'. It also has the stylistic advantage of providing a rhyme, as in 'Tony's cronies'. A Labour Party donor has been alleged by the *Daily Mail* to have been given preferential treatment in a bid for a medical contract. It is a script which prompts an interpretation of the Labour government as corrupt.

Peerage for the 'crony' who gave Labour £100,000

Tony Blair was facing a fresh cronyism row last night ...

(*Daily Mail*, 1 May)

The following example demonstrates how a rhetoric of siding with the commonsense views of ordinary people can be built up in the language characteristic of the tabloids so that the newspaper appears to side with an implied populist chorus of condemnation of the ills of society and the implication that a return to some form of harsh regime of discipline is the solution. It demonstrates that the tabloid agenda is one all too often predicated on an authoritarian populism (Hall, 1988a). Conclusions are printed literally in bold type, which highlights the preferred emphasis for the reader and is in itself a common rhetorical device embedded in tabloid typography. Such rhetorical and indeed political predispositions which can be found across the spectrum of the popular tabloids do tend to compromise any potential for a contemporary radical voice within the overall pattern of the tabloid press in Britain. The *Daily Star* opinion page comments on the news that David Hart, the Headteachers' Union leader has a 'lesson for Blair' and claims that he has given parents 'six of the best'. In keeping with this metaphor of school-based violence he is said to have 'lashed out at failing mums and dads'. The paper stresses the point that it shares with the speaker:

> Mr Hart offered his own cure – good old-fashioned discipline.

> and gives the Prime Minister its own advice ... give teachers the power to get tough.
>
> *(Daily Star*, 4 May)

Metaphors and politics

Politics are often depicted in metaphorical terms in newspaper language in general. It is a tendency which calls into question the objective and neutral claims of newspaper language, given the emotive nature of much metaphorical association. Yet some linguists claim that non-literal language, including metaphor, is the rule not the exception (Lycan, 2000: 209). Lakoff (1987) and Goatly (1997) consider metaphorical language as having the structure of a bridge between the factual world and ideological persuasion, and according to this hypothesis, metaphors have an important role in establishing common associations within newspaper texts. The tabloids draw upon a range of metaphor which is very much in keeping with the other popular references of their coverage. This can be seen as we move – with an example of bathos – in a story about Tony Blair, from a simple Canute-like metaphor of 'waves crashing around him' to a popular sporting simile which compares his struggle with the leader of the opposition, Michael Howard, to the rivalry between two Premiership football managers.

> Tory waves sink Blair

> Tony Blair looks like a drowning man.

> More waves were crashing about him yesterday...

> Mr Howard is becoming more confident by the day.

> *He's like Arsene Wenger plotting the downfall of Sir Alex Ferguson.*
>
> *(Daily Star*, 5 May)

The vulgarity of political debate is continued in discussion of the voters giving Blair a 'kicking'.

Blair in fear of voter backlash

I'M IN FOR A KICKING

Worried Tony Blair yesterday begged fed-up voters not to give Labour a kicking.

(*Daily Star*, 5 May)

Military metaphors are always a good standby when discussing politics in the tabloids (Kitis and Milapedes, 1997):

LABOUR AIMS ITS BIG GUNS AT HOWARD

(*Sun*, 5 May)

The language of violent encounter continues in the *Daily Mirror* on 5 May where Blair and Brown are said to 'gang up' on opposition leader, Howard. The piece includes 'savage onslaught', 'slapped down' and 'ripped into' as extensions to the metaphorical field drawn upon here. Sport, military engagement by other means, we might say, can also be drawn on to provide the link between politics and metaphorical violence. The earlier, oblique reference to football is full of metaphors of physical conflict, providing a continuing rhetorical background to the reporting of politics as a process of conflict.

The tabloids' treatment of politics is marked throughout by a rich variety of vernacular devices which have the paradoxical effect of reducing the complexities of political debate to a narrow range of familiar positions which are embedded in compact phrases. The complexities and pragmatism of politics are often reduced to a simple binary of moving forwards or of moving backwards with the implication that it is often because of pressure from the tabloids themselves that change occurs and that any change in direction for a political party is a climb-down. Blair knowingly claimed that he had no reverse gear as a variation on the well-known claim by Margaret Thatcher that 'this lady's not for turning', but the tabloids see U-turns everywhere in a familiar pattern of colloquial political referencing. Popular language merges with populist debates and never more effectively than when they can in addition combine distrust of politicians with fear of foreigners.

BLAIR U-TURN ON MIGRANTS

(*Sun*, 28 April)

Spy chief who saved Blair's bacon is rewarded with top job at MI6

(*Daily Mail*, 7 May)

Economic decisions are also presented within the vernacular discourse of 'hiked up', 'whack up', which places individuals as the focus of the story and invites a reader response which can subsequently be further woven into the newspaper's populist position on the subject, thus championing itself as the supporter of the ordinary British reader.

> **MILLIONS of homeowners face growing mortgage misery after interest rates were hiked up again yesterday**. ... Cheltenham and Gloucester was first to whack up its lending rate. ...
>
> IS IT RIGHT TO RAISE INTEREST RATES?
>
> > (*Daily Star*, 7 May)

British politics are also treated within the overlapping and complementary frameworks of familiarity and the discourse of dishonesty.

> **BLAIR MUST GO SAY HIS MATES**
>
> ... his close pals and ex-allies urged him to stand down ...
>
> > (*Daily Star*, 10 May)

The Labour government and Blair in particular are portrayed as 'greedy' and 'sneaky':

> **End of the road, Tony**
>
> **MOTORISTS are to be hit with yet another sneaky tax**. ... Greedy ministers ...
>
> > (*Daily Star*, 10 May)

This tone of address with all its familiarity is not restricted to the news pages but crops up in the *Daily Mail* even in its finance section.

> **Pull your finger out Gordon**
>
> > (*Daily Mail*, 12 May)

Salacious storylines

There is a continuity in the delight which the tabloids display in vulgar and salacious humour which they share with many forms of popular culture down the centuries. Ribald humour in the first printed forms of English literature such as *The Canterbury Tales*, music halls, saucy postcards at British seaside resorts, the popularity of Benny Hill and the *Carry On* films all testify to the resilience of this kind of popular humour. No opportunity is missed in their eye and ear for innuendo and this desire for the vulgar is an important feature of their news values and of their popularity. It represents an element of the rhetoric which to a large degree defines the parameters of tabloid Britain in its tastes and its sense of humour. Apart from standing alone as an important feature of tabloid rhetoric, it also works, as with other aspects of their news agendas, with the way in which sex and gender are represented overall in the paper with important cumulative consequences which have clear political implications on occasions.

In the *Sun* on 4 May we read:

CUPSIZED

Boat tips over as 60 ogle nude beauties

This seems like a throwback to the days of saucy postcards at British holiday resorts and certainly indicates a lightly moral perspective which suggests that the 'oglers' got what they deserved. Yet there are other examples which indicate that it is not just the naughty innuendo but explicit sexual material which makes up much of the tabloid content. This has led to what some have called the sexualization of popular culture (Holland, 1998) and the representation of women is centre-stage.

In a typical example of titillating photo-play the *Daily Star* continues its gratuitous exploration of sexuality in the 'Just Jane' series, entitled

AM I A LESBIAN? Day Two:

JANE O'GORMAN SOLVES YOUR PROBLEMS TODAY AND EVERY DAY

(*Daily Star*, 11 May)

A story in the *Sun* provides medical assurance that chocolate may provide the ultimate pleasure:

CHOCS WAHEY

Sweet treats will give you an orgasm, says doc

(*Sun*, 17 May)

As a variant, there is an interesting tendency to be simultaneously coy and vulgar in terms of language in the tabloids. Expletives and vulgar word play can be found either masked by asterisks or embedded within serious or trivial storylines.

ABOUT F★★★★★G TIME. ...

A Family torn apart by the Potters Bar train crash hit out bitterly last night after rail firms finally took responsibility for the disaster.

(*Daily Mirror*, 28 April)

FAKING IDIOTS

(*Daily Star*, 5 May)

The *Sun* provides an asterisked version of instructions similar to those on a contemporary TV show. At Bonapartes restaurant Gordon Ramsay is portrayed joining in the common joke on his use of vulgar language.

Gordon's recipe for The F★★★★★★ Perfect Omelette

(*Sun*, 6 May)

It is interesting how vulgar language is played with and deleted in contrast to the more infrequent but blunt use of such language in broadsheets such as the *Guardian* when it is using direct quotations which it considers of relevance to the story. The tabloids are also first to report on events which enable them to indulge in smutty jokes about body parts and functions.

YOU'VE GOT NO BALLS

The FA last night showed they have no balls after deciding not to charge Robert Huth with stamping on Alan Shearer's family jewels. ...

The Toon skipper said he had to check to make sure his tackle was still in place after referee Bob Styles overlooked the clash.

(*Daily Mirror*, 28 April)

CAPN'S LOG

Astro poo to power rockets

ASTRONAUTS who boldly go could help power their own mission to Mars. ...

It means that the 'poop deck' could become a useful power source on long missions.

(*Sun*, 20 May)

Normal readers

The readership of the tabloids as inscribed in the rhetoric of the newspapers has its own characteristics portrayed more explicitly and more often than the readership of broadsheet newspapers where the process is more implicit. One of the ways in which this identity is made more coherent and reinforced over time and through a variety of storylines is the portrayal of a certain category of outsider to the community idealized in language. Before considering the range of other outsiders who have their status predicated on ethnicity, nationality or criminality, we can look at the primary assertion in the tabloids that its readers are normal and that they are constantly threatened by outsiders who are described as mad (Philo, 1996). The normative momentum of such descriptors leads to the implication that the insiders who comprise the readership of the tabloids or of the particular tabloid in question form part of an elect upon whose behaviour normality can be grounded: the 'construction of conformity' which McQuail writes about (2000: 469) has strong moral undertones despite the superficial flippancy of popular humour found in the tabloids.

In the following examples, we see slang mixed with the narrative of madness which always tends to reinforce the casual flippancy regarding mental health issues and which serves to construct outsiders to the assumed 'right-minded' tabloid readership through this blend of language. The story in the *Sun* on 5 May about a reckless driver's 'Lunatic's 150mph' while using a mobile phone is amplified by quotations supporting the assertion of lunacy: '... branded a "madman". ... "It's absolute madness..." '. The boss of an ice-cream firm is reported imprisoned for setting fire to an intruder in the following terms:

FIRE NUT IS CAGED

(*Daily Star*, 11 May)

The rhyming potential of the name of the latest football sensation cannot be resisted: 'Rooney: Looney or just childish?' (*Daily Mirror*, 3 May).

When an intruder breaches security at the Queen's residence in Windsor he is referred to as the 'Castle loon' in the *Daily Star* (19 May). The world outside the tabloid community of language is represented as madness indeed, peopled as it is by 'nuts', 'maniacs' and 'crazed' individuals. It appears that the tabloid itself and its readership are the definitional guarantors of mental normality. The excess and abnormality of outsiders appear to confirm the intrinsic safety of the internal community of the tabloid.

In the following, we have an example of when ordinary people become news through behaviour which puts them temporarily beyond the bounds of normal behaviour. Here a court has heard how an infuriated commuter parked his car across a railway line in desperation after being told that the train would not be making its scheduled stop at the station. There is still the binary of ordinary reader and extraordinary protagonist identified as mad (LOCO) but here it is implicitly tied to the script of the long-suffering commuter on public transport, disregarding of course the political and economic questions of how the British rail system got to this impasse in the first place.

HE'S GONE LOCO

Angry commuter parked on line to stop train

(*Sun*, 21 May)

The banal and bizarre can sometimes combine as in the following encounter of fast food and the hostile outsider where a pizza delivery man turns stalker and is referred to as:

PIZZA NUT

... besotted nut ...

(Sun, 25 May)

The individual in tabloid news

The tabloids specialize in a variety of news which has been categorized as the 'other news' (Langer, 1998), full of strange happenings, freak events, larger than life characters, endearing eccentricity or the grotesque. Such stories have always formed part of the news agenda from earliest times but the tabloids have refined their presentation and taken them to a more central position within the news than ever before as news agendas shift more towards an integration with other areas of popular media culture (Harcup and O'Neill, 2001). It has been argued (Bromley, 1998; McLachlan and Golding, 2000) that the gravitational pull of these news values distorts the spectrum of news in Britain. The national community which the tabloids assist in representing is one in which these news items play a significant role. The presence of such stories diminishes the weight of political coverage and helps engender a non-rational worldview where humans are at the mercy of strange and incongruous events. The logic of this world has a corresponding politics, according to which improvements in life come from individual effort or the workings of fate. Politics are simply an irrelevant game and the Thatcherite nightmare of a nation with no such thing as society is frequently paraded in the 'anarchic existentialism' (Langer, 1998) of their pages.

Some of these stories can be categorized as simply bizarre, as in the following three examples. In the first, in the *Daily Mirror* (3 May), a teenage girl is thrown into the air in a gas explosion and remains unharmed in bed, giving the reporter the opportunity to joke that not even an explosion can get a teenager out of bed. The story comes complete with a picture of the scene of devastation and the bed! A second deals with the tale of a 'dad-to-be' who was asked by the ambulance driver to pay £50 for petrol to get to the hospital.

CASH ON DELIVERY

(Daily Mirror, 3 May)

Finally a large picture accompanies the story of a goose who has spent three weeks sitting on a golf ball trying to make it hatch:

Egged on by a ball

(Daily Mirror, 5 May)

Puns can be used to reinforce the humour of certain stories which are included for their novelty value and for their potential to generate language play for the readership's pleasure, as in the tale of a dog found twenty miles away from its home after being lost for three years:

Pooch went walkie-bout for 3 years

(*Sun*, 13 May)

The *Daily Mail* can also provide its own brand of bizarre pun-led news when a celebrity fashion shoot dog is accidentally given a severe haircut:

Short bark and sides

(*Daily Mail*, 27 May)

Yet often the agenda within stories of the bizarre can be more complex when they mesh with the individualism which the tabloids appear to revere. In an editorial, the *Sun* praises the commitment of a man who has spent a fortune trying to prove that his daughter was murdered in a Kenyan game reserve.

For 16 years, John Ward has conducted a one-man crusade. ...

But you must admire the kind of father who would go to the ends of the earth for his daughter, even after her death.

(*Sun*, 5 May)

In an article from the *Daily Star* (21 May), we have the individual action hero taking on, almost by accident, an ineffective council and improving his own environment through his own personal endeavour. Harry Sas had complained to the council about the state of his street and they sent him equipment to clean it up himself, which is what he did. He is categorized in tabloid fashion as an ordinary man, a 'stunned dad-of-two', yet is nevertheless compared to the Hollywood individualist vigilante cop, 'Dirty Harry', whose picture from the film illustrates the story. His rejection by an arrogant local council is reinforced in the punning headline 'BRUSH OFF' and yet this humble hero takes on the work of clearing up the streets in a 'one-man campaign'.

Transitivity

Transitivity is the technical word in linguistic analysis which describes who does what in a sentence and often to whom (Iwamoto, 1995). The transitivity of the tabloids, how they foreground the attribution of agency and process to the participants in a story, is one which is typically emphasized by hyperbolic verbs which highlight the actions and speech acts of individuals in a contest of wills, the louder the better. The selection of verbs can also demonstrate how individuals are treated or how they respond to outside forces.

LEE BLASTS RUMOURS …

(*Daily Star*, 3 May)

COPS QUIZ BURRELL THIS WEEK

(*Daily Mirror*, 4 May)

This selection of powerful verbs, to which we might add 'exposed', 'revealed', 'blasted', 'slammed' and 'KO', also has a reductive function which collapses the complexity of events as they fit into a relatively predetermined syntactic map which ties into the range of news values of the tabloids. This map is one upon which individuals figure prominently in verbal expressions either as victims or subjects and are represented as dominating over social and institutional acts. It matches the worldview of the tabloids who see news values almost exclusively in terms of personalities and reduce political and cultural processes again to focus on a few individuals. This selection of verbs is a highly efficient way of processing aspects of a complex world into a set of linguistic formulae which simplify as much as possible. Tabloids are not unique in this in the news environment but they do take the process further towards one end of the linguistic spectrum of a sensationalized and simplified set of explanations of the world.

Intertextual cultural references

Despite the intensification of global media brands and personalities, in their selection of intertextual references from other areas of contemporary culture, the tabloids are highly dependent on British examples for their targeted readership. A particular event within British popular culture can be described in terms of a range of other popular references reinforcing the national-descriptive role of these papers. The figure of Alan Smith, crying as his team Leeds United were relegated from the Premiership, led to a series of interventions from the tabloids who exploited the image in a variety of ways which demonstrated how this intertextuality can draw on a selection of local cultural references.

First the *Sun* trades on the assumed common knowledge of the catchphrase of the 1966 World Cup triumph and now the name of a popular sports quiz show:

They think it's bawl over

(*Sun*, 3 May)

This is supplemented by the headlines in the *Daily Mirror* on 3 May, which cross from pop music references to a pun on the colloquial 'Cheerio'.

Tears for fears

TEARIO LEEDS

Tabloids are adept at exploiting references to stories which have appeared in other parts of the popular media, especially when they can be deployed to fit into some humour-driven copy as here in a story from *Bliss* magazine based on a survey of secondary school pupils, which has been given the grotesquely humorous touch of the tabloids.

I CAN'T THINK …

TEACHER STINKS

Nearly half of all teachers PONG, according to teenage pupils

(*Sun*, 4 May)

So important are other popular media, particularly television, to the tabloids' agenda that they often, as in the *Daily Star*, make regular explicit claims that their television coverage is the best, or in popular punning mode, the 'most switched-on'.

CHARLIE CATCHPOLE

HE'S BRITAIN'S MOST SWITCHED-ON TELLY CRITIC

… ALL THE LATEST TELLY GOSSIP

Running stories concerning the coverage of Reality TV shows in the tabloids draw upon all the rhetoric of popular involvement as each vies to be identified as the paper that will bring you the best coverage of, in this case, Big Brother Five.

Big Brother 22 Days to Go

(*Daily Star*, 6 May)

BB5 – 6 DAYS TO GO

(*Sun*, 22 May)

Not to be left out of an area which is clearly a prime site of interest for the lower end of the tabloid market, the *Daily Mirror* on 24 May also claims to be the 'OFFICIAL BIG BROTHER PAPER … FOUR DAYS TO GO' and joins in the countdown to the start of the series.

Yet there is on occasions an interesting subversion of the pattern of popular television coverage which shows that there is never anything entirely predictable in the tabloids as they try to outmanoeuvre each other. They must retain a freshness despite the limitations of their agendas and their concentration on a fixed range of language devices. Here the novelty is provided by a spoof TV reality show – the hoax courtesy of the *Daily Mirror*. The newspaper had launched a competition for a show called 'Quarantine' where contestants would compete to spend a week in a lab exposed to infectious diseases, on live TV, to see who could stay healthy the longest. The *Daily Mirror* delights in the fact that the show claimed to be produced by the 'Mentior' production company which they reveal now is 'Latin for wind-up'. Despite their own enthusiasm for reality television shows, the newspaper takes a highly judgemental stance based on the avalanche of applications for the hoax show:

> This spoof advert for a sick reality show exposes the people who will stop at NOTHING to get on television
>
> (*Daily Mirror*, 11 May)

The ever popular televised lottery is also rife for intertextual borrowings when the story aligns with a 'love rat' agenda and can be made to fit with puns on the 'roll over' and the visuals of numbers on coloured lotto-style balls.

ROLLED OVER

Lotto rat dumps wife No4 for wife No1

(*Daily Mirror*, 29 May)

Self-referentiality

Popular journalism has never been timid about selling itself. This is hardly surprising given the close links between the formation and development of the mass popular press in Britain and the techniques of advertising in the late nineteenth century (Conboy, 2004a: 166). Part and parcel of its tradition is the way in which individual newspapers make claims about being the biggest, the best, the most up-to-the-minute. It is a world of superlatives where the mediocre and the mundane are avoided at all costs. The hyperbole of the tabloids is reinforced by their self-promotional claims about their own columnists or their own record for the most sought after tabloid story, the 'scoop', which fits the novelty agenda and in the era of instant news, takes on a particular style of news value.

The *Daily Star* flags its sports columnist Rodney Marsh under the strapline:

> Love him, loathe him but you just can't ignore him
>
> (*Daily Star*, 1 May)

On the back of scoops on a failed bullion robbery and the dismissal of Liverpool football club's manager, the *Daily Mirror* claims of itself:

TOP SCOOPS ARE IN DAILY MIRROR

(*Daily Mirror*, 25 May)

This is underlined in the sports section on the same day when it claims:

100% RIGHT

100% SACKED

(Daily Mirror, 25 May)

Self-congratulation can also be drawn from the reported support from loyal readers in a reciprocal movement:

WELL DONE, OUR SUN

HUNDREDS of readers last night congratulated The Sun for saluting Our Boys …

(Sun, 10 May)

Tabloid lists

Lists are a significant part of the syntax of the tabloids. They contain their own rhetorical dimension and fit within the set of expectations that readers have of them. Lists act in the tabloids to reduce complexity and bring a levelling equivalence to the topics which they systematize. They may literally not be joined-up thinking but they do make a series of connections for their readers. Lists can be implicitly compared across news categories and the very process of listing means that a pop star can be treated with the same technique as a major political issue. Listing brings a false sense of ease to subjects and is sometimes used to provide a pseudo-democratic point of access to a topic in the news.

The *Daily Mail* uses a listing of characteristics in a battle of the sexes view of gardening to fit in with the Spring Bank Holiday weekend:

Growing apart in the garden

Women work with nature. Men want to tame her.

WOMEN LIKE	MEN LIKE
Ornaments	Power tools
Co-ordinated patio furniture	Barbecues and heaters
Pot plants	Patios
Herbaceous borders	Lawns
A natural approach	A geometric layout

(Daily Mail, 3 May)

The centenary of Rolls Royce and trivia about the World Snooker Champion Ronnie O'Sullivan brings the familiar '20 things' list:

20 things you never knew about Rolls Royce

(*Daily Mirror*, 4 May)

20 things cue didn't know about Ronnie O

(*Daily Star*, 5 May)

In its more middle-brow fashion the *Daily Mail* brings its readers a front page advertisement for its spring guide to hay fever:

Your A–Z guide to beating hay fever

(*Daily Mail*, 4 May)

The *Daily Mirror* each Saturday continues in the style of listing, as it has a regular feature, 'Sound Bites – The week in quotes', which includes snapshots of 'Hero of the week' and 'Villain of the week'. On 1 May the hero was HMS Trafalgar sonar operator James Metcalf, who refused to return to the 'death trap' nuclear submarine, and the villain was Tory leader Michael Howard, who had been scare-mongering on the subject of European integration.

Tabloid as actor in the news

The tabloids are keen to be seen by their readers as themselves playing a prominent part in making the news. Part of this process is to single out individuals for their own distinct brand of populist praise. This can take the form of the tabloid salute, as in the case of the one-legged marine Jim Bonney:

Captain Courage, we salute you.

(*Sun Says*, 25 May)

There is almost an echo of imperial Rome in this exhortation and the 'salute' is a common expression in the tabloids, especially the *Sun* when an individual achieves their ultimate respect. 'Saluting' characters which it selects from the everyday is a tabloid speech act which demonstrates how involved the newspapers are in activating news stories which foreground themselves as protagonists as much as the personalities they single out for praise.

There is nothing more indicative of the nature of tabloid rivalry as protagonists in their own news agenda than when the different newspapers begin to criticize each other. The faked photographs purporting to be from Iraq were one recent moment where one tabloid and its editor in particular became the news. The *Sun* called on the *Daily Mirror* to '**Say sorry**'. Claiming that the editor had 'turned it into a laughing stock' … it demanded in a double display of righteousness that:

In the interests of fair and accurate journalism, Trinity Mirror should admit it was wrong.

And apologize to our troops.

(*Sun*, 7 May)

This style of criticism forms part of a tradition of historic disputes between these two newspapers in times of armed conflict (Chippendale and Horrie, 1992: 123–4). Under the headline 'BLOOD MONEY' the *Daily Star* 7 May highlights the profits that *Daily Mirror* has made from publication of the photographs because of their impact on circulation.

It comes then as no surprise to read of the delight of the *Daily Star* when the editor of the *Mirror* is 'frogmarched' out of his office and out of his job.

MIRROR EDITOR IS AXED

Fake torture pictures became recruiting ground for al-Qaida say Army top brass

SHAMED Daily Mirror editor Piers Morgan. ... **The disgraced boss ... slurred their men ... frogmarched ...**

(*Daily Star*, 15 May)

The sacking of the *Daily Mirror*'s editor, Piers Morgan, was the most indicative example of how the events within the tabloid world can be drawn upon within other tabloids in a celebration of the importance of their own affairs within their own news agendas. Such coverage also places the *Daily Mail* firmly in the tabloid camp. If you're a tabloid then you are into the finer points of rivalry and mockery of those you identify as your rivals. This explains the mocking delight within the article on Morgan's sacking. It gleefully reports that he was:

frogmarched out. ...

The egomaniac editor who was brazen, bold and fatally flawed.

CONTEMPLATING how Piers Morgan would have covered the news of Piers Morgan's demise is intriguing. How about: 'End of the Piers Show'? Or: 'Snap, Crackle, Pop – Ed Axed in Fake Photo Storm'?

(*Daily Mail*, 15 May)

More often though the tabloids act explicitly as definers of the news agenda in the way they launch and maintain campaigns. Campaigns have a long history within all forms of journalism in Britain; the *Times*' 'thundering' for reform of the voting system in the 1830s to the *Daily Telegraph* on prostitution in the 1860s to the Maiden Tribute of Babylon in the *Pall Mall Gazette* of 1886. Today, campaigns remain an important part of the identity of the tabloids and their populist ambitions. The hyperbolic language of campaigns allows many of the linguistic and promotional features of these papers to be co-ordinated and attempts a popular involvement connected to the self-promotion of the paper.

On 3 May, the *Sun*, with the words, 'Thanks 4 everything', informs us that it has arranged for a luxury holiday for four ill boys before they undergo major surgery. Echoing the title of a popular television programme 'Jim'll Fix It' the *Sun* claims, 'We fixed it', and asks readers at the end of the report to contribute to a charity which researches the disease which the boys are suffering from. This links in with the 'heartwarming' phone connection of the interactive news desk agenda mentioned previously. It presents the benevolent *Sun* which has 'fixed it' in popular parlance acting on behalf of the 'sick' (twice) brothers who are simply described as 'brave'. In keeping with the anarchic existentialism of the 'other news' these boys are described as 'stricken'. Both elite 'doctors' and the readers of the *Sun* are participants in this charitable campaign. This sort of circular relationship between readers and newspaper constructs a communal identity, an 'interpretative community' (Fish, 1994) which is very much one of the tabloids' strengths.

At times, the campaign can feature a category of person already clearly demonized by previous scripts within the newspaper. All it needs to do is flick the semiotic switch and add a novel ingredient. In this case we have nine locations pictured in a typical tabloid mnemonic with clocks and timings.

TRAFFIC WARDENS GIVING MOTORISTS HELL

Who gives the quickest ticket?

(Daily Mirror, 15 May)

A mother uses the *Sun* to get a parking ticket withdrawn which she had been given for overstaying her limit while giving birth in the hospital. As well as being full of categories which fit the tabloid *dramatis personae*, cops, mums and traffic wardens, the paper also manages to indicate discreetly that it has itself intervened in a crusading fashion to help the woman to resolve her dispute against the bureaucracy:

> A Poole council spokesman told The Sun: 'We'll be happy to reconsider the case.'

(Sun, 6 May)

In another story along similar lines a reader in May draws on an exposé of over-zealous traffic wardens from the *Sun* in February to overturn a court decision. Here the newspaper is used as a material weapon in the campaign and is waved in triumph by the victorious reader.

Disabled OAP uses The Sun to beat fine

… Delighted Vashtine said: "I have to thank The Sun. Traffic wardens are a menace.

(Sun, 7 May)

The opponent to the victimized woman 'martyr' is characterized as a 'meanie council', in itself a minor classic of a compressed noun phrase, linking to reinforce a longer script on local councils whose genealogy can be traced at least to the campaigns in the popular press from the 1970s against the 'looney left' in London chronicled by James Curran (1987) and more recently by Curran, Gaber and Petley (2004).

Sometimes tabloids put their rivalry to one side and are unified in their rhetoric against a common enemy. On this occasion the hyperbole is prompted as their shared practices of intrusion and vilification appear to be threatened by a judgement in favour of Naomi Campbell against the *Daily Mirror*. They join in a chorus of self-interested warnings about threats to the freedom of the press which they purport to hold in high esteem.

Bodyblow to press freedom

(Daily Mirror, 7 May)

Naomi Campbell drove a stake through the heart of Press

(Daily Star, 7 May)

Political correctness is also a common enemy to the tabloids, given that they appear to perceive it as monitoring the use of language and possibly heightening public awareness of language abuses and discrimination expressed through language (Williams, 1995; Cameron, 1995). A Punch and Judy performer was banned from a school because of fears his portrayal of domestic violence was unsuitable and the condemnation fits neatly into the lexicon of the newspaper on such matters:

This is political correctness with a capital P and C, says puppeteer

(Daily Mail, 5 May)

The *Sun's* editorial on 25 May blames the 'Politically Correct Brigade' for the decision to remove a woman working on a course for young offenders because of her use of the word 'Petal'.

Sometimes even the typography can be used to highlight an emerging tabloid campaign in melodramatic fashion, as with the cross-page headlines, the use of the newspaper's logo alerting readers to the explicit association of campaign and paper and most frequent of all strong and evocative language as a paper sets out its stall in its campaigning, which leaves readers in no doubt about where the paper stands. In what turned out to be an extremely ill-advised strategy on the issue of the photographs purporting to show the abuse of Iraqi prisoners by British soldiers, the *Daily Mirror* (10 May) used a huge font to announce: '**FILTH**'.

The undercover investigation into a corrupt immigration officer is hailed:

SUN probe gets officer **BUSTED**

(*Sun*, 13 May)

The *Mail's* campaign on genetically modified foods provides a powerful rhetoric of popular involvement. Campaigns such as this are cut to fit the competitive space between the different newspapers and are editorially highly distinctive. It claims, capitalizing the modal verb, that involvement of the news-paper in this debate proves that 'ordinary people CAN defeat conglomerates and politicians' and announces in a tone not altogether in keeping with the general politics of the paper on other issues of social and political solidarity:

VICTORY FOR THE PEOPLE!

It features a series of self-referential former *Daily Mail* headlines: 'POLLUTED FOR GENERATIONS', 'THE SEEDS OF DECEIT', 'NIGHTMARE OF THE GM WEEDS' (*Daily Mail*, 12 May)

There can also be subtler, longer running and more oblique styles of campaign which blend with the broader values of a particular tabloid newspaper. At times one has to wonder whether there is a point to a particular story beyond the hyperbole and the need to conform to a sensationalist agenda. Yet often the hyperbole masks a script such as that which follows where there seems to be an oblique call for a return to simpler, less complicated times. The implication being that the modern world is too complicated. New rules for postage charges draw the assertion in the *Daily Mail* of 15 May that 'SENDING a letter will require a maths degree if plans for a shake-up of the postal system' are implemented, and the report comes complete with a mathematical formula sketched onto an envelope as illustration of the alleged absurdity of the new system.

The *Daily Mirror* on 18 May takes issue with the expense of new consultancy work which purports to elicit what patients want from the NHS.

THE PATIENT EXPERIENCE DEFINITION

It points out that the cost of stating the obvious was £625 per word or, even more pointedly, £40,000, and this is calculated to be the wages of two nurses for a year.

Campaigns link with other areas of tabloid agendas, not only the hotly disputed moral or political. Here we have a key, low-brow populist campaign complete with supportive and integrative quotations. Building a picture of a lost English idyll, the *Sun* launches a campaign to save deckchairs at Blackpool which are threatened characteristically by a 'tourism big-wig':

WE RESCUE A BRITISH SEASIDE FAVOURITE

Page 3 Girls are enlisted to make the Churchillian point: 'Nikkala, from Greenford, Middlesex said: "We fought 'em on the beach and won. Getting rid of the chairs was a crackpot idea …" ', and once again a reader is quoted in congratulatory support which links the bastion of British culture with the role of the newspaper in striving to maintain it as a patriotic gesture.

> Sunbather Paul Allan… "This is our culture – and The Sun is right to protect it."
>
> (*Sun*, 18 May)

Campaigning for their own populist variety of justice is a favourite *leitmotif* for the tabloids. At its most effective such campaigning can combine populist language and address to politicians as well as various forms of inter-activity each time a tragic story is covered by the paper. This is highlighted in the possessive adjective which leads off this particular example, and later on readers are provided with a *pro forma* letter to write to the politician responsible:

OUR CAMPAIGN FOR JUSTICE

NAIL THE DANGER DRIVERS SUN CAMPAIGN FOR JUSTICE

Dear Mr Blunkett …

This careless driver killed a mum-to-be and her unborn daughter … his punishment

£1,250 FINE

(*Sun*, 21 May)

The agenda setting of the tabloids can often invoke recent memory as an implicit call to action. It is interesting to consider in the following exactly who believes that fears of unrest may be sparked and whether the tabloids might play any role in heightening that possibility themselves by their style of reporting. There is in this case a disassociation of the petrol price from wider politics and the global security situation.

DRIVERS' FURY AS PETROL PRICES HIT RECORD HIGH

FURIOUS drivers faced record petrol prices last night, sparking fears of more fuel protests

(*Daily Star*, 14 May)

The *Daily Mail* of 15 May refers to its own story of the previous Thursday, 'Summit on "petrol panic" ', and has quotes highlighted in the article – 'Grimmer than in 2000' and 'Jittery about civil unrest' – as the report reviews the protests of 2000. While in the *Daily Star* the 'you' of the piece is an indication of the implicit ideological bond in such campaigns, implying an almost atavistic individualism. The agentless verb "emerged" displays a disembodied flow of communication which may heighten the sense that this is information which is never directly transmitted to people by politicians but which leaks from the system.

SPEND OF THE ROAD

Motor tax costs you £1,600

BRITISH families pay an average £1,678 in motoring taxes a year, it emerged yesterday.

(*Daily Star*, 21 May)

Finally, in a report in the *Daily Mail* on the installation of new speed cameras, we have once again the ordinary people as victims of underhand politicians and tax-gatherers acting almost in a robber-baron mode. The common and anonymous people are pitted against a named official with the common people portrayed as victims – and the newspaper discursively on their side:

1,000 new cameras set to trap drivers

… Richard Brunstrom, the man behind the controversial cash-for-cameras offensive … further misery to beleaguered motorists …

(*Daily Mail*, 25 May)

Conclusion

This chapter has considered the ways in which rhetorical features are used in the popular tabloids and combined to generate a tone specific to their market ambitions to appeal to a particular section of newspaper readers. The patterning of these features plays a big part in providing the ideological cohesion important for any newspaper's sense of editorial identity. With the tabloids, this identity is predicated on an exclusively populist set of assumptions about their target audience. A systematic examination of these linguistic features across a range of common themes will enable us to identify patterns in the routine representation of important aspects of the dominant, naturalized articulation of the version of contemporary Britain inscribed in these newspapers.

3 The semantics and narratives of nation

Having considered how the language of the tabloids is composed of its own range of rhetorical devices, designed to appeal to a particular readership, we can now move on to see how that rhetoric is deployed to provide a relatively consistent view of the national community which it seeks to reinforce. Stability must be achieved against what is in reality a volatile cultural background: 'while representing itself as fixed, natural and eternal, national identity is continually in process' (Brookes, 1999: 249). While agreeing broadly with Schlesinger (1991a; 1993), who has cautioned against claims for any direct relationship being posited between the media and national identity, this study aims to show less the effects rather than the attempts to construct that community of readers; what the readers do with that textual construction and its wider social and cultural effects are, as usual, the business of the readers themselves. This community, because all the tabloids are explicitly proclaiming themselves as its champions, gains further textual cohesion through the cross-media concentration on its symbols and themes which can be seen across their pages. Daily newspapers and most explicitly the popular tabloids can be observed performing a crucial semiotic role in cementing the national form (Law, 2001: 299). This chapter will consider moments when the lexicon of the nation is presented in a 'banal' fashion (Billig, 1995), enabling it to retain a background but daily presence as one of the key structuring norms of the newspapers. This study therefore seeks to move away from a reification of the nation to an engagement with the dynamics of discourse construction within the tabloids. In addition, it will examine moments when nationalism explodes into vigorous prominence on specific occasions which are central to the nation itself and overwhelmingly endorsed by the tabloids.

The link between nation and language is a crucial one. Benedict Anderson has written that it was the style of representation, principally in print, which allowed the modern nation to become a plausible construct rather than any concrete reality (1987). The diurnality of news and its creation of nation require a simultaneity of experience to build the abstract empathy necessary for nation to be imagined in the text of a newspaper and its projected audience (Anderson, 1987: 30). As any ideology, a sense of nation needs institutional support and if it is to spread it must be organized through specific channels of communication (Mann, 1996). This essential link between language and nation which the daily press provides is encapsulated in Billig's observation: 'Just as a language will die for want of regular users, so a nation must be put to daily use' (Billig, 1995: 95). This still holds true today in the language of the tabloids, as this language of representing and addressing a national community is a very large part of their appeal. Tabloid Britain is something which is based on an appeal to the imagined community of its readers. One reason for this remains a market motivation: the importance of national audiences even within the global network of communications as both newspapers and nations depend for their continued success on a 'daily plebiscite' (Renan, 1990: 19).

Nationalist news media have an important if paradoxical role in the contemporary global environment as, it must be stressed, the nationalist-orientated tabloids are in turn a part of global media corporations themselves. They fit one of the defining patterns of contemporary identity formation in the intensified awareness of difference brought about by the latest phase of globalization in which: 'The driving imperative is to salvage centred, bounded and coherent identities ... it is about the maintenance of protective illusion, about the struggle for wholeness and coherence through continuity' (Robins and Morley, 1995: 122). This is particularly true of popular media such as the tabloids whose political economy serves to hold together cultural continuities as markets in a time of fragmentation and cultural fragility (Alabarces *et al.*, 2001: 663). The comments of Brass on how national identity can be created by organized elites within specific societies have great resonance with the political economy of the tabloid press in Britain. He writes:

> Ethnicity and nationalism are not 'givens' but are social and political constructs. They are creations of elites, who draw upon, distort, and sometimes fabricate materials from the cultures of groups they wish to represent in order to protect their well being or existence or to gain political and economic advantage for their groups as well as themselves.
>
> (Brass, 1991: 8)

Yet the content of these papers must be based within the parameters of what a national readership is willing to recognize as belonging to its own narratives and traditions of nation. National news may exist within global communications conglomerates, but it needs a strong local resonance for its continued success. Tabloid Britain is not created as an elitist intellectual activity but as part of a populist, market-driven engagement with the pre-existing myths and language of a popular nation.

News values – the elite British nation

The vast majority of newspapers are sold on a national basis, have a strong national bias to their news values and in Billig's words, 'flag the homeland daily' (1995). Yet this bias is even more pronounced in the tabloids as they exaggerate the nationally specific, while in the main ignoring international news. Some have observed this as one of the defining features of the tabloid newspaper (McLachlan and Golding, 2000). The only exception is when it has a very obvious connection to the dominant British news agenda.

A typical example would be when the global threat of terrorist attack only becomes a significant item when it emerges that according to a report Britain is not braced for attacks on its own territory. Then it is dealt with in characteristic, punchy, hyperbolic style.

OUTDATED, INCOHERENT, IRRESPONSIBLE

TERROR CHAOS

BRITAIN'S plans to deal with a major terrorist strike were last night condemned as outdated.

(*Daily Mirror*, 15 May)

The scripts implicit in foreign coverage when it does break into the tabloids are straightforward. The coverage of overseas news is so rare that it can only be read in terms of other agendas such as when a form of 'Little Englanderism' is at its most marked. Hall has pointed out the complex associations around the nation and the popular in the context of Britain's imperial history, which have implications for the tabloids' appropriation of these terms, particularly in relation to overseas news: 'it is exceedingly hard, given the history of imperialism to disinter the idea of "the British people" from its nationalistic connotation' (Hall, 1981: 34). As an illustration of this tendency, we can read how in the following example, the *Sun* is drawn to echo agreement of the words of Tony Blair, a rare enough event in itself. It reinforces the image of Africa as blighted and unresponsive to Western help and unable to contribute to the wealth of the developed world. Its triple repetition of 'too' underlines what a mean response this is. The *Sun* is with the Prime Minister, at least when he is hectoring the poverty of an Africa devoid of any meaningful historical context and criticized in terms of its lack of contribution to post-colonial affluence.

It still has too many dictators, too much poverty, too many dying of Aids.

Anything that can be done for Africa not only makes life better for millions, it also has the selfish benefit of increasing world trade and increasing security.

(*Sun*, 5 May)

This fits the Manichaean worldview of the tabloids within a post-colonial perspective illustrating how:

The dependent peoples … reappear as the starving peoples of the Third World, passive and waiting for the technology or the Aid to arrive. … They are not represented as the subjects of a continuing exploitation or dependency, or the global division of wealth and labour. They are the Victims of Fate.

(Hall, 1981: 42)

'Brits' and 'Britons' are common, collective tags which reinforce the national community in populist form. Their usage is overall a strong indicator of newsworthiness in the tabloids. This holds true whether used in a story of international significance covered in the rest of the press or in a more trivial affair made newsworthy only because of national interest and the 'Brit' tabloid tag.

One of the primary uses of the term 'Brit' comes in a military context with contemporary references to British involvement in Iraq much to the fore:

'Battered' after arrest by Brits

(*Daily Mirror*, 8 May)

BRIT PICS FURY GROWS

(*Sun*, 6 May)

The implicit hostility of a world divided in populist terms between the Brits and the rest, with all the political condensation that implies, fits well with the simple binaries of tabloid news. It sometimes moves into a fully explicit model as in the following example with the associated agenda attached to the word 'backlash'. The antipathy explicit here between the 'Brit' and the 'foreign' will always be newsworthy given the importance of the national/communal to the agenda of the tabloids and the fact that national identity always seems to be enhanced by any form of conflict:

FED-UP Brits are leading a backlash against foreign call centres.

(*Daily Star*, 14 May)

A blackmail attempt in a Los Angeles supermarket which would otherwise not have qualified because it is relatively unimportant and has happened overseas, can suddenly find itself promoted in the interests of readers' nationalist orientation in their news diet because the protagonists are 'Brits'.

BRIT LACED BABY FOOD WITH ACID

(*Daily Star*, 8 May)

The story highlights this national perspective throughout, going on to refer to the 'British girlfriend' and once again the main protagonist as 'The Briton'.

Likewise, a health story can gain added importance because of its association with this absolutely key agenda-setting word. This recalls the way in which health scares can be used in the tabloids to construct an image of a nation defined through its health problems (Brookes, 1999).

4,000 BRITS INFECTED BY MAD COW VIRUS

(*Sun*, 21 May)

THOUSANDS OF BRITS MAY CARRY vCJD BUG

(*Daily Mirror*, 21 May)

The tabloid mnemonic of listing can contribute to the portrayal of national identity as part of the direct address to the imagined community. In a piece on the contribution of famous immigrants to British culture, the *Daily Mail* uses the enlargement of the EU to flag up how Britain has welcomed and nurtured its immigrants. It is a highly selective and retrospectively flattering view of Britain. It uses a heart symbol, lists ten rich and famous immigrants, and uses the word 'Briton' to refer to the indigenous population who can in turn be proud of their country.

We ♥ Britain

We asked ten famous representatives of the new EU countries why they settled here. Every Briton will be proud of the answers.

(*Daily Mail*, 3 May)

Loyalty to army as loyalty to Britain

The battle for the hearts and minds of the British community of tabloid readers is not static and shifts considerably between papers over time, demonstrating how 'National identity more adequately describes the *process of identifying* with the nation' (Brookes, 1999: 248). One constant in the contemporary tabloids is that they all swear allegiance to the virtues of patriotism and are unequivocal about the bravery of British soldiers abroad. The differences between competing newspapers in the reporting of pictures allegedly of British soldiers abusing Iraqi prisoners of war demonstrate just how this loyalty to the British armed forces is constructed as such an active process. During the main sampling period for the research for this study, the Iraq conflict was the dominant political story. For some of the tabloids, the post-conflict occupation with its heavy dependence on British troops provided a litmus test for patriotism. For the *Sun* and the *Daily Star* the message was clear: an unequivocal support for both the invasion and the occupation especially where it concerned the British troops. The *Sun* was the first to jump to the defence of British soldiers accused of abusing Iraqi prisoners:

FRAMED

Brit soldiers 'torture' pics fake, say experts

(*Sun*, 3 May)

It followed this early defence with a full-blown celebration of 'A nation's heroes' on its front page, with a picture of a soldier against a Union Jack background. Inside, it recounts how this flag flies in Iraq, the Falklands, Belize, Ulster, the Artic and Australia, and 'flutters on ships plying every ocean and sea'. Building to a crescendo it adds:

> And it is The Sun's duty as Britain's biggest-selling daily paper to give them this message:
>
> **You all have the full support of the people of Britain**
>
> (*Sun*, 8 May)

In addition to the rhetoric of tabloid recognition, 'We salute you', its ultimate token of esteem already identified in the previous chapter, we see here a set of explicitly imperialist echoes which locate Britishness very much within a post-imperial glow of satisfaction. Despite its patriotic/military lexis, it is still odd to consider that a tabloid newspaper has explicit duties beyond its legal and economic responsibilities. It is perhaps testimony to the implacable seriousness of the theme that no irony can be detected here. This is clearly represented by the tabloid press as a whole as one of their fundamental responsibilities and none seems willing to go any distance to query it.

The *Daily Star* of 7 May is also adamant that support for British troops is unequivocal, personifying their heroism by the highlighting of the 'face of courage' of a 'magnificent soldier', killed in action in Iraq, and positing his bravery against those who 'berate and belittle' the troops. They too use 'We salute them' as a collective gesture of recognition, spoken on behalf of an imagined readership. However the *Daily Mail* of 3 May is more ambivalent about rumours of abuse coming out of Iraq, and strives to qualify support for the British soldiers with a reaffirmation of doubts about the political decisions which took them there and have kept them there:

> if they are false, it will be impossible to underestimate the gratuitous damage done to the reputation of the British Army.

It is more committed to using the Iraqi conflict to combine several editorial scapegoats, the Labour administration, European legislation and an 'ambulance-chasing', 'poison-tongued solicitor' into an assault on the trust of 'Our fighting forces' on 6 May:

> New Labour is today facing the consequences of its own crass decision to embrace the European Convention of Human Rights with open arms and incorporate it into British law.

There is in the *Daily Mail* a distinct edge to the patriotism which proclaims loyalty to the armed forces while taking every opportunity to take government and solicitors to task for their betrayal of the intrinsic and unquestioned bravery of 'our fighting forces'. The loyalty to troops as an indicator of loyalty to the nation so central to the ethos of the tabloids is also transferable over to opinion on other issues relating to national sovereignty, such as the European import of the Human Rights Act. Columnist Max Hastings reinforces this on the same day with powerful hyperbole in his opinion column comparing the employment of the Human Rights Act into military affairs to be:

> like inviting a Wimbledon umpire to adjudicate in Nero's Coliseum.

The *Daily Star* on 11 May also takes the high moral and patriotic ground and makes the most of associating itself with heroes, pointing out the unpatriotic nature of the 'lying *Daily Mirror*', a 'shabby newspaper' which it claims is 'stabbing our brave troops in the back', implying that it is acting in a cowardly way. This is a perfect rhetorical ploy to score points against a tabloid rival and has a long tradition within tabloid coverage of conflict. The tabloid which provoked the political and journalistic row in the first place, the *Daily Mirror*, through the publication of the photographs which purported to show British abuse of Iraqi detainees, very carefully seeks to maintain its own position of patriotic loyalty despite having cast aspersions on the actions of a minority of the British soldiers. The language of its coverage is carefully crafted to maintain that statement of loyalty, claiming the revelations were part of its patriotic 'duty', and reaffirms its pride in the British army, arguing that the publication of the photos will help prevent the whole of the occupying forces' reputation becoming tarnished.

The 'Voice of the Daily Mirror' editorial on 4 May uses the cumulative rhetoric of national pride to rationalize its revelations concerning the alleged abuse of Iraqi prisoners:

> Why those pictures had to be shown
>
> ... Just as national pride swells when our forces perform great acts of heroism, so we feel badly let down when they behave like this. ...
>
> *It is not in the interests of this country, the army, the regiment or other newspapers to say this is not a true and proper cause for concern and investigation.*

The explicit nation

Greenfield (1992) sees the idea of a 'sovereign people' particularly evident in what she considers to be the first paradigm of modern nationalism, the English variant, and given this longevity of associations around the distinctiveness of the English nation, it is therefore unsurprising that it can draw upon a range of myths and symbols with at least an aura of ancient authenticity. It is certainly a set of images and narratives which the tabloids draw upon enthusiastically. The flag of St George appears in a variety of relatively banal, everyday contexts in the contemporary tabloids. It is as common a sight on the front pages accompanying stories about the EU as it is on the back pages when following the fortunes of English sports teams. There was recently even one example which contributed to the general knowledge of the readership of the *Daily Mail* on the queries page of that paper on 8 May, illustrated by a photograph of England's World Cup-winning rugby captain, Dallaglio, holding up the said flag.

Answers to Correspondents

Flagging up the traditions of our country

Question: What are the origins of the flag of St George?

The *Sun* on 24 May showed the England football team flying off to the European Championship preparations with their children, 'Lion cubs', and had the cross of St George filling in the 'o' in 'lion'. It is only because of the constant presence of such an iconography and symbolism that the tabloids can move into a more explicit mode on set occasions, in full confidence that they are articulating sentiments which are familiar to their readers. There is no better example of this than on the annual round of St George's Day celebrations. The *Sun* and the *Daily Star* in particular share a desire to see this day become a formally recognized celebration of English identity or even a national holiday, and use all of their rhetorical resources to campaign for it. On 23 April the *Sun* calls upon its readers to:

CELEBRATE YOUR NATION TODAY

The newspaper calls on *vox pop* pieces representing a snapshot of 'patriotic Sun readers' including a cab driver, a grocer and a policeman, from Carlisle to Chichester, in an interesting circularity to stress how:

You back St George Campaign

The paper exploits its Page 3 culture ('SAINT GORGEOUS DAY') by featuring two women posing and transferring a metaphor into the literal in the 'NEWS IN BRIEFS' section as they proclaim they are 'proud to wrap themselves in the English flag'. Trevor Phillips, head of the Commission for Racial Equality, an organization often castigated in the pages of the *Sun* on other occasions, is called upon to give a key-note commentary on the significance of the day: 'we are a nation of many faces and many faiths, but being English binds us together'. His piece is the main feature of a centre page spread with flags and mini-interviews with school children under the headline:

I ♥ MY COUNTRY

Equally patriotic but more self-consciously vulgar, the *Daily Star*, with the double entendre characteristic of popular British comedy, proclaims:

It's Saint PHWOARge's Day

IT'S St George's Day, girls, so get your flags out!

It then points out that 'patriotism can have its advantages' and introduces the best of 'the nation's fave fellas … cream of the English crop … our hottest hunks'. Aware of its reputation and making the most of its popular vulgarity the *Daily Star* announces the gift of a free St George's Day flag in the paper and calls on readers:

STICK IT IN YOUR WINDOW AND BE LOUD 'N PROUD

In the tradition of the tabloids, what better way to encapsulate everything which the *Daily Star* wants to emphasize about the day than with a self-congratulatory list which includes:

10 REASONS TO BE PROUD

1   Winning the Rugby World Cup …
4   Fish and chips …
6   William Shakespeare …
9   Everyone speaks our language so we don't have to learn theirs
10 The Daily Star

In its editorial that day the *Daily Star* uses the national celebrations of its selection of ordinary readers and 'patriots' to contrast with growl concepts such as 'officialdom', 'asylum seekers', 'poets' and 'lesbians' in a powerful statement of national exclusivity as pride in a community which has forged an identity from the lower sections of a patriotic society. The repetition of the word 'we' amplifies this sense of a community of the 'ordinary folk', those outsiders to the 'power bloc' (Fiske, 1992) which is very much a part of the ideological consensus that insists that the nation is represented as coming from below, from the common people themselves (Seton-Watson, 1977):

Together we created the world's greatest democracy and fought wars to defend it.

We've produced men and women who've shaped this planet in every conceivable way …

officially, we don't do a damn thing.

It's left to ordinary folk to get out the bunting, hoist up the flag of St George and organise a knees-up.

Lottery grants are thrown at asylum seekers, daft poets and lesbian support groups.

But not a penny goes to those who shout for England. ...

Ashamed for once having an Empire, for being prosperous, for having military might.

Well, the Daily Star and our readers are not ashamed – in fact, we're brimming with pride.

One key point here is the way the use of the pronoun 'we' suggests a conjunction of the newspaper and its readership in an 'implied consensus' of national community (Fowler, 1991: 189). As the campaign for St George's Day has become more prominent in public life, so too has the flag and its potential to act as an ideal rallying point for tabloids to demonstrate their nationalist credentials within this linguistic framework. The *Daily Star* picks a fight opportunistically with the flag as its battle-ground to emphasize its place at the head of the patriotic tabloid pecking order. It appears that some pub landlords had been instructed to ban the display of the flag of St George. In the ensuing campaign, the *Daily Star* works around a set of binary distinctions: loyal fans and patriots against the pub bosses, women and louts. The story broke on the front page and was reinforced by the rhetorical listing of the argument as a set of bullet points.

PUBS BAN OUR FLAGS

Cross of St George 'too offensive' say bar bosses

- Pub bosses have banned the England flag from a chain of sports bars during next month's Euro 2004 football championship.
- They claim the flag of St George offends women drinkers and might attract louts.
- But the decision has angered loyal England fans.

(*Daily Star*, 20 May)

When the ban is finally lifted it is translated into the language of the football result. The newspaper has been able to create a rhetorical bond with its readers in its campaign and the language of inclusivity emphasizes this. Finally the paper has justified its right to chant 'In-ger-land' with the fans of the popular game.

We're No1 for football

DAILY STAR ... 1

PUB KILLJOYS ... 0

We're a winning team

The Daily Star named and shamed a pub chain that had barred the English flag during Euro 2004.

You responded with howls of outrage at the decision ...

the irresistible force of The Daily Star and our readers in action ...

So get those flags waving and let's hear you shouting: In–ger–land
(*Daily Star*, 21 May)

Europe as a common external opponent

Hyperbole concerning the EU is threaded through with emotive language and scripted agendas alluded to economically in a demotic, populist tone of persuasion. This can be employed across the tabloid spectrum from the *Sun* to the *Daily Mail*. In the *Sun*, an opinion poll conducted among employers in Britain is presented under the headline,

BOSSES: EUROPE ISN'T WORKING

The interpretation is that 'failing' Brussels ... is a threat to wealth and jobs and that:

Bosses fear the EU is bad for business and want its bureaucrats banned from having any influence in the boardroom.

(*Sun*, 28 April)

The *Daily Mail* picks up on a comment from European Trade Minister Pascal Lamy which suggested that Britain could end up in a 'rearguard' of insignificant nations if it did not sign up to the EU constitution. He is referred to disparagingly as a 'Eurocrat', a non-British bureaucrat with the accumulation of negative implications throughout the rest of the newspaper's discourse on both bureaucracy and Europe. This emphasizes how the comment should be interpreted as a deliberate insult to the British:

Eurocrat's swipe at Britain

(*Daily Mail*, 3 May)

On occasion the EU can be used more subtly as a counterpoint to the policies of the government on asylum and immigration. On this occasion, the *Daily Mail* cherry picks arguments from a political organization which the newspaper is usually only too quick to criticize. The occasion is the expansion of the EU and in celebrating the enrichment this will bring, it employs the opportunity to foreground criticisms of the government and those eager to exploit the systems supported by British taxpayers. The benefits of economic migration are contrasted to the familiar rhetorical threats of those who 'leech off the state' and the failings of the government's reform of 'our sclerotic benefits system':

> But there will be others who will be less welcome in Britain … those who see our benefits system as a soft touch − those who prefer to leech off the state.
>
> This week, at the eleventh hour, Mr Blair finally seemed to wake up to this harsh reality. But mustn't New Labour take its share of the blame?
>
> It has failed to reform our sclerotic benefits system and, unlike almost every other EU state, did not send out a clear message that those arriving without jobs could expect no support.
>
> (*Daily Mail*, 1 May)

The ideal pairing of the EU and an intrusive bureaucrat in the condensed political representation characteristic of the tabloids provides one powerful hate figure of an EU bureaucrat. This is built upon by its coupling within a *Sun* campaign which adds the final insult by implying that he is worse than traffic wardens. This is perhaps the ultimate insult in the context of this newspaper's characterization of traffic wardens as pathological bullies and meddlers. It starts with a restrained but vernacular command to the EU:

Clear off, EU

The report claims that a European directive will seek to impose random breath tests on British drivers, yet points out that there are far lower levels of road death in Britain than in many other countries of the EU. The official who has proposed this is alienated in the language used to present him:

GIVE a pumped-up EU bureaucrat an inch and he will try to take a mile.

The British driver is represented as 'already over-taxed and harassed by zealot parking wardens and speed cameras' and raises the spectre of a European nanny state, 'Doesn't Europe trust us to do **ANYTHING?**', before turning to a parochial Little Englanderism in its final command:

It's time you lectured the Greeks and the Portuguese, not us.

(*Sun*, 24 May)

What is not as predictable in the following example is that this is the *Daily Mirror*, which is normally more measured on European issues, taking advantage of the Eurovision Song Contest to strike an anti-European corruption note.

Predictable as ever, the Eurovision song con ...

WHAT A LOAD OF BALTICS!

... The Greeks don't vote for us. The Elgin marbles can get the blame for that.

We can't count on Spain or Iceland, which we can blame on Gibraltar and the cod wars ...

(*Daily Mirror*, 17 May)

The language of the criticism of the European Union in the following example, as something narrated as being profoundly at odds with the interests of the British people, includes the weight of corrupt politicians, the EU and MEPs counterpoised to the plight of overburdened British taxpayers. Once again, the little people whose interests the *Sun* claims to articulate are inscribed in the rhetoric of this piece as the authentic inhabitants of the imagined community of tabloid Britain. The cumulative effect of the following litany of insult is a powerful assault and comes combined with the traditional impact of a tabloid investigation which singles the issue out for more serious attention than is normally offered in these newspapers for foreign news:

SUN INVESTIGATION: Brit MEPs digging deep in EU expenses trough

ALL ABOARD GRAVY TRAIN

Today we expose the greed of Britain's Euro MPs whose expenses claims are costing taxpayers a fortune.

Dozens of snout-in-the-trough politicians are accused of 'clocking on' at the European Parliament for a cash handout then leaving quickly ... fat cats ... scamb ... vast army of MEPs, hangers-on and translators ...

(*Sun*, 13 May)

National decline

Narrative is very much at the heart of Bhabha's analysis of the construction of the nation, but just as important as the narrative itself is the imperative to ensure that it acts: 'to produce the idea of the nation as a continuous narrative in national progress' (1990: 1). To this end, even alerting the collective community to anxieties of decline fits with a sort of progress or a desire for it as fundamental to the continuity of the narrative of a nation with all its peaks and troughs. They too provide a marker of hope in the transcendence of the nation (Hall, 1992) through adversity. For all of their patriotic pride, the tabloids are quick to jump on various populist bandwagons. One of these claims that the country is in decline. It fits with many of the scripts of a community under attack from various forces within and without. It is therefore no surprise to read a report which quantifies the disillusioned of the national community. It is once again led by the tag of 'Brit'.

HALF OF BRITS WANT TO QUIT UK

(*Sun*, 28 April)

The otherwise patriotic *Daily Mail* is quick to develop the idea of an 'alcohol-sodden Britain'. Reporting on government proposals to extend licensing laws to allow round the clock drinking, the headline is representative of the general hyperbole of the piece and predictably enough it is the politicians who it is claimed will be to blame with their insistence that more flexible opening hours will allow round-the-clock licenses for pubs and clubs.

Bingeing Britain

… drunken yobs and bloodied brawls, young girls vomiting in the gutter, raucous disorder, an atmosphere of menace …

(*Daily Mail*, 12 May)

The *Daily Mirror* (21 May) joins in with the narrative of declining public behaviour by embroidering upon Blair's warning:

BOOZE IS THE NEW BRITISH DISEASE

Perceived threats to national stability appear to trigger a range of narratives which act as a cry for assistance in maintaining the resilience of the national community under attack. The merest whiff of rising fuel prices is enough for the *Daily Star* on 15 May to recall 'nationwide blockades' and to provide a handy set of archive photos to prompt memories of previous fuel protests. Here, it is keen to build up a set of expressions which indicate the imminence of military intervention. Despite the air of panic and the implied danger of martial law, the next chapter in the fuel protest never took place.

TROOPS will be ordered onto the streets to smash petrol protests under secret plans drawn up by ministers.

Sport is another area which allows narratives of national decline to flourish, despite the inflated expectations of the country's sportsmen and women in the tabloids. Hobsbawm has seen them as 'primary expressions of their imagined communities' (1992: 143). Sport can also act as a style of commemoration similar to the long-established ceremonies that can perform a 'symbolic reaffirmation of national greatness … a collective longing for past glories … a requiem' (Cannadine, 1993: 105). Not only do defeats on the field act as part of a narrative of threat and decline for a nation constructed as having such a strong historical tradition of victory, but also, off the field of play, British sports stars are seemingly perennial targets. Supporters of the national football team receive similar treatment. This was encapsulated in the characteristic treatment of the release of a film called *The Football Factory*, and its association in the *Sun* on 5 May with the problem of English football hooligans:

CAGED YOBS STAR IN FOOTIE MOVIE

… England have been warned the team will be expelled if the fans riot.

A couple of stories in the lead-up to the European football championships in 2004 indicate how the general sense of moral decline emphasized in the tabloids on a regular basis moves into more specific reporting on the behaviour of the English captain, David Beckham.

So is Beckham still fit to lead England?

(*Daily Mail*, 18 May)

The piece deals with Beckham's threatened refusal to talk to representatives of various national newspapers because of their coverage of his private life, and places it along with 'his most petulant tantrums', contrasting his stance with what the paper considers 'the duty of a national captain to give press conferences' and contrasting him with the demeanour of 'Steven Gerrard – as crew-cut and demonically old-fashioned as they come'. Clearly the latter places Gerrard favourably because he seems to be reminiscent of an older tradition, a more straightforward patriotic pride in country and with the bonus of a haircut to match! In another tabloid, Beckham is explicitly linked to the sort of moral decline reported on as a general British phenomenon elsewhere. A picture of the player during an angry altercation with a linesman stresses that this is 'no lager-fuelled yobbo from the terraces' but the English captain and insists from within the rhetoric of the collective community:

England expects better than this, Becks.

(*Sun*, 18 May)

The glow of a golden age is so much a part of the retrospective of a national narrative. It transfigures many representations of the contemporary state of the nation as an implicit call to recover past glories for the present. In the same edition of the *Sun* another explicit reminder of the putative ideals of a previous generation, a better time, are recalled for readers by drawing upon the most popular of football icons and one of the most famous of sporting moments, wondering what Bobby Moore would have made of it had he still been 'with us'. This was the English football captain of 1966 who had the presence of mind to wipe his hands before accepting the World Cup trophy from the Queen in what is clearly for the newspaper a sublime moment of deferential instinct and nobility on a par with Sir Walter Raleigh and his placing of his cloak at the feet of the first Queen Elizabeth.

A contradictory aspect of much of this reporting becomes apparent when the fans are treated appropriately to the way they are portrayed in the British press. The only objection, implicitly, is that they are being treated like this not by our own British police but by a foreign police force. In the *Daily Star* of 25 May there is a strong military association in the headline: '**BATTLE STATIONS**'. This is followed by a punning reference to the affliction which the English fans are said to be labouring under while wearing the national flag, which is consistently paraded in the tabloids as an absolutely integral part of English national identity: 'CROSS TO BEAR'. Resistance to this labelling as hooligans by outsiders culminates in the thuggish demotic expression 'Come on, if you think you're hard enough', emphasizing that, if nothing else, our hooligans are tougher than foreign riot police, in the opinion of the *Daily Star*. The response to this, reported in the same paper the following day, is '**FURY AT THUG TAG**'. The piece includes details of the phone lines being 'flooded' and a poll indicating that 86 per cent of readers believe that the police tactics intended to curb hooliganism will in fact trigger it.

Binary nation

National politics on the international stage is often reduced to a stand-off between binary choices or oppositions. There is little complexity to debate in this political universe, just a desire for quick solutions to match the shifting daily agendas of newspapers at the extreme end of the spectrum of sensational reporting and the daily attention span of its assumed readership. Tabloid coverage of such political machinations certainly makes no attempt to broker any of the complexity of world politics or reduce the amount of dependence on sound-bite political gestures. The 'them' and 'us' divide defines to a large extent the community which the tabloids are constructing. Building on its consistent criticism of the Labour government and its relationship with America, the *Daily Mail* of 8 May encapsulates the issue as: '**Blair's folly, America's shame**'.

In the *Sun* of 11 May, the photographs of desecrated graves are provocatively framed by the binary distinction between 'Arab fanatics' and the 'British war graves'. The vandalism is said to have been provoked by the publication of the torture photographs in the *Daily Mirror*. The impact of the story is highlighted by the amplification of descriptors, 'shocking', 'shocked' and 'sickening', leaving readers in no doubt what they are intended to infer. The story has the additional benefit of being able to reinforce the *Sun* as the patriotic and responsible paper and to condemn what it claims is the irresponsible behaviour of the *Daily Mirror* in its publication of what turned out to be faked photographs of abuse.

BRITISH war graves have been smashed and desecrated by Arab fanatics in revenge for the fake torture pictures.

The accumulated semantic significance between 'British troops' and 'Shia fanatics' – 'Brits battle Basra fanatics' in the *Daily Star* (10 May) maintains the divide between them and us and makes the task of understanding the world from a British perspective a much more troublesome one. Such binary divisions make the world a simpler place to understand, yet paradoxically a more difficult one to inhabit with any degree of empathy.

In many ways, the ideological compact between reader and tabloid is constructed as we have seen above, by the unswerving confidence in the loyalty and bravery of the British armed forces. The compact between reader, newspaper and community is expressed within a syntax of solidarity, and never more so than when dealing with British troops abroad.

FAKE PICS

Death threat to our brave boys in Iraq

(*Daily Star*, 4 May)

In this example the abbreviation/slang of the headline adds to the vernacular appeal of the outrage and the noun phrase compression into the familiar tag of 'our brave boys' cements the ideological compact between reader and newspaper. The *Daily Mirror* of 12 May takes up the offensive against Defence Secretary, Geoff Hoon, positing his 'smarmy lawyer's tactics' as a danger to 'our troops' and 'an insult to the British people', thus drawing in the imagined community into common cause with the soldiers who are clearly beyond the possibility of reproach against a member of the 'power bloc'.

TERROR NERVE GAS ATTACK ON TROOPS

TERRORIST fanatics ... sarin ... Nazi nerve gas

(*Daily Star*, 18 May)

The *Daily Star* here uses an emotive, historical reference to enable the gas to be located in popular cultural memory. In identifying the gas as 'Nazi' it immediately puts it into the same semantic territory into which Saddam Hussein had been placed by reference to the Nazi leader, Hitler (Keeble,

1997: 65–8). Such terms allow no fine distinctions and no argument and therefore short-circuit rational debate. The *Daily Star* also calls on the familiar rhetorical 'salute' and the communal identification of the soldiers as 'our brave boys'. Decca Aitkenhead, herself a journalist, has written perceptively of this tendency in the British news media, using identical terms for her critique: 'Our Brave Boys. Their Lunatics' (1999). Such slogans impair other possible interpretations of the soldiers, e.g. as employees of the British state or unquestioning servants of American imperialism. The repetition normalizes our expectations of their function in the rhetorical strategies of the tabloid press and the binarism of their opponents as 'Islamic fanatics' consolidates this polarity.

Salute our brave boys

… outnumbered five to one by Islamic fanatics …

(*Daily Star*, 18 May)

Football as popular national metaphor

In the build-up to the European football championships of 2004, individual English players are called upon to endorse the national ambition in military rhetoric, sometimes vague or attached to popular contemporary media cross references but sometimes couched in extremely specific historical terms. It is a practice which fits with Smith's claims that the press is essential in reinforcing and popularizing the elements of what he terms the 'myth–symbol complex' necessary for older forms of ethnically rooted nationalism (1986: 18).

DEFOE CAN LEAD SVEN TO GLORY

(*Daily Star*, 17 May)

Cole: We must dig deep to bury the French. … The phoney war began in earnest …

(*Daily Mirror*, 17 May)

Once David Beckham's wife agrees to a tabloid truce for the duration of the Euro 2004 competition, the well-known Victorian cliché is called into play:

And now – England expects

(*Sun*, 21 May)

In an interesting historical cocktail of imagery, Ericsson's team are represented as a team of '23 gladiators' in England shirts, with standards adorned by the cross of St George at their sides. Ericsson himself has 'all his weapons charged and fully loaded' (*Daily Mirror*, 18 May). The *Daily Mail* of 19 May chooses a much more specific historical reference when describing the

French midfield for the opening game as the 'Maginot Line' from World War II:

We will breach Maginot line, insist England

Readership as nation

On occasion, the tabloid's nation is addressed explicitly and this style of articulation clearly assists in the symbolic confirmation of the existence of this community. It confirms the suspicion that, 'a nation exists when a significant number of people in a community consider themselves to form a nation, or behave as if they form one' (Seton-Watson, 1977: 5). It must be stressed that the consent of the whole community is not necessary, merely a symbolic quorum. The following example is instructive in the way that language is used to create that direct address. The editorial from the *Sun* reports on proposals to create new laws to curb terrorism. The address to Britain as a nation draws parallels between the way that the issue is being dealt with in France. The capitalization of key moments of the argument for emphasis is a typographical feature of tabloid argumentation:

Don't worry, Britain, there IS a plan to deal with Muslim fanatics who live here.

... But hang on. These laws won't come in until AFTER a terrorist attack on our country. ...

We need to boot out the enemies in our midst, like Abu Hamza and Sheik Bakhri Muhammed, TODAY.

Before an outrage is committed.

If France can do it, so can we.

(*Sun*, 5 May)

In a different context, a campaign to control the rise of dangerous driving calls explicitly upon that same national community. The piece combines the rhetoric of nation with its articulation of the 'public anger' which is so often claimed to be the fuel of tabloid debate and meshes perfectly with populist claims of the tabloid to represent the public.

The nation demands proper justice.

(*Sun*, 26 May)

Here the national community is embodied rather than merely represented by the *Sun*. The readership becomes the ultimate rhetorical arbiter of the national good. The appeal to a national community blends easily with the tabloid campaigning style and helps the newspaper maintain that appeal across various parts of its editorial bringing a consistency to it. At moments like this, Britain is addressed as a very tangible community.

A day of shame for British justice

(*Daily Mail*, 6 May)

WHEN a copper is murdered on duty, the whole nation mourns
(*Sun*, 22 May)

In another example of explicit correlation of readers with the British people, the *Daily Mirror* confesses its own shortcomings to its audience and calls on the government to do the same:

SORRY … WE WERE HOAXED

… Our mission is to tell the truth.

That is something this newspaper has been doing for more than 100 years and will always strive to do so. If ever we fail, we are letting down the people who mean most to us. Our readers. …

It is not an honourable way to behave and is leading to growing disenchantment among the British people.

(*Daily Mirror*, 15 May)

National variation – Scotland

The nation is an almost exclusively English version of Britain in all of the popular tabloids apart from when they are being sold specifically to a regional audience within the UK. When it comes to covering the news in other constituent parts of Britain, the English-based tabloids are often keen to highlight a degree of national or regional specificity. The most fertile area for this is also that with the most developed infrastructure for national autonomy, namely Scotland. English-based tabloids 'cover themselves in Scottish paraphernalia and give a certain prominence to "Scottish issues" … a repertoire of Scottish signs and content' (Law, 2001: 304).

This is particularly noticeable when sport is being covered, as this has an already higher correlation to the specifics of nation. Sport in the tabloids sold in Scotland has an exclusively Scottish appeal reinforced by the vernacular of nicknames for the local football sides: Jags, Gers, Accies, Celts, Pars, Hibees, Hibs, Dons and Livi all feature prominently.

The *Daily Record* of 14 May, as part of a special series on 'Violence in Football', has a particularly Scottish angle:

HATED MAN IN FOOTBALL

It's not sectarian – it's just me says Lennon

Sectarian is not a word that would ring many bells in English sports coverage. Yet it is a distinct feature of discussions of football in Scotland, particularly in Glasgow. Lennon, a protestant from Northern Ireland, plays for Celtic with its traditionally Catholic fan base. The Scottish *Sun* of 20 May displays its local diversity by featuring a story about Rangers player Bob Malcolm, who had signed an autograph 'FTP' ('F★★★ The Pope') and provides a familiar tabloid list of similar cases of 'bigotry'.

Hard news has more of a local emphasis: 'Yob in drunken spree in Perth' is covered on 27 May by the *Sun* and the *Daily Record*. In another local variant to its English mainstream publication, the *Sun* on 13 May provides an exclusive and in-depth eight-page account with pictures and reports of the Stockline factory fire in Glasgow.

The use of a recognizably Scottish vernacular variant of tabloid language is evident as part of an enhanced regional appeal. For example, on the *Sun*'s front page of 21 May the tour of the Scottish Parliament is referred to twice as 'Parly'. However, it is Joan Burrie in the *Daily Record* on 28 May who shows how the Scottish-based tabloid can use an extended form of this demotic:

We are breeding a generation unlikely to survive their parents
... 'Every time I see some wee lard bucket waddling into school, I want to take his or her mother firmly by the neck and ask her what the hell she thinks she's doing allowing her kiddie to get to that size.'

The *Daily Record* demonstrates the political economy of a local–national press by the flagging of its own unique place in the symbolic landscape of Scottish popular media, complete with the paraphernalia and linguistics of tabloid promotion elsewhere:

Daily Record car stickers GOOD MORNING SCOTLAND

Welcome Back Folks

Our family of readers is growing

The Daily Record is the best-performing paper in Britain. Official.

... in March ... biggest rise of any national newspaper. ...

More and more of you are saying there is only one paper that truly reflects the values and opinions of real Scots. ...

We're No 1 because we give you unrivalled coverage of local, national and international events – written and edited from a Scottish perspective.

Last month we revealed the horror of elder abuse in Scotland's care industry and launched a campaign to root out the culprits. We travelled to China to expose the scandal of workers who are paid £1 a day to churn out expensive High Street lingerie ... big names in Scottish journalism ...

(*Daily Record*, 15 May)

The *Sun* demonstrates on its front page that the generic gender representation in the tabloids can be shifted into the specifics of national appeal with no problem and the *Daily Record* can also claim sexual notoriety for a local man:

Scots babe in good Nic for Telly

(*Sun*, 10 May)

A RANDY Scot entered the Big Brother house last night boasting that he had bedded 250 women.

(*Daily Record*, 29 May)

The Scottish tabloids still use the 'Brit' lexis when referring to Iraq, with the same tendency to categorize along British national lines against the common enemy of Iraqi insurgents, reduced to the familiar shorthand of 'fanatics'.

SCOTLAND'S thoughts are with the family of oil worker Michael Hamilton. ... Like other British workers ...

Scot shot dead by fanatics

(*Daily Record*, 31 May)

Conclusion

After drawing on theories from left and right, Spencer and Wollman (2002: 2) conclude that nationalism has no reserved place on the political spectrum other than one which is forever attended to by a high degree of ambivalence.

We have come to accept the arguments of those who suggest that fundamental to all forms of nationalism are processes of categorization that create and reproduce as enemies, strangers and others those who do not fit inside the nation, just as they also seek to provide a sense of 'deep horizontal comradeship' (Anderson, 1987: 7) for those who are included inside the nation.

The sort of material connection to the nation which Bauer (1996), for instance, identifies can only be grasped as transmitted through the language and narrative of identification with a specific place in time. The material connection between the language of the tabloid newspapers and the longer narratives of the nation provides an essential element in enabling the imaginary community of the nation to retain its cultural and political authority. As one commentator has observed, 'the only way that imagined community ... can be constructed in modern times, especially at short notice, ... [is] through the instantaneity of the media, press ...' (McGuigan, 2000: 13). The speed of this process in the accelerated flows of the current phase of globalized capitalist media culture is quite remarkable. Britain might be, in the words of Seton-Watson (1977), the oldest of 'old, continuous nations', but in its tabloid manifestation it is able to reformulate and revise itself at prodigious speed to retain its claims to authenticity in the modern world.

4 Tabloid history

Following on from discussion of the role which language concerning the nation plays in constructing an ideal reader community within the tabloids, we can move on to consider the ways in which the tabloids integrate a popular version of history into this language to ensure that the national community represented is not merely one suspended in a constant present but one which comes with all the authentic appeal of a national past and one which is negotiated on a daily basis with the readership through a variety of editorial and linguistic strategies. These strategies reinforce what Samuel has observed, acidly: 'The decline of nationality in the present, and the growing uncertainty about its future, have been offset by an enlarged sense of the national past' (Samuel, 1989: xlii). This process of galvanizing a national past as it is inscribed in the tabloids is key to the way that 'nations … are represented in the minds and memories of the nationalized subjects' (De Cillia *et al.*, 1999: 153). This chapter will consider what the implications of such a populist history are in forming a distinctive version of the British collective past.

Despite criticisms that tabloids do not engage often enough in locating news within historical contexts (Conboy, 2004a: 409), they are adept at the maintenance of a particular sort of history. Indeed, Smith has claimed that

> Images and cultural traditions do not derive from or descend upon, mute and passive populations on whose tabula rasa they inscribe themselves. Instead, they invariably express the identities whose historical circumstances have formed, often over long periods.
>
> (Smith, 1990: 179)

The signs and narratives of this variety of British history match the broader nationalist inclinations of the tabloids. This history can be presented in either straightforward narratives or in more oblique references to the past. Sometimes these latter references can be folded within the rhetorical strategy of what we have already referred to as 'scripts'. Scripts are extremely valuable in the densely pressured space of popular newspapers as a subtle insinuation of historical reference points. They assist in the process of creating the necessary continuities within national memory outlined by Smith:

> Traditions, myths, history and symbols must all grow out of the existing, living memories and beliefs of the people who are to compose the nation. Their popular resonance will be greater the more continuous with the living past they are shown to be.
>
> (Smith, 1993: 16)

Tabloids employ their rhetoric to enhance the community of national readership and ensure that as this rhetoric crosses generations and news categories they create a longer narrative of nation in which their readership is invited to participate. This banal history provides an important part of their marketable identity. Its representational mode can be didactic or it can be interactive. Involving readers in the reconstruction of the past works best in conjunction with direct appeals to take part in the maintenance of national community. The *Daily Mirror* asks readers to send in photos and a sixty-word description from yesteryear for the *Daily Mirror*/HP National Photo Album. The winners each week will get a digital camera as a prize.

> Your pictures will make up a unique history of the nation, showing how the British lived, worked and played over the last century.
>
> (*Daily Mirror*, 3 May)

Also on this page we can see another explicit draft of history in the regular column 'On this day', which highlights significant dates from history.

What is of great relevance to this study is the didactic role of the tabloids in constructing such a history – their 'significant role as a social educator' (Hall, 1975: 21), which through selectivity, emphasis, treatment and presentation, enables the tabloid press to itself interpret social change as an active process on behalf of a clearly articulated and nationally located readership. The history lessons of the tabloids can range from hyperbolic celebrations of D-Day to the background set of references upon which they draw for much of their narrative continuity. The heroes and villains which are thus created suit the binarism of the overall tabloid news agenda perfectly as well as indicating the symbolic nature of much of this historical creativity, which is a point endorsed by Rafael Samuel's seminal commentary: 'A national gallery, if it were to attempt to reflect popular memory, would need to give as much space to the figures of national myth as to real life historical personalities' (Samuel, 1989: xvii). Before engaging with specific examples from the contemporary British tabloids, it is worth noting what one outsider to the pageant of British national narratives has pointed out from outside the patriotic discourse of history:

> No nation has ever produced a military history of such verbal nobility as the British. Retreat or advance, win or lose, blunder or bravery, murderous folly or unyielding resolution, all emerge alike clothed in dignity and touched with glory.
>
> (Tuchman, 1971: 557)

The tabloids develop their construction of a common history for their readers by integrating selected episodes from the past into their already powerful, rhetorical strategies of popular imagination, forming a significant element of what Halbwach has called 'a collective memory' (1985). Nationality is therefore, in the context of our study, not just 'a story which people tell about themselves in order to lend meaning to their social world' (Ram, 1994: 154) but one which can be powerfully amplified by the mediation of these stories through the pages of the popular press, entering into an extended dialogue as they do with millions of readers every day with the symbols and the narratives of community imagined historically. This process enables the 'national socialization' (De Cillia *et al.*, 1999: 153) necessary for the fullest inter-subjective participation in the national project.

One of the clearest recent examples of the determination of the popular tabloid press to recreate a chronicle of national history as part of its core activity was in the preparations for and the coverage of the sixtieth anniversary of D-Day in May and June 2004. This was manifested not only in using history to create a picture of the British past but as importantly using it as a context to criticize and celebrate the British present. Before looking at the specifics of this coverage, it is worth considering for a moment just how important the historical referent of World War II is for the continuing discursive formation (Foucault, 1974) of Britain. Since national heroes are an essential ingredient of any national past then clearly the 1939–45 conflict provides some of the more memorable figures of national historic memory. These are particularly important to popular historical memory as they coincide with the lived experience of a significant number of people, directly or vicariously, through the many popular cultural re-imaginings of this period.

One of the most effective media for the popular dissemination of such vicarious experiences of this period of history recounted from a British perspective is the tabloid press. There are strong reasons why this should be the case. Although popular newspapers have always been extremely contemporary in their focus, in common with most other aspects of popular media culture, their identity also depends to a large extent on being able to generate and perpetuate a sense of their own longevity and indeed tradition. This identity becomes reinforced within a sort of communal identification with a clear sense of readership and perspective. The importance of such long-term communal identity is evident when considering the fortunes of popular newspapers after World War II. Smith (1975) demonstrates that it was the inability of the *Daily Express* to adjust its own historically located identity in the face of the challenge from the *Daily Mirror*, which enabled the latter to take on and triumph over its rival. Apart from the extremely important financial restrictions, this need to provide a distinctive location within the spectrum of traditions of the popular press in Britain is one of the main inhibitions to growth in the market. There is only room for a limited number of popular identities within the symbolic space of the nation. Selective recollection of national history is one of the ways in which popular newspapers align their readership with an institutional as well as an historical past.

Promoting memories of D-Day

The weeks leading up to the 60th anniversary of D-Day on 6 June witnessed a range of traditional tabloid strategies which would enable them to recall for readers the significance of the invasion in terms of British history, and to identify the newspaper vicariously and patriotically with the heroism of the event. As well as the banality of daily low-key coverage, we are reminded that, 'The great days of national celebration are patterned so that the national flag can be consciously waved both metaphorically and literally' (Billig, 1995: 45).

The tabloids are quick to make connections with other media which match their agenda. One of these broader connections with contemporary popular culture was a set of tie-ins with a TV series called *Destination D-Day: The Raw Recruits*. This series featured twenty-four recruits from the present day who underwent four weeks of intensive training to prepare them for a simulation of what would have been expected of them in 1944. The coverage was interspersed with interviews with veterans and the feelings of the recruits for the series. The whole thing was predicated on the familiar hypothesis that today's 'youngsters' couldn't hold a candle to the men of yesteryear. It is interesting to note the lack of reference to the veterans of yesteryear as ever having been 'youngsters', which is used here as an implicitly pejorative term. In another commercial tie-in, the *Sun* provides extracts from a book produced to commemorate the D-Day landings which includes interviews with participants. The book, *D-Day By Those Who Were There*, is on special offer to *Sun* readers. One of the first extracts comes from Sergeant Major Stanley Hollis, and is adapted from a talk he gave about the day – he died in 1972. A picture of the oldest D-Day survivor is inserted, Major George Young, 93, commenting on Hollis. The story is illustrated by archive pictures. It is presented in characteristic rhetoric connecting the past with the tabloid present and using the familiar 'Brit' tag.

> 60 YEARS ON, ASTONISHING STORY OF ONLY MAN TO WIN VC ON D-DAY
>
> **BRAVEST BRIT ON BEACH**
>
> (*Sun*, 6 May)

Later in May, the *Sun* moved to associate itself and its readers in a communal and graphic way with the forthcoming celebrations. It produced within the paper a form to fill in with a message to the combatants and a Union Jack with 'THANK YOU' written across it. This combines a patriotic sign with a gesture of thanks, designed to reinforce the bond of community between these men, 'our D-Day heroes', the community of '*Sun* readers' and the newspaper itself. All are orchestrated to provide an end product of a beach in Normandy spectacularly decorated, with messages wrapped around thousands of miniature Union Jacks, commemorating the dead of the first day of the Normandy landings, as much a testimony to the pact of solidarity with readers, tangibly displayed by campaigns such as this, as a tribute to the war dead. In order to bolster its own place in this process, the *Sun* claims that it has '*teamed up with the Royal British Legion*', the representative body of former service men and women. The newspaper asks readers to send their own personal messages of thanks in a powerful gesture attempting to link the readers, newspaper and 'D-Day heroes' within a rhetoric of national memory. Phrased like this, it seems an offer the reader cannot refuse:

TODAY we invite Sun readers to fly the flag for Britain's D-Day heroes.

(*Sun*, 17 May)

The next method of associating tabloids with the heroes of that historical event is to provide a juxtaposition of the veterans with accounts of bungling incompetence by the organizers of the celebrations. To personalize the story, we have a picture of medals on the chest of 79-year-old Albert Rogers, his career summary and a mini-interview. Part of the rationale for the outrage expressed in the paper is, of course, that their attendance at the celebrations is something which the *Daily Mail* has been involved in organizing. The language of the article stresses the status of the men by repeating the word 'heroes' and by describing their journey of remembrance as a 'pilgrimage'. These individuals are clearly marked as the central point of this historical memory. In a secular society such as Britain and particularly in the language of tabloid newspapers, the elevation of these veterans to a level approaching religious respect implied by the word 'pilgrimage' is emphasized by the use of this metaphorical language. We would do well to recall however that the linguistic traffic of metaphor is no one way street. The reader is clearly inscribed in this process:

> Metaphor, however, can only be fleshed out in complicity with the obliging reader, whose active involvement is required not only in the construction of meaning and significance, but also in the intertextual process of activating other texts and discourses (mythological or otherwise) which are part of his/her background knowledge in constructing the appropriate myth(s).

(Kitis and Milapedes, 1997: 585)

The tabloids in their use of metaphor are amplifying the readership's assumed knowledge across a range of cultural experience and memory, which already locates them within the national community.

In the populist criticisms of 'old corruption', the enemies are bureaucrats, the organizers and, by implication, the 'dignitaries', and the fact that 'the

Government failed to warn them in time' draws politicians into the fray as well. The transitivity of the lead to the story deploys the passive voice which has the effect of highlighting the heroes as victims and in tabloid fashion how they have been 'hit' by 'farce':

D-Day heroes hit by security farce

(Daily Mail, 17 May)

The *Sun* provides a characteristically binary perspective on the events of the day, this time from the enemy side in the language of pulp fiction. It has an account from 'THE OTHER SIDE' of how a German infantryman shot 300 Allied soldiers in a day '**in the face of gunfire and flamethrowers spitting death**' but providing an account which can be folded neatly within the dominant narrative of British bravery:

Courage of Allies astounded us

(Sun, 22 May)

D-Day 2004

In the run up to the celebrations of the sixtieth anniversary of the D-Day landings, many of the tabloids which were in existence, whether in broadsheet or tabloid format, in the 1940s, produced souvenir facsimiles of their D-Day editions marking the continuity of the newspapers themselves as well as their intimate connection with the longer history of the country. Whereas not all newspapers could compete in this patriotic display of their own archives, all the tabloids developed a strong sense of the arrival of the key date in June some time before the anniversary itself. As a complement to the reproduction of pages from the newspaper's own archives, the *Daily Mail* on 1 May produced a 'Special Souvenir Weekend Magazine', which added to the range of its 'blow-by-blow account' and 'gripping stories' of the day with its illustrations and photographs, a magazine version of the day from a much more media-orientated and intertextual perspective.

In the supplement, there is an abundance of features based on both factual and fictional accounts of the period which all match the magazine format, as opposed to the more common location of this coverage in the news sections of the other tabloids. There are detailed references to a contemporary retro-TV programme, *Foyle's War*, complete with stills from the series which indicate how often recollections of the past are constructed by contemporary representations and remind us what a key feature of our media-centric postmodernity this sort of programming is. Here we have an example of how the contemporary popular media provide us with something of the heritage necessary to 'redeem' the past and rescue it, 'from a denigrated everyday life and its restaging or display in certain sanctioned sites, events, images and conceptions' (Wright, 1985: 69). Famous personalities of the time are represented by reference to the memories of their descendants: both Churchill's grandson, Nicholas Soames, and Montgomery's son, David, contribute to features on these national heroes. In a less literal manner, Poppy and Eloise Fraser, granddaughters of the 'dashing' Lord Lovat, who led the commandos into battle on D-Day, recreate the fashions of the 1940s with a spread of photos and details on period accessories. The traditionally female readership of the newspaper continues to be clearly inscribed in a piece on allotments and women. There is a special retro-version of a regular contemporary consumer/fashion feature, 'take two', which contrasts the 1940s with 2004. There is a D-Day cooking special feature entitled, punning on the words of a wartime song made famous by Vera Lynn, 'We'll eat again', with wartime recipes for lentil soup and Lord Woolton Pie which substituted root vegetables for meat. There are many reproductions of advertising posters of the time to enhance the overall atmosphere of the magazine. Indicating the fact that an interest in sexual scandal is nothing new to the popular press nor to the contemporary age, one piece is headlined 'The Naughty Forties' and proclaims it 'wasn't all rationed sausages and Dad's Army. It was a hotbed of love and lust that changed our lives forever.' Celebrity news is not a phenomenon confined to the recent past and there are examples of the genre from that era to confirm this. We have stories about Vera Lynn, Princess Elizabeth, the honours list Alexander Fleming categorized in terms of his 'penicillin' knighthood, together with an account which demonstrates the ability of a celebrity focus to bring an otherwise trivial story to the headlines of the popular press. The actress Bebe Daniels is reported as receiving a fine of £3/5s at Marlborough Street court for allowing her dog to worry rabbits in the Dell in Hyde Park. The accumulation within this glossy representation of the era for contemporary consumption indicates the accuracy of Samuel's observation of heritage trends in general and their impact on how we receive the past: 'The vitality of the national idea ... can flourish in the most unpropitious circumstances. ... Denied satisfaction in the present, it can take refuge in a glamourised – or prettified – version of the past' (Samuel, 1989: lx).

The *Daily Star* on 26 May produces a variation on a familiar tale of Germans, stereotypically playing on the tabloid-generated myth of their early-rising, aggressively possessive behaviour around holiday sunbeds. The story reports that all the hotel rooms are booked to German tourists as the French authorities had banked on less visitors from Britain, and continues that local people are helping to sort out the crisis. The D-Day anniversary means that the report can take the stereotype back to the source of World War II and posit the victims not as tourists but as 'D-Day heroes':

NOW GERMANS START WORLD WAR 3 – STAR

They nick beds off our D-Day heroes

Another example of how during the build-up to the anniversary celebrations a simplified model of history can be used by a popular media celebrity to amplify criticism of those he disagrees with in the present comes in the Sun's 'CLARKSON ON SATURDAY' column on 29 May. He comments on the historical irony that it was the Nazis who first banned smoking on Germany's trains in 1944 and claims it was this kind of 'government interference' which Allied soldiers fought to resist. He locates the piece precisely in terms of the historical celebrations, '**SIXTY years ago**', and exclaims in outrage:

We got rid of the Nazis ... then we got this lot

Max Hastings, a columnist and historian of World War II recounts some of the background and the issues which continue to inform D-Day as an historical event, attempting to rescue from cliché the observation that this was 'truly Britain's finest hour' and praising the 'fine and mighty things' which the veterans achieved in that war. He also uses this historically informed piece as a means to attack contemporary politicians who wish to associate themselves with the heroism of the soldiers.

> What a pity that politicians are also attending. Yet such men as George Bush and Tony Blair will always be eager to find a place on the stage, to associate themselves with heroes living and dead.
>
> (*Daily Mail*, 29 May)

This strategy of using the past to underscore contemporary political points continues as a cohesive strand through the same newspaper's coverage. On 5 June, it explains why the German Chancellor should have stayed away from the remembrance ceremony, not in terms of political memory or residual xenophobia as implied in the question it poses to its imagined audience: 'Is this a moving act of reconciliation or a kind of sacrilege?' Instead it focuses on the personal historical memories of those who took part, dismissing the political manoeuvring of this gesture and saying that the German Chancellor should stay away, 'as long as there is a single British veteran who opposes it'.

On the same day, this respect for the memories of the ordinary men, these 'proud old soldiers' who sacrificed so much in their youth is eloquently contrasted with the machinations of contemporary European politics. There are stories of individual soldiers who are returning to Normandy and the collective power of these individual stories is amplified in the stress on how many they add up to:

They came in their thousands to banish their ghosts

The piece emphasizes that the memorials are 'not just about the big parades' but are made up of 'little' delegations and 'little' scenes at a colloquially imprecise 'umpteen ceremonies'. This is historical memory on a national scale conducted editorially on behalf of the little men of history. In their experience of such an iconic moment of the nation's history, they have become the subjects of Deep England:

> To be a subject of Deep England is above all to have *been there* – one must have had the essential experience, and one must have had it in the past to the extent that the meaningful ceremonies of Deep England are above all ceremonies of remembrance and celebration.
>
> (Wright, 1985: 85)

The *Daily Mirror* of 31 May, in its leading article, draws two conclusions about the relevance of the D-Day anniversary to contemporary Britain. Both are placed within narratives which the newspaper is promoting as part of its editorial identity and therefore also as part of its relationship with its readers in a national framework:

> There are two lessons to learn. One is that war is never easy or sanitised. It is not like the movies or a computer game. If today's young generation think it is, they should speak to the men who fought on D-Day ... those who rail against the European Union should remember what the alternative was.

On the same day, it provides a set of easily accessed accounts of the day and the celebrations through a range of familiar tabloid devices, designed to popularize and to facilitate understanding of this historical event for a contemporary readership. First, there is a four-page hour-by-hour account of the day which is accompanied by a photograph of a soldier from 1944, with his kit labelled as a sort of visual mnemonic to indicate something of the physicality of the weight of what they had to carry with them. There is then a timetable of all major events concerned with the anniversary and details of how to travel to France and where accommodation might be available. It is rooted back into the centrality of the ex-soldiers themselves in these celebrations with the following words: 'How you can honour our D-Day heroes'.

The following day, the *Daily Mirror*, as if to confirm how united the tabloids are when it comes to issues around national identity and the nation's heroic past, leads the criticism that a survey of a thousand under-25s it has commissioned has revealed a total lack of historical knowledge of the key facts of World War II, particularly among the young. As a corrective to this situation, it launches a mini-campaign which ties in with its coverage of the anniversary in an example of populist pedagogy. It seems to be attempting to revive the conceit articulated by Samuel, that the British are more historically minded than other people, and that 'Britain is an old, "tradition-loving" country' (Samuel, 1989: lv). The outrage at the lack of historical knowledge of young people seems rooted in an outmoded belief in this fallacy and a refusal to accept any cultural responsibility apart from blaming the usual suspects as well as the young people themselves. As far as the tabloids are concerned the

Normandy beaches very much form a part of the 'sacred geography' (Wright, 1985: 199) which reinforces the status of the national past.

The campaign connects lack of knowledge about this history to a general lack of intelligence in a forceful condemnation: '**BRITAIN is a nation of D-Day dunces**'. It describes the results of its survey as 'extraordinary and frankly, depressing' while pointing the finger of blame at, '**A sad failure by teachers and parents**'. As a gesture implying involvement with its readers, the paper prints extracts from the survey in a question and answer format: 'What is D-Day? ... What is the date of D-Day? What happened? Who was the American President at the time? Who was the British Prime Minister? During which World War did it happen?' The piece concludes in the hope that we have not become a nation that knows more about 5–1 victory over Germany at football, although clearly there is a strong possibility that this is the case, given the obsessive popular media interest in couching contemporary sporting rivalry with Germany in terms of war and the fact that such cultural elisions have led to the fading of accurate historical memory. It seems to exculpate the role of the popular press in any of this by pointing out that the ignorance comes, 'despite massive coverage'.

As a contrast to the lack of historical memory among certain sections of the younger generations, the *Daily Mail* of 2 June uses a direct link between a writer on the newspaper and his own family connections. Edward Heathcote Amory has lost a great-grandfather and grandfather in World War I and World War II and asks 'Would I have their courage?' It is an approach which is strongly personalized through the inclusion of letters, personal reminiscences and family photos. It is also tied with the aspirational social class perspective of its idealized readership. The didactic tone cautions his own peers: 'Their calm courage set a frighteningly high standard against which to measure my own generation and its petty concerns' and stresses the lack of European military antagonism, for which 'we can thank Ludovic, Gerald, and those other young men from two generations of Britons for the sacrifices that they made'.

Having outlined how the tabloids work effectively to provide a series of historical contexts for their reports, we can now consider something of the dynamism involved in the process as it evolves, indicating how 'Newspapers provide a daily index to shifts within the nation/media problematic' (Law, 2001: 314). Two tabloids pick up the story of a tired English football team to make an historical contrast with the events of 1944 which are so prominent in the news agenda, and once again the 'script' fits with the narrative of a moral decline in the youth of today:

Tired? Think about those poor lads on D-Day, Becks

... exhausted by months of severe training ... paid enough to buy a packet of Woodbines ...

(*Daily Mail*, 5 June)

The *Sun* of June 5 has a report threaded through with military metaphors directly echoing the vocabulary connected to the real combatants of sixty years ago:

D-DAY FOR ENGLISH FOOTBALL

ON the eve of their own D-Day, the England football squad complain they're tuckered. Well, boo-flippin'-hoo.

The boys are too pooped to fight according to their Commander-in-Chief Mister Eriksson. ... Forget the spirit of '66, the English football squad needs the force of '44.

The piece goes on to contrast the 'modest survivors of June 6 1944', saying in contemporary idiom that 'These are Britain's real idols and superstars' and that Beckham and his fellow footballers appear to have little fight or grit in them.

Unflattering comparisons with the general youth of today continue in the *Daily Mirror* on 7 June:

It is to those people who did not [experience the war] – and especially young people – that the message must be drummed home. ...

Today they worry about jobs, girlfriends, money, getting homes and their cars. Sixty years ago there were different problems.

The main worry was staying alive.

The *Daily Mail* of 5 June, in its 'COMMENT' section, contrasts the sacrifices made for the country sixty years ago with the social problems it sees today, using the past, and the national past in particular as a didactic tool:

The invasion that saved the world

... the disintegration of communities and a corrosive lack of confidence in traditional moral values. ... Much is right about this country, but much is wrong too.

Melanie Phillips a few days later on 7 June in the same paper takes up the theme, 'Today our nation faces a new lethal threat', and points out that we need the collective will of the soldiers from sixty years ago to survive. The major threat that she sees for contemporary Britain is no less than the survival of: 'the coherence and identity of the nation itself'. In a strange and certainly unintentional echo of the war years, she advocates strong leaders unafraid to take risks. All the above is eloquent testimony to the potential of the national narrative to be linked with other motivations: 'Could we ever narrativize without moralizing?' (Whyte: 1984: 23).

The *Sun* also continues to build its preparations for the anniversary, and on 1 June produces a three-page special in which, 'we explain the events that led up to the invasion'. This style of explicit exposition of past events can be seen as a veritable popular history lesson. The difference with much of the other media coverage is its shift into the tabloid lexicon which has been drawn from other popular cultural traditions such as boys' comics, and which maintains a certain set of attitudes to the history of the war: 'JERRY HAD HIS PANTS DOWN'. The *Sun* of 2 June provides a range of visual rhetoric to support its exposition, with a full colour centre page spread of the battle fields of the Normandy coast, complete with illustrations of defences and Allied forces. D-Day is literally flagged in a display of large colour flags of the USA and the UK.

In keeping with the populist position towards the soldiers who had fought on that day to be found in all the tabloids, each of the newspapers provides a wealth of personal anecdotes from surviving veterans:

I played the bagpipes. A Sgt said, You mad bastard

(*Sun*, 1 June)

VET, 100 GETS A D-DAY MEDAL

(*Daily Mirror*, 2 June)

The accurate eye-witness accounts of the details of invasion and its aftermath do serve to provide a genuine feeling of gratitude to these old soldiers, occasionally independent from the political and moral agendas of the tabloids:

EVER SO HUMBLE HEROES '... through the youthful eyes of those who lived to tell the tale ...'

(*Daily Mail*, 3 June)

This is complemented on occasion by the inclusion of a personal recollection of a token enemy from the German forces on the Normandy beaches sixty years ago, which provides human interest from the other side and therefore a richer narrative of this composite history, such as on 2 June in the *Daily Mail* interview with 80-year-old Hein Severloh, '**The Beast of Omaha**', now living near Hannover.

Often, there is a downside to the concentration on stories of soldiers as this leads to a militarization of war memories despite the impact of war on civilians and their own massive loss of life. As a slight corrective to this general trend which also sees women eclipsed, the *Daily Mirror* on 3 June includes Stephanie Kerans, a plotting officer in Portsmouth, amongst its list of war heroes, asserting correctly that, 'the role of women in the war is scandalously overlooked' and asking for readers to make donations to the Royal Star and Garter Home in Richmond where she lives with other veterans. This gesture broadens out the exposition and the personalization of this period of history in a way which invites readers to play a very direct part in contributing to the well being of these former military personnel, thus demonstrating the role of the newspaper in consolidating this aspect of national history in a material as well as a rhetorical manner.

The *Sun* seems to want to take on a didactic role itself in bridging the generations by using photographs of young men then and now, recounting their tales as 'Eyewitness stories' under the explicit headline 'D-Day Heroes' on 3 June. In order to place itself in the forefront of attempts to teach the history of the D-Day landings, and to bring a direct experience of history, the *Sun* takes this cross-generational history to a more literal level when it teams up Royal British Legion veterans with eleven girls from Abbey Grange Church of England High School in Leeds. These girls won the trip after producing work which showed the importance of learning about the sacrifices made by the World War II generation. It finishes off with an appeal to make a donation to the British Legion, again seeking to make a tangible contribution as a complement to its rhetoric.

The *Daily Star* 5 June is also keen to expand the popular reach of its coverage with pictures of children laying flowers and one 79-year-old veteran holding a 4-year-old boy's hand and represented as explaining the landings to him in a powerful but simple statement of generational responsibility:

'WE DID IT FOR YOU SON'

Even the *Daily Mirror*, perhaps in a further attempt to counterbalance the historical ignorance of British youth, revealed in its survey findings, provides on 7 June a story from France which includes, rare in a British tabloid, a poignant quotation in French (with English translation).

THE FRENCH CHILDREN TAUGHT NEVER TO FORGET

Parce qu' ils sont morts pour nous

Charlotte Lesueur is only five … in her home town … dozens of French children … white roses

On the Saturday before the memorial celebrations, the *Sun* elevates the veterans to the position of a '**Nation's pride**', and in exhorting readers to '**Remember them this weekend**', it provides a schedule of events and a check on TV listings of the coverage. On the following Monday, 7 June, the *Sun* has an 'Historic Souvenir Edition', a sixteen-page pullout. The front page has a 'Tommy' emerging from the water off the Normandy coast, which has been superimposed on a mass of commemorative poppies floating on the water. It strikes a visually memorable summation of the newspaper's historical account over the previous month. Inside, it reports on the Sunday celebrations on behalf of the 'glorious heroes', and there is a significant amount of retelling of the events, with statistics and battle names. All newspapers provide a full narrative of the day. There are copious archive photographs, re-enactments of air, sea and land troops' actions, memories of veterans, descriptions of the pageantry of the formal commemoration itself, and all show pictures of the Blairs singing. Beyond all the retrieval of the past and its blending with the political personalities and issues of the present, there is still in many places a simple respect paid in powerfully demotic language and images of what it meant to the men who were there:

> Barrel chests, ram-rod backs, jutting chins … the finest generation of men any of us will ever know.
>
> > (*Daily Mirror*, 7 June)

The *Daily Mirror* on its front page shows a picture of a weeping veteran on Juno Beach:

> One hero's tears …
>
> One nation's thanks

The Daily Mail on 7 June also poignantly displays on its front page an eloquent and simple image of Union Jack flags on the beach, and states unequivocally:

A FLAG FOR EVERY HERO

Intertextual media references make it a very contemporary style of memorial. This is best illustrated by the well-publicized presence of Tom Hanks, the star of the Hollywood feature film which was based on the D-Day landings, *Saving Private Ryan*, pictured present. The Queen is the cornerstone of the reporting of the day's ceremonial. The fact that the Queen is present in the reports is of no particular significance from a journalistic perspective. She was present and she played an important part in the ceremonial proceedings. What is noteworthy is the way in which all of the tabloids deal with her contribution and enclose it within a rhetoric which places her at the symbolic centre of this celebration of the nation's past. On 7 June the *Daily Mirror* represents her as having a uniquely privileged personal perspective to bring to national history and prioritizes her words:

> The words which best expressed what this moving ceremony stood for came from the Queen. For hers was a personal message.

The *Daily Mail* chooses to highlight, 'the moving moment when the Queen and other elders rose to their feet in spontaneous tribute to men who gave so much' while the *Sun* gives prominence to the part of the Queen's speech which seems to echo the populist appreciation of the central role of the history of World War II in British memory, and certainly in its collective memory of its own identity:

One of the proudest moments in our national history. I take it upon myself to express the immense debt of gratitude we owe to you all. I salute you and thank you on behalf of our whole nation.

In these reports we can see history not only as a repletion of the past but the explicit location of this past within the discourses of royalty and patriotism. The familiar setting of the celebrations within the rhetoric of the tabloids enhances the implicit conversation between tabloid and reader as one between nation and subject, in ways which Billig has observed enable the activities of the royal family to be quite literally turned into conversations which act as a bridge between the domestic and the public (Billig, 1992). In the process of the recollection of these events towards the end of World War II, the monarch has a secure place as a vital source of historical security. The centrality of the role of the Queen acts to reconcile a stable national identity out of the differences often on display in the 'mirror in which competing versions of Britishness as well as everyday gendered and family identities are overlappingly articulated' (Chaney, 2001: 208).

The *Sun* adds a contemporary coda to the celebrations, returning to generational comparisons in an interesting variation on the them and us formula: this time not marking insiders and outsiders but indicating the difference between two communities both divided by and united in a common history.

THEY DIED TO KEEP US FREE

… ARE WE AS BRAVE?

This comparison is also deployed politically to bring the questions specific to World War II into a contemporary frame, indicating once again the ways in which a national history can gain contemporary relevance in the hands of a newspaper with a particular editorial perspective. History is collapsed into a Manichaean binary between good and evil and metaphorized into darkness and light with religious and even racial overtones in an explicit didacticism:

D-Day: A lesson in fighting evil

We will always remember those who fight for freedom.

… shone the light of hope into the darkness of a beleaguered Europe held hostage by the Nazis …

In those dark days we stood four square with America as together we liberated the world from tyranny.

Just as we do today … the terrorists of Al Qaeda and the dark forces trying to deny Iraq the democracy it craves.

… If we have courage and perseverance, good will always defeat evil.

(*Sun*, 7 June)

History – political and politicized

More recent history than World War II can be presented with all of the political controversy of recent memory. In contrast to the 'euphoric articles' in the *Daily Mail* and the *Sun* which it criticizes, the *Daily Mirror* provides a more militant view of the anniversary of the election of Margaret Thatcher as Prime Minister in 1979. This perspective is articulated as being that of *Daily Mirror* readers and it is supported by a range of characters from the historical narrative themselves. There is a strong collective tone to the response starting with the use of 'us', which includes both the imagined collective of the readership plus the assembled characters selected to provide the recollections of their time while she was Prime Minister. The whole thrust of the piece is to justify by example and personification that this collective is the readership of the *Daily Mirror* and that they continue to be unified in their opposition to all she stood for.

25 YEARS SINCE THE RISE OF THE IRON LADY

What Thatcher did for us

The list of those invited by the newspaper serves as an abbreviated and personalized roll-call of those years:

> Miner's Wife, Poll Tax Rebel, Greenham Common Protester, Stop and Search Brixton Boy, Falklands Veteran 'Right to go to war though he lost a leg', Yuppie who bought her handbag.
>
> (*Daily Mirror*, 4 May)

An associated piece starts with a cultural reference to an expression which spans kitchen-sink playwright Osborne to contemporary rock band Oasis and emphasizes the popular nature of the retrospective. The rhetoric is underlined by the championing within the article of 'ordinary people' and 'vulnerable people'. It is a brief political history lesson from the idealized editorial perspective of the *Daily Mirror*, and remarkable is its deployment of a mythical British hero, Boadicea, as the antithesis of Thatcher in that the former is associated in popular memory with fighting for her people.

Thatcher: Look back in anger

A Battery of adulatory, euphoric articles has marked the 25th anniversary of Mrs Thatcher becoming Prime Minister.

That is not how most Mirror readers will celebrate the day.

Margaret Thatcher certainly had an impact, though not in the way her admirers mean. She was not some modern Boadicea, fighting for the people she ruled. Her battles were against ordinary people.

(*Daily Mirror*, 4 May)

In the following example we can see another, more subtle induction of readers into a politicized version of history and its contemporary implications. The *Daily Mail* takes the reader through a micro-account of Nelson, Trafalgar and its implications for Britain's subsequent place in the world: 'his victory laid the foundations for the Royal Navy's sovereignty of the world's oceans for a century'. Here we are invited to see both the script indicated in the emotive word 'beg' as indicative of the assumed state of public attitudes to our naval heritage and the didactic gloss of the meaning of Trafalgar and its place in British history. The Royal Navy are presented as reduced to begging for sponsorship to fund celebrations of a famous national historical event.

Sponsors needed to bale out Nelson's celebrations

SOS to big business over Trafalgar tribute

Defence chiefs have been forced to beg private sponsors for funding in order to mark the anniversary of the Battle of Trafalgar.

(*Daily Mail*, 13 May)

A more recent historical moment is presented in political form when the *Daily Star* reports that bayonets were used for the first time since 1982 by British troops – 'Our Boys' – under the caption '**GET STUCK IN**'. The incident is reported very much in line with the tabloids' binary agenda in support of a nationally orientated perspective:

OUTNUMBERED British soldiers. … Iraqi rebels …

(*Daily Star*, 18 May)

Sport and national history

Sport is another area where flashes of the past are recovered for a new generation familiar with the iconic moments of the nation's history in the tabloid archive. The Argentinean footballer, Diego Maradona, scored a decisive goal using his hand against England in the World Cup of 1986. After the game he claimed that the goal had been assisted by the hand of God. This goal is continually threaded across contemporary references to create a solid moment familiar to all readers of these papers whatever their age because of its intertextual amplification. This ranges in the following examples from the literal coverage of Diego Maradona, the culprit, contextualized and made newsworthy through this association, to references to a goal scored in a contemporary match also involving an Argentine's handled goal.

Diego setback

… The fallen 43-year-old soccer legend, who helped Argentina beat England with his Hand of God goal in the 1986 World Cup …

(*Daily Star*, 6 May)

HAND OF GOD II

Heartache for Ranieri as Argentine's dodgy goal KOs Chelsea

… as another Hand of God goal by an Argentine … evoking bitter memories of the goal by his compatriot Diego Maradona which helped end England's 1986 World Cup campaign …

(Daily Mirror, 6 May)

The European football championships were also put into an historical context in the *Daily Mirror*, which drew upon events in World War I. Playing on the name of the band chosen to sing the anthem for Euro 2004, the *Daily Mirror* provides a full historical gloss of the events from 1914 when British and German soldiers declared a Christmas Day truce in order to play football in no man's land. It provides a small picture of the key event and the tabloid 'Brits v Germans' strapline, complete with the lyrics of the song referring to the wartime football match. It also puns on the Barmy Army, the eccentric band of supporters who follow England, usually on tour and traditionally in sports where English teams have not been too successful.

FARMY ARMY

Anthem for Euro 2004 inspired by WW1 game

(Daily Mirror, 8 May)

The championship was an opportunity to indulge in some of the most popular football memories to make connections for the tabloid readers between moments of past success and also draw attention to promotional stunts tied in with these memories of 1966 reconstructed in other contexts.

SPIRIT OF '66

BA names new jet for England's Euro 2004 stars

… new jet named Spirit of '66 … in memory of the team that won the World Cup 38 years ago.

Contemporary stars can be located in the pecking order of national sporting heroism with pictures of goals from the past.

WAYNE ROONEY'S eyes light up when he thinks of England.

He was just ten when he marvelled at Paul Gascoigne's goal at Euro 96 and only 12 when Michael Owen made him start to dream with his stunning effort against Argentina.

(Daily Star, 26 May)

Anniversaries and individuals in sporting history are in the following examples drawn from both triumph and tragedy.

> **HIS record lasted less than a month but Roger Bannister's name has been etched in history forever.**
>
> Fifty years ago today, Bannister ran the mile in under four minutes – and smashed one of the great sporting barriers. ... Sir Roger Bannister is an international icon ...
>
> (*Daily Mirror*, 6 May)

In the case of the Bannister sub-four-minute mile, the picture itself of the athlete crossing the finishing line in his record-breaking run, reproduced here, is as famous as the person. The tabloid binarism is in perfect keeping with the story ('less than a month ... etched in history forever') together with the hyperbolic statements: 'smashed', 'international icon' of British sporting achievement.

The memory of sporting disaster is also an important component of national recollection through the pages of the tabloids, especially when threaded through with a poignant personal story of one victim's son. The son of one of the victims of the Hillsborough football tragedy eventually seems set to get his chance to play for Liverpool on a day referred to with all the potency of a collective, national rite of mourning:

> THE LEGACY OF HILLSBOROUGH
>
> ... the darkest day in British football history ...
>
> (*Daily Mail*, 15 May)

References to the national past can be used in sporting terms to provide a simultaneous combination of patriotism and collective memory. In this example, a football manager's reference to Churchill is drawn out and emphasized, and through this emphasis it is thereby continuing to contribute to the resonance of the war-time leader in vernacular culture. In a pre-match talk Ian Holloway is reported in the *Daily Mirror* of 10 May to have said: 'I gave the players a bit of Winnie – "we'll fight them on the beaches" and all that type of stuff.' The report itself highlighted this by using the headline '**BULLDOG SPIRIT**' and stressing that he had taken 'a leaf out of Sir Winston Churchill's book'.

Popular memory and the recent past

Tabloids will often refer to their own recent histories in an attempt to emphasize their idiosyncratic scoops and editorial perspectives. This is no better illustrated than in the self-promotional but deeply ironic report on a government inquiry into breaches in royal security exposed by the *Daily Mirror*. It refers to an exclusive report which was originally revealed on 19 November 2003 and quotes the editor as he claims to be providing a public service in his paper's underground exposé of lapses in royal security.

THE INTRUDER REPORT

(Our man Parry)

... Mirror editor Piers Morgan said last night: 'Ryan Parry performed a valuable public service in highlighting how woefully lax the system was'.

(*Daily Mirror*, 7 May)

Selective recent memory is also stimulated, for instance by running stories of child murders with the pictures of the children as advertised during the murder enquiry, illustrating the later stories as if the tabloids are keen to keep the personalities in these dreadful cases clearly in the public eye because of all of the populist frameworks of retribution, moralizing and sensationalizing which the tabloids map onto. A report on Maxine Carr in the *Daily Star* on 7 May is accompanied by pictures of the children killed by her boyfriend. In reviewing such terrible cases, 'evil' is a common word. It is a word which simply closes down discussion or reflection on events and the pictures are a poignant reminder fixed in the past.

In other circumstances, a different form of mnemonic can be used as in the phrase 'summer of discontent', which calls upon popular memory of how the phrase has been used in the past by the right-wing press as a 'winter of discontent', to drum up the threat of a return to a type of industrial militancy demonized in recollections of 1978. This is added to by the general lexical choice which feeds into an alarmist representation of possible industrial action which draws in vocabulary such as 'nightmare', 'chaos loomed' and 'wildcat action':

RAIL STRIKE TO ADD TO FIRE WOE

SUMMER OF DISCONTENT

(*Sun*, 21 May)

Borrowings from film and other popular media can also be used to prompt a review of a particular historical moment or personality, as in the following example which typifies the *Daily Mail*'s style in these cross-over tales. The feature concerns a revelation that the character on whose life the film *The English Patient* was based turns out to have been far from a conventional film hero and had espionage dealings with the Germans in order to rescue his lover from the desert.

The Nazi English Patient

'Hero' played by Fiennes was scruffy, ugly ... and gay

(*Daily Mail*, 21 May)

The report is completed by the juxtaposition of archive pictures of real-life character Almasay and Fiennes in the Hollywood film, connecting feature film with archival documents in a formative fusion of popular historical memory.

On the launch of the disaster movie *The Day After Tomorrow*, the *Sun* prints a series of features on the memories of survivors of real-life disasters in the not too distant past, such as Aberfan and Piper Alpha. These fit with the popular national demand to 'produce heroes' and are in keeping with the individualized emphasis on how 'tales of survivors can be an inspiration to us all'. The series runs from 24–28 May as 'DISASTER WEEK' and offers a bathetic 'FREE SURVIVAL GADGET' which incorporates an eleven-feature torch, screwdriver, compass and food peeler.

History of war

The history of World War II tends to appear quite randomly in the tabloids unless it can be matched with specific anniversaries or events, but it is tied nevertheless to the wider news values of individual papers. The following two examples give a flavour of the boys' comic style of prose which often accompanies the heroic exploits of the armed forces of a previous generation. The bodies of pilots lost in an exchange over the Netherlands, having been discovered last year, were laid to rest in an official ceremony with full honours and their relatives present.

> After 63 years, a farewell to lost RAF bomber boys.
>
> On the night of May 11, 1941, the Stirling bomber roared into the skies over southern England. Its target the heart of the Nazi empire. ...
>
> Flying over the Netherlands, they encountered one of the Luftwaffe's most feared aces. ... Prince Egemont zur Lippe-Weissenfeld, who notched up many allied 'kills' in his career.
>
> His Messerschmitt's cannons scythed into the slow-moving Stirling. Dutch villagers below looked on in horror as the bomber erupted in a ball of flame and broke up in the air as two of its 1,000lb bombs detonated, before plunging 18,000ft into a field ...
>
> (*Daily Mail*, 12 May)

The second example further emphasizes the preferred rhetoric of battle by including a cartoon depiction of another wartime event in colour on the same page as the report. This details the excavation of a Hurricane used by a pilot who is now 89 to defend Buckingham Palace:

PILOT WHO SAVED THE PALACE

> In a breathtaking act of reckless wartime bravery, Ray Holmes flew his fighter into a Nazi bomber attacking Buckingham Palace.
>
> (*Daily Mail*, 1 June)

Yet military service can also be employed to emphasize a history which those in authority would prefer to forget. It is no coincidence that this following story appears most prominently in the *Daily Mirror* with its long association with support for the ordinary military which does not preclude condemnation of superior officers, an association which was forged during World War II and led to its period of greatest popular success as a self-styled proletarian spokespiece (Cudlipp, 1953).

Airman Maddison believed he was helping to find a common cold cure ... he died from a massive dose of sarin in a biological weapons experiment.

There are two points of historical contextualization here. First, we have a picture of the airman aged 20, shortly before his death in 1953, and then we have an extract from the coroner's report which is clearly intended to provide a context for understanding the historical circumstances of this case.

> He described a post-war world, divided into East and West by the Cold War, of hydrogen bomb tests in the Pacific and in Russia, and the death of Joseph Stalin.
>
> (*Daily Mirror*, 6 May)

There are times also when the gestures of ordinary readers are used to flag the patriotic virtues so approved by the tabloid press. 'Big-hearted' is certainly a characteristic which the *Sun* would claim for itself, and it uses the popular storyline of lottery winners helping out 'men who have served their country' as an exhortation to readers to be generous when the annual Poppy Day memorial comes around in November. Ray and Barbara Wragg are presented as popular exemplars of patriotic behaviour 'rekindling the residues of ancient beliefs' (Samuel, 1989: xxx) for a contemporary and future national readership:

Proud gesture

WHAT big-hearted folks Lottery winners Ray and Barbara Wragg are.

They happily paid £12,500 so 90 old soldiers could go to Italy to mark the 60th anniversary of the battle of Monte Cassino.

It's a wonderful gesture towards men who have served their country.

You can be generous, too, by giving when Poppy Day comes round.

(*Sun*, 15 May)

History and individuals

Occasionally there will be a story of an individual whose life itself can encapsulate a sort of living history. A report such as the double page spread on Hanna Barusevitch from Belorussia fits with many of the rhetorical features of the tabloids as it draws upon a personality who has triumphed against the chaos of the world to be able to tell her own story. It fits well with the tabloid worldview of the individual against the world and can summarize the success of such a life in suitably trite terms.

WORLD'S OLDEST WOMAN ON THE SECRET OF LIVING 116 YEARS

My husband and lover were shot but gherkins, pork fat and vodka keep me healthy

(*Daily Mail*, 12 May)

It is juxtaposed with a summary of the world in 1888 as an historical gloss for interested readers.

Scripts, history – the good old days

As Wright (1985) has reminded the British, we live in an old country. One of the characteristics of the tabloids is that they reinforce a very popular sense of this 'old country' in aspects of their coverage of history. Although in the contemporary media market, the historical is increasingly marginalized by an instant, celebrity-driven culture, there is still a sense that the past is a place which the tabloids need to maintain as a sort of definitional discursive boundary (Foucault, 1974) if they are to maintain their broadest popular appeal. There is another use to which the tabloids put their versions of history in order to retain this sense of the past. It belongs to a script that we might term 'the good old days'. This script pictures a past in which the world was safer and simpler and by association it implies or sometimes explicitly states that the world today should try to turn back the clock to such a mythological past. It is of course a subtle and revisionist view of the world which takes the past very much as a rose-scented vision of perfection which we cannot aspire to other than by moving back politically and socially. It implies a world in which people knew their place and which was governed by simplicities of social and cultural hierarchies. The world was never this simple so we cannot be anything other than highly suspicious of this particular use of national history. The following story is accompanied by a picture of short-trousered boys playing in the 1950s.

The children who are too frightened to play outside

FOR previous generations, the streets around their homes were playgrounds to explore.

But for many children of the 21st century, the outside world has become a dangerous place.

According to research, most ten and 11-year-olds prefer to stay in the safe environment of their home because they are afraid of being kidnapped, attacked by a paedophile, run over by a car or caught up in terrorism. ...

The report by the Blairite think-tank Demos and the Green Alliance. ...

'It is a scourge of our times'

(*Daily Mail*, 24 May)

The final quotation is taken directly from the report as a summary. It fits in consciously with a range of stories which all conjure up the simple binary of 'old world safe', 'new world dangerous'.

Conclusion

The treatment of the D-Day anniversary celebrations illustrates many things about the complexities of the relationship between the tabloids and British history. This is a relationship which is crucial in defining the readership. It is also a key feature in the creation of a coherent set of characters, dates and features which can be used to determine the wider scope of Britain as an elite nation in terms of what both Galtung and Ruge (1973) and Harcup and O'Neill (2001) have defined as decisive in the news values of these newspapers. The tabloids both reinforce a kind of historical knowledge for a very specific popular audience as well as flagging up pride in national history as an important element in their own identity, a feature which is in turn integral to a nationally specific readership. History may not feature on a daily basis but when it is covered it provides an important element in the cohesion and argumentation strategies of the tabloids in defining their identity and their take on the world. The sort of history which the tabloids expect their readers to be familiar with forms a very important part of the ideological compact they share with them.

The narrative elements which the tabloids choose to emphasize in constructing a continuity in the representation of the nation are an important part of the ideological cohesion which they present to readers. We can observe in the patterns and repetitions of these historical accounts much of what Anderson has identified as the cultural roots of nationalism (1987: 17). One of the functions of nationalism when represented in this way is that it portrays what is, in material terms, a national population stratified by status and class as essentially homogenous (Greenfield, 1992: 7). This is of particular importance in newspapers which are sold predominantly to blue collar and lower-middle-class readerships; they represent the nation as something which transcends class divisions and which is therefore able to call upon all members of the national community regardless of status. The tabloids are not subtly indicating the parameters of the national past and implying political positions. They are powerful vectors of an overtly didactic approach to this history, and it is an educational project which is profoundly marked with political intent. Tabloid Britain is to a large extent predicated upon the narrative of British history which these newspapers promulgate. To a large extent they encapsulate Hayden Whyte's aphorism about narrative: they translate knowing into telling (Whyte, 1984: 1).

Munslow has observed that although history is written by historians, it may be best understood as a cultural product existing within society as part of the historical process itself (1997: 10). In our terms, it is the tabloids who are writing this contemporary form of popular mass-marketed history, not the historians or political elite, and this may form one part of its appeal to ordinary readers. The tabloids are extremely effective in combining the issues of language, memory and history which 'bulk large in discussions of the relationship between culture and national identity' (Spencer and Wollman, 2002: 73). The tabloids may turn history into what Barthes has described as myth, connecting it to the present in a highly significant and politically charged way, yet myth can be brought up against real experience of the past, as in the case of the soldiers of World War II. Their authenticity provides a complexity to the political and editorial use of the history of the war for readers who remember the sacrifices of members of their own families. At moments such as this there is a powerful bond between the popular press and the popular memory of very real readers drawn together across geography and history to form an imaginary community and something more tangible even. The tabloids are clearly keen to be involved in this process of authentication and do all they can to flag up their active role. Smith always sees in contemporary nationalism a version of its ancient origins.

> For ethno-symbolists, what gives nationalism its power are the myths, memories, traditions and symbols of ethnic heritages and the ways in which a popular living past has been and can be rediscovered and reinterpreted by modern nationalist intelligentsias.
>
> (Smith, 1999a: 9)

The memories of World War II may not be ancient but they are articulated in a language which claims them very much as a core element in vernacular versions of a British ethnic past.

It may be stretching a point to call the tabloid journalists an 'intelligentsia', but the tabloids do work through their use of narrative and language on making the recent historical past appear both more ancient and more contemporary at the same time. In their use of history tabloids are acting very much as agents of national construction.

5   Outsiders and the national community of readers

The cohesion of the imagined community of nation within the tabloid newspaper is not only established and reinforced by reference to insiders and indigenous narratives of nation but also by a consistent patterning within the representation of outsiders to the community. This patterning forms part of the 'style of representation' of national communities in print (Anderson, 1987). They may be geographical outsiders, ethnic outsiders or those placed for other social or economic reasons beyond the parameters of the implied normal readership of the tabloids. Race and ethnicity are significant features in identifying these norms. Van Dijk (1984) has argued that racism is a cognitive phenomenon which has the social function of protecting the interests of the in-group. Gilroy has identified the way in which talk of nations can be used as a substitute for some of the more provocative aspects of older racist discourse: 'Its novelty lies in the capacity to link discourses of patriotism, nationalism, xenophobia, Englishness, Britishness, militarism and gender difference into a complex system which gives "race" its contemporary meaning' (Gilroy, 1987: 43).

The language used may have been moderated over the past twenty years with regard to race (Searle, 1989), but a certain exclusivity based on ethnicity is certainly apparent in the very construction of British or even English identity (Kumar, 2003). It is still very much the case as when Hall argued that, 'a culturally-contrasted sense of Englishness and a particularly closed and exclusive form of English national identity. ... Is one of the core characteristics of British racism today' (Hall, 1988a: 29). A form of 'inferential racism' is reinforced within the nationalist preferences of the popular tabloids. The language of this representation has a strongly normative inflection which aims to reinforce a sense of reader identity and in turn a strong sense of national community based not only on a sense of what is shared in common but also on what is shared as a common perception of external challenge or threat to that community. There is a great deal of parallelism in the language which the tabloids use to represent outsiders, threats and moral panics, and this reinforces the projected ideal reader (Cohen, 1980; Critcher, 2003; Chan *et al.* 1987). Some of these language patterns will be explored in this chapter and assessed as to their congruence with the broader rhetorical strategies of the tabloids.

Writers such as Van Dijk (1991) have pioneered analysis which demonstrates how news values are the values of the white establishment since they are predicated on the views of elite groups of society and elite views of history. He argues that it is not just the use of overtly racist or exclusivist language but also a whole series of institutional discourse around what is normal which reinforces racist practices, drawing attention to the linguistics of racism by stressing that it is 'not only in *what* journalists write about ethnic affairs, but also *how* they do that' (Van Dijk, 1991: 209). Gary Younge, from the perspective of a black British journalist, echoes this point in his article on 'The Badness of Words' (2000), reinforcing the claims that Van Dijk makes that it is often in the lexical associations that such prejudice can be seen at a surface level:

> An analysis of these examples shows that the invectives tend to be chosen from very specific style registers, those of mental illness and irrationality, political and ideological intolerance and oppression, and finally that of threatening animals.
>
> (Van Dijk, 1991: 214)

Asylum

The issue of asylum has become one of the most controversial within the tabloids and its over-representation is significant in cultural and journalistic terms. 'Over-lexicalization as a means of encoding ideology in news discourse. ... often has a pejorative effect as it signals a kind of deviation from social convention or expectation' (Teo, 2000: 20–1).

The *Sun* manages to present itself and its views as moderate while continuing to use language about asylum seekers, which can be categorized as inflammatory, and about the government, which may contribute to a populist denigration of political efforts to deal with the issue; a language which may have the potential to further compromise the public perception of asylum seekers and their rights. While reporting that Blair has come 'as close to an apology yesterday as we're likely to see', seeking vindication for its claims that its editorial policy is not racist, it describes its own coverage as 'cautious' while using the familiar provocation of 'thousands of asylum cheats flood into this country'. It is worthy of note that metaphors of flooding, along with those of disease, are regularly overemployed with regard to outsiders in newspaper discourse (Van Dijk, 1987; Wodak and Matouschek, 1993). The language, particularly the over-lexicalization around asylum seekers echoes the latent xenophobic sentiments and attitudes that resonate beneath the surface of a democratic, egalitarian policy in a predominantly 'white' society' (Teo, 2000: 9). The article referred to also uses the word 'racist' in inverted commas to further display its disagreement with the application of this term in relation to its own coverage:

And he also agreed it is not 'racist' to feel alarmed that thousands of asylum cheats flood into this country.

Yet 'racist' is the word Home Secretary David Blunkett used to describe the *Sun's* cautious coverage of this crisis.

(*Sun*, 28 May)

Day by day, the language of this coverage is as consistent as it is relentless. The government being represented as incompetent and ridden roughshod over by the judiciary fits the confrontational stance towards the establishment favoured by tabloid rhetoric. In addition, it also veers towards a dangerous impression that the asylum situation is out of control, thus fanning potential hostility. This section will analyze a range of extracts selected to display the range of lexis and argument as well as the occasional moderation and the attempt in the *Daily Mirror* to focus attention on the tactics of the other tabloids in a noble but limited gesture. Overall the picture painted by the language of the tabloids is of a community under attack, with common complaints of: 'abuse of free handouts', '*clampdown on asylum cheats*', '*benefits tourists*', '*to milk the system*'.

Beyond this, the government, often personified by Blair or the then Home Secretary, Blunkett, is castigated as it is counterpoised to lawyers and judges who are presented as undermining whatever system there appears to be in place for dealing with asylum applications and economic migration in general. The net result is a complex one in which the only certainty appears to be that the much derided government is unable to fulfil the plans so often represented as inadequate because of the meddling of venal lawyers or high-minded judges counterpoised to the reasonable expectations of the 'taxpayer' whom the tabloids claim as their shorthand champion. The policy makers can never win within this scenario, pressed as they are from all sides. The Home Secretary David Blunkett is often the populist scapegoat:

BLUNKETT ASYLUM POLICY IN TATTERS

(*Sun*, 22 May)

CLUELESS

... DAVID Blunkett faced a new asylum row last night after claims the cost of jobless migrants to the taxpayer has been covered up.

(*Daily Star*, 26 May)

Benefit fraud is a favoured target for sensational scaremongering in the tabloids. It is an easy and often anonymous target on which to pin a variety of economic and even moral anxieties. To bring asylum seekers into the debates around benefit fraud is an extremely provocative move and one which structures the community of readers as victims in a desperate war of attrition, clinging to their modest but hard-won economic advantages. The *Sun* claims that immigration is becoming a 'cash-rich' growth industry and produces a two page banner spread with the words '**ASYLUM INC.**' illustrated as a road sign, reducing Britain to a stereotype of a company dedicated to providing asylum. The *Sun's* investigation reveals an '**asylum gravy train**'. In capital letters it lists, 'LAWYERS', 'LANDLORDS', 'SECURITY FIRMS', 'TRANSLATORS', 'ADVISERS' and 'HELPLINES', all represented as growing rich from what it terms a 'crisis' now alleged to cost '**£5 MILLION A DAY**'. The verbs are characteristic of the treatment and have a cumulative semantic effect: '... pocketed ... cashing in ... raked in ... guarantees a very nice cheque ... crammed with refugees ...'. And those dedicated to helping to deal with the situation are categorized as 'an army of advisers' whose role is reduced to 'now help illegal immigrants try to beat the system' (*Sun*, 11 May).

The *Daily Star* on 26 May takes the discussion on, highlighting one particular profession which it claims is doing very well out of this 'industry'. In an echo of populist scandals which focus on the pay-offs and pensions of an elite of wealthy entrepreneurs, the legal profession is accused of 'ripping off the legal aid system':

FATCAT LAWYERS IN ASYLUM RIP-OFF

It claims that government figures show that a quarter of firms specialising in asylum advice have 'continually overclaimed' – often for 'hopeless cases'. And that there has been an 'Eightfold increase ... rocketed.'

The language of alarm and exaggeration is generated across various popular tabloids and is maintained not only through remaining within a certain lexical register when it comes to reporting stories about asylum, but also by encouraging readers to become actively involved in reinforcing these terms of reference. The language serves as a series of speech acts – assertions, questions, promises, threats or accusations – demonstrating and enforcing the ideological terrain as a sort of 'cognitive machine' (Van Dijk, 1991: 37) on behalf of the readership. After the emotive accumulation of criticism in the article, readers are asked a question and invited to become interactively involved in commenting on the newspaper's editorial line, and thereby are drawn into a network of cohesion with the repetitive language of representation on this issue. Unsurprisingly these set-piece opinion polls are overwhelmingly more likely to deliver a verdict which supports the editorial position of the paper in a circular confirmation of opinion within this community, and not only because of the loaded colloquial term 'RIPPING OFF' which skews the debate from the start:

ARE THESE LAWYERS RIPPING OFF THE SYSTEM? Yes/No
Phone and text

(*Daily Star*, 11 May)

The *Daily Star* echoes the famous slapstick comedies, paraphrasing a legal judgement on asylum regulation to mean:

YOU CAN CARRY ON SCROUNGING

... The shock ruling has left David Blunkett's bid to crack down on foreign scroungers in tatters ... citing new 'human rights' laws imposed by Europe ... kicked out his tougher measures.

(*Daily Star*, 22 May)

It is made clear that in the newspaper's opinion a familiar structuring outsider, 'Europe', is the culprit undermining Blunkett here in the Law Lords' decision.

The picture is not as one-dimensional however and part of the complexity of the coverage of these debates in the tabloids is that they often shift tack to avoid an unrelenting barrage of negative coverage which could rapidly become boring to readers. Despite the weight of negative coverage of the issue, one tabloid is also able to indulge in characteristic humour at the expense of asylum seekers. In a tasteless variation on football squad rotation the *Daily Star* produces a report, complete with picture of a football team of asylum seekers, which enables the paper to indulge a sense of humour even on this issue which the tabloids rarely find worthy of any coverage other than outrage:

ASYLUM UNITED

(TROUBLE IS THEIR BEST PLAYERS KEEP GETTING BOOTED OUT OF BRITAIN)

(*Daily Star*, 24 May)

This variation in tone can be used to demonstrate the wisdom of what Said has written on the 'whole range of positions ... which give the Westerner a positional superiority' (1978). On occasions even the *Sun* can voice moderate and qualified support for the government's policies, here incorporating a classic liberal statement of vernacular acknowledgement, 'give them credit where it is due'.

Looking up

THERE have been few fiercer critics of the Government's asylum policy than The Sun.

So we're happy to give them credit where it is due ...

The Government has done well – but can still do better.

(*Sun*, 26 May)

The *Daily Mirror* as a lone voice uses its leader column of this day to provide what it claims is a corrective to 'right-wing newspapers' and 'small-minded racists'.

Calming fears

ASYLUM has become one of the biggest issues in the country.

That is mainly due to hysteria whipped up by right-wing newspapers and racists, but it has still presented the government with a serious problem. ...

This country needs immigrants who are useful to the economy. And we also need to keep our historic reputation as a haven for the oppressed.

But immigration must be managed and that is what the government is doing.

In doing so, they will starve the small-minded racists of fuel for their fires of hatred.

(*Daily Mirror*, 26 May)

Yet, as if to perpetuate a debate which is located to the far right of the political spectrum, it is left to the *Daily Mail* of 26 May to air its potentially alarmist views of the situation facing the country. It chooses to explain 'Why asylum figures don't tell the full story', highlights sections on 'Missing refugees', 'Deportations' and 'Free housing' which it reports do not show up in official figures, and hypothesizes 'hundreds of bogus refugees officially listed as having been deported could still be in Britain'. The linguistic strategy of 'generalization' refers to the extension of certain characteristics or activities to a specific and specifiable group of people. Here the whole lexical area of asylum seekers is extended to incorporate a much more general set of attributes such as illegality, bogus and free and unearned access to social benefits. The selection and repetition of particular generalizing attributes also hint at an underlying ideology that might have motivated the selection of language in the first place, which is often symptomatic of stereotyping or cognitive prejudice (Teo, 2000: 16).

On the same day it takes the government to task under the headline: '**This mockery of asylum "success"** ', using a wide semantic selection of the terminology reserved for these cases to build a compelling portrait of a nation under attack from an outside threat to its integrity: 'illegal immigrants', 'our porous borders', 'burgeoning black economy', 'glaring hole', 'whole army of illegals ... live in the shadows'. Three days later, normal service is maintained as a *Daily Mail* reporter compiles a portrait of impending disaster. Playing on the second meaning of 'asylum' as madhouse, the report presents a scene of chaos and despair. It is designed to make the community anxious for its own continued existence against what is presented as a failing system and one which is leeching money off the readers as taxpayers.

WELCOME TO THE ASYLUM

A Mail reporter spent a week in our asylum courts. What he found there was stupefying inefficiency, profligacy, incompetence and deceit on a massive scale. A truly despairing picture of a system on the point of total breakdown. And, guess what, you're paying for it.

(*Daily Mail*, 29 May)

Economic migrants

Following on from asylum and not only sequentially, the treatment of all issues of economic migration blurs uncomfortably with issues of race and ethnicity as represented in the tabloids, indicating how our analysis can contribute to 'not merely … identifying instances of racist discourse in the newspapers … but to show how they are embedded in a much larger, but less transparent structure of power discourse that disguises dominance in naturalized discourse' (Teo, 2000: 8).

We can note in the following the lexical progression from 'tidal wave' to 'foreign freeloaders', leading to the familiar accusation that Britain is a 'soft-touch', a script which implies the need for a toughening of attitudes and policies as a rational response to the problem and which reaffirms what Van Dijk has written concerning the ways that rhetorical figures, although independent of meaning in themselves, are still able to draw attention to and therefore indirectly emphasize particular meanings (Van Dijk, 1991: 217). Blair is referred to as a modern day Canute and Britain compared unfavourably to countries such as France and Germany:

Tony can't turn the tide

A tidal wave of economic migrants is moving across Europe and is about to crash onto our shores.

Why?

Countries such as France and Germany have set up water-tight laws to ensure their welfare handouts cannot be creamed off by foreign freeloaders. …

But Tony Blair's government has only introduced a handful of feeble last minute safeguards. …

But Blair's blundering has made soft-touch Britain the No. 1 destination for everyone who does not.

(*Sun*, 3 May)

The piece deploys a whole range of devices, including typographical features of italicization, underlining and bold type. It uses elements of a question and answer format and finishes with a crescendo of abbreviated political sloganeering in 'soft-touch Britain' and an expression borrowed from the register of holiday advertising, referring to Britain as the 'No. 1 destination'.

In the following examples, we see further evidence of the abbreviation of complex problems relating to the admission of migrants, newly entitled to enter Britain after the expansion of the European Union:

NO PASSPORT? NO PROBLEM

Migrants demanding to be let into Britain were waved through yesterday – WITHOUT passports.

(Sun, 3 May)

The *Daily Star* on the same day seems to prefer the vocabulary normally associated with weather forecasters' reports on rainfall, a lexis which emphasizes the scale further by extending the metaphor to the migrants who 'poured' into the country in their thousands. This extract reinforces what has already been claimed about the role of metaphor. It is not simply an embroidering after the facts of reports on race and ethnic issues, but a central part of the way that the story is composed and is intended for interpretation. The metaphor gives a strong indication of what Hall has called the newspaper's 'preferred meaning' and assists the reader in this (Hall, 1973).

WE GET YEAR OF MIGRANTS IN 2 DAYS

An incredible 15,000 immigrants have poured into Britain in the last two days – that's as many as the tally for a whole year.

The EU provides a narrative bridge to another asylum story to tarnish the EU further by this juxtaposition and the implied association with an illegal racket:

FAKE PASSPORT GANG SMASHED

EU identities for illegal refugees

A scam to provide thousands of illegal immigrants with fake EU passports has been smashed.

(Daily Star, 4 May)

The on-going reports on the expansion of the European Union are embroidered by the style of the coverage of the claims of the Polish President, a leader of one of the accession states himself, represented in tabloid punning tradition. The whole issue of economic migration slips temporarily down the scale of seriousness, into a comic register, as a celebrity tinge is brought to the table when the President reveals that he worked illegally in a London pub as a student:

THE POLE TRUTH …

Polish president: I was an illegal worker in London pub as student.

(*Daily Mirror*, 7 May)

However, despite the individualized take on the past of a political celebrity, it is the exaggerated scale of the current situation which is woven into both stories as the newspapers report on and amplify popular concerns that the expansion of the EU will bring thousands of Polish and other Eastern European workers to Britain looking for work. The following piece takes the standard migrant conspiracy to baroque depths of tabloid sensationalism and dubious raucous humour to illustrate a story which blurs into the asylum debate. The use of the terms 'bogus bride' and 'black economy' provocatively locate the story within familiar patterns of coverage but this time there is the opportunity for the *Sun* to integrate it in a wider range of its bizarre agenda.

HOUSE MARRIAGE SCAM

Till death us do chapatti

The story has a '**BOGUS bride**' being married bigamously to a chef in a 'curry house' to allow him to stay in the country to 'curry favour' with her lover, the restaurant owner. The puns accumulate in the format of a mock menu which serves to reinforce both the absurdity of the story and the prejudices and stereotypes on which it builds and thereby which it further propagates.

MENU

Wedding Breakfast

Starters

Popadum the question

Union Bhaji

Main courses

1 vindaloo

Here kormas the bride

Chicken Honeybhuna

Served with

BEST NAAN

PILAU SPLICE

(*Sun*, 6 May)

There is arguably nobody more of an insider to Britain than a prisoner detained behind bars in a British prison and whose release may be years away. However, the *Daily Mail* is quick to point out the differences between 'our' prisoners and 'foreign' prisoners as contrasted in their different approaches to the small amounts of money earned for work undertaken in prison in keeping with traditional tabloid binarisms. In this account, the thrifty practice of saving money is turned to their disadvantage as they are represented as exploiting a perk, once again at the cost of the British taxpayer and by strong implication the reader of the *Daily Mail*.

CRIME DOES PAY

How foreign inmates send their £40-a-week prison 'wage' home while we pay for them to stay behind bars

(*Daily Mail*, 8 May)

In the following example, the *Daily Mail* launches its own provocative campaign to make news which it can then tag onto its predetermined agenda, beginning with its slogan: '**OPEN-DOOR UK**'. It tells of a journalist from the paper who had paid £700 for a fake passport and travelled to Britain. This form of 'tagging' enables a cohesion to be maintained across a range of stories. It acts as a narrative cue to readers to categorize it and the language it echoes along with similar reports. It explicitly preys on fears of the scale of such practices and the possibility that terrorists might gain access in this way, accentuating the overstretched officials at the end of the line in Britain:

After flashing my passport at a harassed official. ... There is little to stop people – who knows how many? – following in my footsteps.

(*Daily Mail*, 8 May)

The *Sun* can go one further however, planting an undercover journalist among immigration officers on a tip-off, to get its story of corruption. One attractive feature of this story for the tabloid is that the immigration officer in question is alleged to be a lesbian, adding an opportunity for further punning in the headline. The story allows undercover photographs to be published in sequence like a film shoot – 'THE MEETING', 'THE PAY-OFF', 'THE PASSPORT'. It draws favourable comment thanking the *Sun* from the Immigration Minister, Des Brown, and calls upon the readers to reinforce this community of scandal tip-offs by calling the paper.

BENT IMMIGRATION OFFICER'S BOAST TO SUN INVESTI-GATOR

It's £500 for a passport ... I can get more for your pals

- DO you know a scandal? Call The Sun ... or email ...

In the above campaign, the *Sun* itself is the chief motivational factor, determining the news agenda proactively and seeking to include its readers in the development of this coverage of the presumed widely available evidence of other corruption.

Those who have in the past been outsiders to the British community and who are atypical of the core readership of the tabloids can sometimes be drawn in as honorary insiders if they confirm a point being made by the newspaper. These occasions are as erratic in their patterning as they are in number. Here, in this example, a Polish soldier who was already a 'war-hero' on the side of the Allies in World War II and therefore already high on the tabloid list of respect, became 'A BRIT' in taking up citizenship, and is used as a model for new immigrants.

> THE POLISH WAR HERO WHO BECAME A BRIT ON WHY WE MUST EMBRACE THE NEW EUROPE
>
> (*Daily Mirror*, 28 April)

The exceptional outsider to the community can also become newsworthy when he can be presented as an aspirational model in an idealized British meritocracy:

> **Bowling for Harrow, the Afghan boy who fled from the terror of the Taliban**
>
> ... But he has been plucked from the obscurity of a North-West London comprehensive and awarded an Outstanding Talent scholarship at £20,985-a-year Harrow thanks to his extraordinary prowess with both bat and ball.
>
> (*Daily Mail*, 13 May)

Evil outsiders

The tabloids create categories of evil outsiders to contrast with the inner community of their own readers, and use a wide range of emotive terms to emphasize both the nature of the outsiders and the stability and health of the insider community (Wykes, 2001). There is a paradox here which the sensationalist tabloid press has always needed to deal with, keeping threats to the community and the solidity of that community in balance so that it may appear under threat but nevertheless in constant process of reaffirming its resilience. There is a great amount of uniformity in cases of moral outrage across the popular tabloids. The individual in question here is Maxine Carr, dubbed 'hated Maxine Carr' by the newspaper. She is a 'Child killer's moll', an 'Evil liar' or 'the Soham liar'. In the following example, the *Sun* also flags up its own intervention in this and uses the photos as a demonstration of its hands-on role in getting access for its readers to the details about a particular individual's circumstances. She is calculated by a rough estimate as costing the same in security as the Prime Minister, and to consolidate her outsider status, it is stressed that readers as 'taxpayers' will have to pay.

CARR GETS 'SAME SECURITY AS PM'

Gun guards for Maxine will cost us £1m a year

(*Sun*, 4 May)

The *Daily Star* on 6 May remarks how 'angry inmates' have already protested over her 'VIP treatment in nick' and are now furious over her 'heading for a cushy new life in Sweden'. It too stresses the 'taxpayers' expense'. Even Maxine Carr's dog gets the pariah treatment and its new name is revealed in a ploy designed to disseminate enough about her new identity without falling foul of the law. Maxine's dog gets a new ID, renamed Cody instead of Sadie, which is revealed in a front page insert in the *Sun* of 7 May. A 'hate-filled protest' of fellow prisoners is presented in the *Daily Star* of 6 May as a legitimate response to her release. By implication, ordinary criminals seem to have popular license to behave like this with the implicit approval of the readers who are drawn in by editorial perspective and pictures to tacitly take the side of their newspaper. Coverage of her hearing on charges of minor fraud and deception was filled with implications of mob justice.

STUFF JUSTICE

Fury as deal lets Carr off new jail stretch

… Fellow inmates staged a furious demo last night over the plan to sneak her out of prison early …

(*Daily Star*, 8 May)

This intimation of approval for a harsher form of revenge is reinforced by the inclusion of comments in the *Sun* of 15 May from the mother of James Bulger, the small child who was killed by older children who similarly had their identities changed for their protection on release from prison. She claims Carr has been 'let off' and the papers generally depict her as having been able to get off on the sympathy of a court by shedding a few tears. The *Daily Star* features a prominent photograph of prisoners at the jail where Maxine Carr is being held shortly before her release.

BURN THE BITCH ON THE STAKE SHE IS PURE EVIL

(*Daily Star*, 13 May)

Part of the hyperbole of this on-going campaign is to represent her as the ultimate antithesis of the tabloid community – witch burning indeed of a tabloid twentieth century variety. Each era may be defined by the way it treats its 'witches' – here we have symbolic death by tabloid campaign. In summarizing its view of the case, the *Sun* is quick to set itself up as the voice of the community, repeating in a rhetorical flourish the phrase '*The public should know*' as a key device in its argument about why the whereabouts of Maxine Carr should be public knowledge.

> **THE cloak of secrecy thrown around Maxine Carr sets a dangerous legal precedent.**
>
> … What if she gets a job at a school?
>
> The public should know. …
>
> The public should know. …
>
> **The law is wrong to protect her.**
>
> (*Sun*, 15 May)

Individual as evil

In the following examples, sexism and disgust at the lower classes conflate into a portrait of behaviour which is predicated solely on the individual; in the tabloids more than anywhere else in Britain there is certainly no such thing as society and certainly little understanding of corporate or collective responsibility apart from the symbolic rhetoric of the nation. This coverage fits with the individual, isolationist view of the world where people are the victims of their circumstances and the fates in an 'anarchic existentialism' (Langer, 1998) common across other tabloid coverage. There are also strong elements of melodrama (Gripsrud, 1992) in the persistent use of the word 'evil' to describe these characters; a word which extracts events from the scrutiny of rational enquiry and places them beyond the vocabulary of explanation. This sort of vocabulary amplifies the tendency of tabloid newspapers to place people outside the sphere of the rational and at the mercy of the elemental forces of fate (Curran *et al.*, 1980). Lynndie England, an American volunteer in Iraq accused of abusing prisoners of war, certainly seems a victim of fate and is represented as entirely dependent on her miserable circumstances. The implication is that Lynndie England is evil because she comes from a poor background and her low moral standard seems confirmed through implication by the combination of her sexual behaviour and her pregnancy. Accompanying a 'sickening' photograph of the accused parading a naked Iraqi PoW around a Baghdad jail on an animal lead comes the headline:

> **WITCH**
>
> **Evil soldier Lynndie in new torture photo**
>
> … The former chicken factory worker from a dirt-poor town is pregnant by one of the other brutes pictured torturing prisoners. … Trailer trash torturer who shames US
>
> … a pregnant divorcee from a trailer park.
>
> (*Sun*, 7 May)

Evil can also be used in the same way to apply to groups of individuals such as the much demonized paedophiles. A special *Sun* report gives details of the day release of sex offenders from a mental hospital and stresses the proximity – 'inches' between these inmates and unsuspecting people going about their daily business. 'Mums', 'kids' and 'kiddies' are juxtaposed with 'sex beasts', 'beasts', 'evil's path' and the captioning of photographs of sex offenders in three photos – 'PAEDOPHILE', 'PAEDOPHILE' and 'PSYCHOPATH' show the offenders in the proximity of young children. The effect is to suggest an atmosphere of panic to ordinary readers.

Sun Investigation

… Kids inches from sex beasts freed for shopping trips

Eleven beasts have been allowed out of a secure mental hospital to mingle with mums and kiddies.

(*Sun*, 4 May)

The device of the compressed noun phrase is frequently used as an emotive trigger for a familiar script concerning sex offenders:

KIDS' AUTHOR JAILED FOR MOLESTING GIRLS

Pervert children's author William Mayne was jailed for 2½ years yesterday for sexually abusing his young fans.

Paedophile Mayne, 76 … used his fame to lure the girls.

(*Sun*, 5 May)

On other occasions it is enough to deploy words or phrases which attempt to capture the hostility of the imagined community of tabloid readers: 'Porno paedo', 'child porn pervert', 'fiends', 'pervs', 'sex beasts', 'convicted pervs'.

A persuasive method of bridging criminality and general deviance with the bogeyman of the EU is deployed in the *Daily Star*, reporting on a decision to allow freedom of movement across the newly expanded EU to those with criminal records:

EU BEASTS ON THE WAY TO BRITAIN

Ban lifted for 60,000

MURDERERS, rapists and other criminals from Eastern Europe …

(*Daily Star*, 6 May)

Outsiders to tabloid Britain are not restricted to sexual pariahs but are also drawn from those outside the assumed work ethic of the honest and hard-grafting *Daily Star* readers. The following story fits well with the overall agenda of bizarre news and with the script that we are undermined financially by the habits of the occasional 'scrounger' who lives off the state and therefore the hard work of others. Such isolated and spectacular cases are emphasized to suggest that this is a bigger problem than it actually is and to indulge in a grotesque form of mockery of the individual concerned. A deluge of negative expressions are hurled at Susan 'Gimme' Moore by the *Daily Star* on 13 May: **'Britain's laziest woman'**, 'lazy slob', 'super-scrounger', 'whining excuses ... bone idle ... work-shy'. It is represented as a victory for the newspaper as it follows on from its own story of 'BRITAIN'S LAZIEST SCROUNGER', which it had run in February and in which it revealed the woman to the authorities, who have now taken action by stopping her Jobseeker's Allowance. This is fully in keeping with the self-promotional tendency within the tabloids.

Outsiders to the imperial nation

The normativity of the British perspective at the core of the tabloids' news values and encoded in their language is integral to the coverage of ethnic and geograph-ical outsiders. This is particularly true when the outsiders have associations with an aspect of Britain's imperial past or neo-imperial present, as British culture is rooted in a history which is indelibly marked with the associations of empire and cultural presumptions of superiority. This has created a set of engagements with outsider groups which have been described in the following terms by Stuart Hall:

> Subordinate ethnic groups and classes appeared, not as the objects of particular historical relations (the slave trade, European colonization, the active underdevelopment of the 'underdeveloped societies'), but as the given qualities of an inferior *breed*. Relations, secured by economic, social, political and military domination were transformed and 'naturalized' into an order of *rank*, ascribed by Nature.
>
> (Hall, 1981: 38)

Ethnic outsiders are frequently highlighted by alliterative phrases which contrast to the projected norms of Western reporters and their readers. Van Dijk has drawn the conclusion that alliteration is a common strategy deployed by the popular press to hammer home its own evaluations of events (1991: 217–18). Reports such as the following not only demonstrate alliteration in action but are doubly significant since they also demonstrate in what circum-stances overseas events or religion become news in the tabloids:

THE MURDEROUS MULLAHS

Few Western reporters are allowed to visit Iran. In this powerful dispatch Ann Leslie paints a horrifying picture of a violent and corrupt dictator-ship run by fanatical Muslim fundamentalists.

(*Daily Mail*, 22 May)

The style of representation of outsiders hostile to the national and dominant ethnic community is key to creating a sense of identification based not only on disputes between international parties and interests but on the basis of binary distinctions around the notion of national community/outsider. In reports of Iraqi protests against the death of innocent members of the public in post-invasion Iraq, this strategy is well exemplified in the hyperbolic call to the memory of readers in building upon the 'OUR'/'YOUR' binary categories assisted by a combination of typographical tricks and strong vernacular mimicry:

Let's not forget ...

There is wrongdoing on both sides and the Islamic fundamentalists should take that into account before screaming revenge.

(*Daily Star*, 6 May)

In the same issue, the paper can also personify its address to the people of Iraq in a rhetorical flourish and gesture of self-regard:

Daily Star message to wailing Iraqis: We won't forget what YOUR mob did to OUR people

SAVE YOUR BLOODY CROCODILE TEARS

Despite criticism in the piece of the Iraqis' 'short memories', the *Daily Star* is working on maintaining the long-term memory of its national community of patriotic readers.

Outsiders are not only ostracized because of their sexual deviance or their sloth, they can also be placed beyond the notional community of readers on the grounds of their religion or their radical behaviour. Abu Hamza, the radical Muslim cleric, has been selected for special treatment as much on account of his extraordinary appearance as for his attempts to radicalize Muslims at a North London mosque. The attention paid to Abu Hamza and the language used to describe him make him a key figure in the personification of Islam as a religion of fanaticism. In the punning frenzy which accompanies all the stories about him in the tabloids it is remarkable that it is possible to combine the notion of 'evil' regularly with familiar and humorous references to him as 'HOOKY', juxtaposed with more sinister descriptions: 'EVIL HOOKY', 'evil Hamza', 'mad mullah' and '**EVIL hook-handed terror preacher**', '**THE preacher of hate**', 'Islamic fanatic', 'Muslim fanatic', 'disgusting stain on this country'.

When it is decided that he can be deported to the USA, the *Daily Mail* uses the news to develop a further binary distinction which fits into its own political opposition to the British liberal establishment. In this the weakness of the British government is opposed to the strength of the USA. Blame for indecision is placed unequivocally at the doorstep of the Labour government. There is a clear expectation, given the severity of judgement, that readers would prefer the more draconian American solution. In addition, the paper counterpoises dissatisfaction with the alleged hypocrisy of the government on multiculturalism, hinting in a tendentiously racist argument that Labour considers certain ethnic minorities above the law.

How U.S. shows up lily-livered Britain

... This is a shocking indictment of the Government. It has grandstanded for years about the multicultural society, and about all Britons being equal under the law irrespective of their race, colour or creed.

Unfortunately, in Labour's eyes some are more equal than others. Equality under the law is crucial to our way of life, our values and our democracy. Yet it has been clear for some time that a man can get away with seditious, treasonable or inciteful acts provided he is a prominent member of a minority community.

(*Daily Mail*, 28 May)

As if to confirm the communal frenzy encouraged by the reporting of the activities of the cleric, there is a picture of protesters outside court with a 'SLING UR HOOK' banner. One of the features of Abu Hamza which makes him such a productive tabloid target is the almost limitless variety of puns and visual references which can be used to weave humour into this tale of extremism and vilification. It is worth noting that the tabloid agenda for poking fun and using gratuitous references to appearance can be woven in unproblematically with claims about the danger which this man poses to Britain's security. In addition, as part of the standard tabloid indexing of outsiders, there is the common calculation of what it will cost the insiders, referred to as 'US', to keep him from being punished by the death sentence if he is extradicted to the USA. To further endorse its position, the *Daily Star*, not normally known for its championing of any Muslim views, seems to include the moderate Muslims in its community of common sense, while at the same time indicating that a little home-grown justice would not have been out of place.

WE HAVE TO PAY £1M TO STOP HOOKY FROM FRYING

... The vast majority of Muslims will welcome his arrest.

We really should have banged this man up ourselves.

(*Daily Star*, 28 May)

The *Sun* on 28 May on its front page hails the success of '**OUR FIVE YEAR CAMPAIGN**' and is at pains to indicate by reference to its own coverage that it first called for him to be 'booted out' in 1999, showing a front page from 31 January 2003 with the banner headline 'SLING YOUR HOOK'.

It makes you wonder how many more dangerous men could be walking the streets of Britain like Hamza was.

We must stop giving succour to the enemy within so we can win the war on terror.

(*Sun*, 28 May)

In addition, it hints that there are more in Britain who could pose a similar threat in an illustration of the parallelism which is part of racist representation in the newspapers according to Van Dijk. Representing such unnamed figures as part of a complex of associations as an 'enemy within' can do little for extending the imagined community of the tabloids beyond the dominant confines of the indigenous white perspective.

> Since the dominant white media and their ideologies are inextricably related to these political, social, and corporate elite groups, and mediate, legitimate, or even directly support white elite power, it is also in their interest to play their crucial 'symbolic' role in the reproduction of the ethnic consensus and, in fact, to participate itself in its (pre)formulation.
>
> (Van Dijk, 1991: 43)

The *Daily Mirror* also joins in the condemnation from a patriotic perspective but without the extreme language of the other newspapers.

Better place without him

ABU Hamza does not deserve to live in this great country and enjoy its great privileges.

(*Daily Mirror*, 28 May)

The *Sun* takes advantage of the news to focus its 'Big Issue' on letters from readers on the subject further contributing to the sense of a community unified by outrage at the time it has taken to get this man the justice which they believe he deserves.

> ... sad indictment of Tony Blair and his spineless government ... loathsome tick. ... Shame on you Mr Blair and Mr Blunkett ... hates us Brits so much ... vile ... the Hook ... our joke legal system and rotten liberal establishment ...
>
> (*Sun*, 31 May)

The *Sun* provides another way of ostracizing him by referring to him here as the 'Bin Laden of Britain'. It is provocative in the extreme by labelling him in this way but it is a familiar comparative device, like comparing Saddam Hussein to Adolf Hitler (Keeble, 1997). This device scores high on emotional intent but lower on analytical accuracy, collapsing particular historical, cultural and geographical differences into personal invective. The enemies of the national community become in this way more metaphorical than real but are no less effective in symbolic terms.

Perfect tabloid villains

Another example of when those constructed as outsiders to the national community become news comes with the report of an 'African asylum seeker', who had exploited his relationship with a gay British diplomat to enter the country and deliberately infect women with the HIV virus while keeping them as 'sex slaves'. It fits with the assertion that there is a stereotypical, naturalized and dominant representation of Africa which can serve to heighten popular feelings of sovereign nationhood, uniqueness, superiority over other societies and resentment towards ethnic groups and foreigners (Brookes, 1995: 487). Feston Konzani is an ideal composite villain, incorporating many of the sensationalist features of an ideal tabloid story about an African outsider who is also a sexual pariah. Konzani had arrived in Britain with the help of a British diplomat, claimed to be his lover and is alleged to have knowingly infected several women with HIV. He is reported in the *Daily Mail* as being from the 'Aids-torn African country of Malawi' (15 May) and in other papers the categorization of Malawi as 'Aids-torn' may not be used but he continues to be reduced to an 'African asylum seeker' without reference to his specific country of origin within Africa. The use of such evaluative epithets as prenominal modifiers are of particular ideological significance as they have become completely naturalized classifications (Brookes, 1995: 480). They supply the frame with which the readers are invited to view news from Africa. It is clearly a process which is distorted by this linguistic mechanism in advance.

This set of reports adds a more xenophobic gloss to the question of when Africa becomes news. The omission of overseas news in general only goes to highlight the negative aspects of the continent when they are given prominence in the tabloids. He is referred to, across the tabloids, in language which draws his nationality together with aspects of their lexicon of sexual outsiders, as 'Evil Feston Konzani', an 'HIV TIMEBOMB', 'A LYING lover', an 'HIV FIEND', an 'AIDS ASSASSIN' and 'A WOMAN HATER'. This perfect tabloid villain can be criticized for not appreciating what is being offered to him in this country, thus encouraging a degree of implicit hostility from readers:

> He regularly appeared at asylum drop-in centres and benefit offices to shout and scream at those who were trying to help him.

> In bile-filled poems and essays he decried the Western values he had dreamed of and attacked the systems that fed, clothed and housed him ... defence funded by legal aid ...
>
> (*Daily Mail*, 15 May)

The whole coverage is a very clear illustration of what Hall has referred to as 'inferential racism':

> By *inferential* racism I mean those apparently naturalized representations of events and situations relating to race, whether 'factual' or 'fictional', which have racist premises and propositions inscribed in them as a set of *unquestioned assumptions*. These enable racist statements to be formulated without ever bringing into awareness the racist predicates on which the statements are grounded.
>
> (Hall, 1981: 36)

Overt racism coverage

Despite the xenophobia and sensationalizing of foreign outsiders, most of the time the tabloids are careful to condemn any expression of overt racism. This was illustrated perfectly in the Ron Atkinson affair where a near unanimity was expressed across the range of tabloids in Britain. Atkinson, a retired football manager and respected television commentator, was heard to utter a brief but explicit racist diatribe against a black player after a game while he believed that the studio microphone was switched off.

The front page of the *Sun* of 22 April shows how a pun, playing on his soubriquet of 'Big Ron', skilfully deployed can deliver a blunt condemnation of his racist outburst in vernacular terms:

BIGOT RON

It continues to describe with all the efficiency of a compressed noun phrase this 'racist slur shame', and calls it a 'shocking bigoted attack' while blanking out syllables from the offensive outburst: '**a f****** lazy big n*****'**. Its leading article combines a recognition of personal responsibility as well as the institutional unacceptability of such language, writing, with typical tabloid modality, that he '**should be deeply ashamed**' and adding:

> There is no room if football – or anywhere else – for attitudes and language like Atkinson's.

Their main article that day calls on opinion from fellow television pundits, Piara Powar of Football Against Racism, the Commission for Racial Equality (an organisation often treated with little more than contempt by the *Sun*) and, interestingly from a populist perspective, the fans themselves: '**Fans blast Atkinson's racist rant at Desailly**'. The tone is however lightened and a familiar tabloid mnemonic put into action with a list of celebrities who have 'put their foot in it' (*Sun*, 22 April).

The *Daily Star* is unequivocal in its leading article on the matter and foregrounds its own television-driven agenda, claiming:

Racist Ron so wrong

BIG Ron Atkinson is famous for his telly bloopers — but his latest just wasn't funny.

Yet in this edition of the same paper there is a minor story about Robert Kilroy-Silk being back on the BBC, if only as a contestant on 'Have I Got News For You'. His departure from his daytime chatshow had been prompted by a well-publicized column he had written in a Sunday newspaper which included his views on Muslims in Britain and the position of Islam in the world. The views had been considered so inflammatory and offensive to Muslims that he was sacked from the show, as it was felt that the expression of such extreme views from somebody so prominent in the public eye made him unsuitable to continue in his role. Yet the *Daily Star* feels able to reduce the gravity of his misjudgement and the response of the BBC to his being 'Forced out of his show … despite overwhelming public support.' This indicates that there is a corner of at least one tabloid, even on a day with such a lead story, which can demonstrate a moderate line on xenophobic outbursts.

In Scotland, despite the traditionally national nature of football coverage in this branch of the British tabloid press, there is a huge front page headline in the *Daily Record* on 22 April, making its own position perfectly clear:

RACIST RON

As a counter to stories that Atkinson was a champion of black players, simply a victim of his own inarticulate anger, the *Daily Mirror* features black footballer Ian Wright on its front page a day later:

Ron IS racist

EXCLUSIVE: HE TAUNTED ME, SAYS IAN WRIGHT
(*Daily Mirror*, 23 April)

In an indication of how tabloids can work within their own traditions to broaden debate on such issues, the *Daily Mirror* uses a piece by former editor of black newspaper *The Voice*, Steve Pope:

Why N word is the worst of insults to black people

The power of any word to offend lies not with its actual meaning but with its history, the mental connotations conjured up by it.
(*Daily Mirror*, 23 April)

In its leading article on the same day the *Daily Mirror* reinforces the historical context of language and racism:

RACISM has been the curse of football since well before the first black player took up the professional game.

At one stage, some terraces were like a parade ground for Nazi skinheads who taunted and chanted their disgusting slogans. ...

Ron Atkinson should be setting an example, not descending to the level of the skinheads.

(*Daily Mirror*, 23 April)

It also runs the story of a complaint by fan Ian Mawson in 1990 about the England versus Cameroon game, where Ron Atkinson is also alleged to have made racist comments on air which were ignored by senior managers at ITV. This highlights the institutional blind spots around racism which allow individuals to operate without sanctions as a characteristic of structural racism.

The *Sun* on 23 April runs counter stories to the *Daily Mirror*'s, with ex-footballers, well-known to readers, Carlton Palmer, Viv Anderson, Tony Daley and Paul Williams ('If Big Ron's racist, I'm a white man') to lend support for the man who they say gave black players their first big break in British football. Yet, it also contributes an accompanying piece from Michael Eboda, editor of *New Nation*, who explains its offensiveness through a historical perspective. The *Daily Star* takes a different perspective and while not wishing to diminish what Atkinson has said, moves to provide a range of mitigating explanations.

Former England star John Barnes called Atkinson's comments 'inexcusable' but questioned whether using such terminology made him a racist. ... Anti-racist campaigners have slammed him but the nation seems divided – even the Commission for Racial Equality praised Atkinson's attitude as a manager ...

(*Daily Star*, 23 April)

A parallel piece in the *Daily Star* by Irvine Wise, Assistant Editor with an Afro-Caribbean partner for his anti-racist credentials, is worth quoting at length:

... good race relations are not necessarily fostered by shock-horror knee-jerk reaction whenever someone says something distasteful ... our society is, by and large, a tolerant and liberal one.

Such a society should be able to voice its disapproval of what Atkinson said, without demanding his head on a platter.

A full, public apology and a hefty donation to an appropriate charity should be enough.

Then a suitably chastened Big Ron should be allowed to go back to what he does best.

Talking harmless nonsense on the telly.

(*Daily Star*, 23 April)

However, on its letters pages it includes a note of support which, though clearly not part of the newspaper's overt agenda, does indicate something of the editorially acceptable range of views on the matter.

Your texts

If that's big Rons opinion hes entitled it, stuff the pc brigade its supposed to b a free country **Phil, Wakefield**

Big ron's got balls he tells it how it is! **Mitch**

The story was revived when another football commentator expressed the opinion that Atkinson's views and the language he had used to air them were not as shocking as had been implied. The *Daily Mail* reported it from an interview he had given to the *Independent* as an example of Hill leading with his renowned chin, but blanked out letters in the offending word.

Jimmy Hill leads with his chin as he joins soccer racism rumpus

JIMMY HILL entered the football racism row last night claiming the word n★★★★r was no more offensive than saying he had a big chin ... 'simply the language of the football field'

(*Daily Mail*, 14 May)

The *Daily Mirror* on 14 May went one step further and referred to the incident as adding to the 'race shame'. In the 'Mirror Comment', the newspaper explained why this was worse than the original:

Hill's own goal

Jimmy Hill's defence of Ron Atkinson's racist remark is even worse than the original.

For he didn't speak in the heat of the moment but with cold calculation.

ITV sacked Atkinson. Sky should do the same to Hill.

(*Daily Mirror*, 14 May)

The clear message that overt racism is unacceptable to the tabloids also extends to celebrities. There is no false patriotic loyalty when a member (albeit an unpopular one) of the Royal Family is accused of expressing racist views in an argument over dining arrangements in a New York restaurant. Nevertheless, the *Daily Star* considers it relevant to add her German ancestry as an implicit explanation for her racist views.

PRINCESS Michael of Kent was branded a racist yesterday after a claim she screamed at noisy black diners. ...

The German-born royal spent her youth in the colonies – Australia – after fleeing Austria with her mum at the end of World War Two.

Her dad, Baron Gunther Van Reibnitz, was in Hitler's SS.

(Daily Star, 27 May)

The unanimity of condemnation for overt racism in British society is applied across the board in the tabloids when it occurs institutionally as well. When a black nurse from Southampton University Hospital is awarded compensation because she had been prohibited from looking after white children because she is black, the *Daily Mirror* is unequivocal:

RACIST SHAME OF NHS

(Daily Mirror, 18 May)

This theme is taken up, developing from the story of the nurse, in Fiona Phillips' Saturday comment column, when explicit advice is offered to readers:

Only cure for sick racists

… next time someone says to you 'I'm not racist but …'. Don't even give them the time of day.

(Daily Mirror, 22 May)

The *Sun* can celebrate the selection of a black officer to lead one of the units at the Trooping the Colour pageant, stressing in a gesture of national inclusivity that 'Our traditions – such as the Queen's Birthday Parade – are his traditions.' The paper celebrates:

A proud day

MORONS like the BNP will be horrified

… That is exactly the kind of Britain we all want.

(Sun, 1 June)

The BNP is also used as the bogeyman for the *Daily Star* when it reports a story concerning the planting of pupils to ask racist questions in schools:

EVIL BNP POISONING SCHOOLKIDS' MINDS

THE far-right British National Party is conning children into helping spread its message of race hatred …

(Daily Star, 20 May)

Yet often it is an integral part of the way that tabloids compress their language which works against any intention to condemn racism in an effective or consistent way. The elaboration of abuse in the following extract leads to an uncomfortable juxtaposition of exposition, repetition of racist abuse and the trivialization of abbreviation:

RACE ABUSE POSTIE BAGS £200,000

AN Asian postman branded a 'spear-chucking raghead' by his racist colleagues was awarded £200,000 yesterday. ...

Only night shift worker ... car vandalised. ... Threats ... sworn at, bullied and called 'Paki' ... daubed graffiti ...

(*Daily Star*, 26 May)

Covert racism as 'political correctness' script

The following shows how the tabloid-generated debate over the alleged practice of political correctness can be invoked in an attack on the way outsiders to the tabloid community are dealt with. The 'PC' argument is that an excessively defensive establishment is reluctant to resist pressure to exercise sensitivity in language and broader cultural matters (Woehrling, 1996) for fear of upsetting liberal, ethnic or sexual minorities. 'Political correctness' is then depicted, particularly in the popular tabloids, as an organized 'lobby' or 'brigade' which is encroaching on the right to free speech of the indigenous majority. The implication is that freedom for this community includes the right to routinely demonize and categorize selected outsiders as scapegoats without fear of legal redress or complaint (Cameron, 1995). In addition, the language deliberately attempts to mimic the vernacular of ordinary readers as a strategy to include them in the critique of what the tabloids depict as an unnecessary interference in cultural affairs. The selection of letters from 10 May illustrates how both the *Sun*'s rhetoric and its continual references to the oppressive nature of 'political correctness' are confident in a receptive and responsive community of readers and include a vernacular exhortation to Home Secretary David Blunkett, indicating that the targeted reader is concerned that he is not up to his job:

Booting out extremists after attack is too late

THE words stable door, horse and bolted come to mind.

... rabble-rousing cleric Abu Mamza and the like ... gutless Government ... these scum ... hate-filled cronies. ... Their race hate and Jihad messages. ... Get a grip, Blunkett ... the UK is so concerned with political correctness ... pathetic bunch ... Muslim extremists ...

(*Sun*, 10 May)

Yet the tabloids still use 'covert' racist strategies to destabilize anti-racist, assertive measures to ensure that racism becomes further marginalized within

British society. We may have less overt racism but we can still see examples of the covert variety, which include the disparagement of formal anti-racist perspectives as if they were as bad as the practice and institutions of racism themselves. Van Dijk points out that for the right-wing press, its main opponents will generally include the symbolic competitors for the definition of the ethnic situation, for example, anti-racist educators, scholars, writers, as well as some politicians (Van Dijk, 1991: 44). The *Daily Mail* was quick to play the political correctness card when black officers refused to co-operate in an investigation which required their giving DNA samples. The expression 'political correctness gone crazy', quoted verbatim, forms part of a self-lubricating linguistic rationale whenever interventions in equality affairs are raised. The matching of the quotation to the standard editorial view of 'political correctness' is a pragmatic closure around protagonists and the idealized community's perspective which the paper purports to champion. It acts as a slogan which attempts to block out questioning the status quo, particularly the social and linguistic. Here, despite the fact that it is, along with other popular tabloids, against overt racism, the *Daily Mail* demonstrates the routine opprobrium reserved for any black people who question the opinions of white society and its normatized community of common sense.

50 black policemen were happy to give DNA to help identify a rapist. But when their union heard, they opposed the idea saying it was politically incorrect. Now the hunt has stalled.

... The hunt for Britain's most prolific serial sex attacker is being thwarted by political correctness in the police force, it emerged last night ... 'political correctness gone crazy' ...

(*Daily Mail*, 19 May)

When a representative for Charter Guidelines for the Bereaved pointed out that regulations recommend that symbols specific to a particular religion should be removed from a crematorium used by many faiths, the *Daily Mail* used the story first to reinforce its views on 'political correctness' and second to highlight other stories, which can provide narrative cohesion for readers. A lexical item such as 'political correctness' can then transcend its cohesive role as a textual linker and assume a role in the ideational function of language, re-shaping and re-conceptualizing meaning and experience (Teo, 2000: 34). It completes this cohesive circle by inviting readers to e-mail an answer to a question which is closed in the cliché of its asking:

Crematorium chief bans Christian symbol 'to spare other faiths'

Cover up, the Cross the PC boss couldn't bear

... Sue Stern of Southwark Pastoral Auxiliary Christian Group said: 'This is political correctness gone mad ...'.

Earlier this year judges were ordered to stop using words such as 'immigrant' and 'Asian' or any gender-based references for fear of causing offence.

And last year Devon and Cornwall police sent out Christmas cards that made no mention of Christmas itself.

Any traditional religious symbols were banned as part of a move to show a more 'community-wide' approach.

- Is this political correctness gone mad? www.dailymail.co.uk

(*Daily Mail*, 26 May)

The *Daily Mirror* is not immune from a similar sort of prejudicial reporting, as became apparent when it was reprimanded for its preview of a television documentary on prostitution in Bradford. It contextualized its report with a brief summary of the riots of July 2001 in Bradford.

'ASIAN PERVERTS' SHOW AXED IN RACE RIOT FEAR

... pulled by Channel 4 from last night's schedule after police warned it could spark race riots.

Edge of the City claims to show how Asian men are targeting white girls as young as 11 for sex and drug abuse (in Bradford) in the West Yorkshire city blighted by disorder in 2001. ... [Y]oung Asian men ... bricks, bottles, petrol bombs ... some of the worst disturbances in Britain for 20 years. ... BNP ... banned from marching in Bradford ...

(*Daily Mirror*, 21 May)

The following day the *Guardian* reported the police response to the *Daily Mirror's* story which was particularly critical of their use of 'Asian Perverts' in the headline. Colin Gramphorn, the head of West Yorkshire police, said:

A Daily Mirror headline, 'Asian perverts show axed in race riots fear', was false and incendiary.

I think it gets very close to the criminal standard of inciting public disorder. What basis is there for the word 'Asian Perverts'? The investigation we have done has arrested both Asian and white men.

(*Guardian*, 22 May)

Categorizing anti-racists who work explicitly to identify and eradicate racist practices which have become ingrained in British society as 'race police' and proposing that London is an idyllic multi-ethnic paradise which has emerged simply through the realization of the benefits of difference does nothing to acknowledge that we have not arrived even in the imperfect place that is contemporary London simply through *laissez-faire*. The cultural tolerance, such as it is, as experienced by *Sun* columnist Littlejohn on a Sunday stroll through the capital has been achieved by the development of policies and their implementation through legal enforcement, by those he would presumably denigrate as 'race warriors'.

> What do the race warriors do at the weekends? … It's time the race police … should get out more. … On Sunday, I took a walk in our local park. There were Second World War veterans drinking tea and eating bacon sarnies alongside immigrant families grilling halal meat on barbies … black and white, Asian, Cypriot – both Greek and Turkish. … There wasn't a diversity co-ordinator, or equalities enforcer in sight.
>
> Just Londoners having a good time …
>
> How very English it all was.
>
> (*Sun*, 25 May)

Once again, the *Daily Mirror* shows that it can also be drawn into the categorization and transitivity strategies which are an integral part of covert racism. It describes Trevor Phillips, the head of the Commission for Racial Equality, as one of the 'race watchdogs' in language similar to Littlejohn's and the familiar 'political correctness' refrain of the *Daily Mail*, and uses the term 'blasted' to indicate the power of this transitivity. The description of Phillips as head of 'race watchdogs' and the publishing of the full text of the song deflate his position, categorizing it as simply opposing a bit of fun and using strong-arm tactics in the verbs of the article, 'blasted', 'slams' and, mockingly, 'rapped':

> RAPPED
>
> Watchdog slams police officer for 'patronising' song to black officers
>
> A POLICE chief has been blasted by race watchdogs for singing a 'patronising' Eminem-style rap to his black officers …
>
> (*Daily Mirror*, 28 May)

Conclusion

The national community functions very much along the lines articulated by Bauman (1997: 190), when he writes that strangers are either assimilated/ eaten or ejected/vomited out of the system of the insider community. The outsiders to this community tend to be portrayed in language which displays a semantic as well as thematic parallelism. This assists in the formation of a sense of cohesion between the attitudes towards various outsider groups. It is inscribed in the reporting of a range of categories of those excluded from the normative readership, whether they be social, sexual or ethnic outsiders. This cohesion, when taken within the general context of the national focus of the tabloids, provides a further core of identification for readers. It provides a strong link between dominant representations of nation and the community of the tabloid audience as a specifically and even exclusively British one where the values of the nation are not only based on a sense of belonging to the national group but also on broader issues of social responsibility and even moral worth. The nation portrayed thus claims for itself a distinctive wholesomeness.

6 Gender and sexuality in tabloid Britain

Readerships within a national framework are also defined in the tabloids through projections of their attitudes to sex. Indeed, Holland (1998) has argued that the leading British tabloid of the age, the *Sun*, has been able to exploit its position to bring about a general 'sexualization of popular culture'. These popular attitudes range from the vigorously vulgar through to prim and prurient and sometimes analysis can demonstrate an interesting shift between the extremes, even in the same newspaper, depending on the subject matter. As with preceding chapters, this one will extend the rhetorical view of the tabloids' linguistic construction of nation and explore how it operates within the area of gender and sexuality while connecting to themes and strategies which extend throughout the newspapers.

According to the established patterns of news coverage, reflecting and contributing to patriarchal divisions in society, women become news with less frequency than men and, as a significant part of the national media landscape: 'our national press presents women as "news-candy" – to please the eye and sweeten the business of reportage' (Wykes and Gunter, 2005: 82). This tendency within the structures and patterns of news is called 'androcentrism' (Van Zoonen, 1994; Simpson, 1993). This is not however the end of the story. When women do become news it tends, particularly in the tabloids, to be in ways which reinforce a sexualized image of women (Fowler, 1991; Harcup and O'Neill, 2001). There is nothing new in this within the patterns of British popular media cultures where there is a long tradition of music hall, saucy seaside postcards, *Carry On* films and the humour of Benny Hill. Translated for a more sophisticated consumer, this tradition has mutated into the comic *Viz* and the magazines *FHM*, *Loaded* and *Zoo*, and shows that the tabloids are not exceptional in their emphasis on sex or their stereotyping of women as a common feature of popular culture. They have to be located within established patterns of expectation to make sense to an audience. What Holland has written about the *Sun* can be applied to much of tabloid culture and its news values in general: 'The *Sun* has openly located its pleasure around sexuality – heterosexuality. Its features and its presentation of "news" are organised around forms of arousal ranging from shock and disgust to thrills or celebration' (Holland, 1983: 86). The *Sun*'s Page 3 Girl has become a tabloid tradition, a marker of the popular tabloid genre with its prominent display of rather prim nudity.

> Page Three is a direct address by the newspaper to its audience. It presents itself as a source of pleasure to both men and women ... it declares how the paper wants to be seen, how it should be appreciated, used, enjoyed. It is the pivotal point of the *Sun's* address to the audience. ... It is part of the *Sun's* discourse on female sexuality which invites sexual enjoyment, sexual freedom and active participation in heterosexual activity.
>
> (Holland, 1983: 93)

A recent ironic addition to this address to the reader is the '**NEWS IN BRIEFS**' which now accompanies the Page 3 Girl. It trivializes both the woman represented and the news it summarizes.

> Anna agrees with the 52 per cent of Britons who want new lives abroad. She said: 'You'd be daft to want to stay in grey and miserable Britain. There can't be one person happy with our weather – I see myself living in sunny Ibiza in five years.'
>
> (*Sun*, 28 April)

Where the *Sun* had taken the lead in the sexualization of popular culture in Britain, the *Daily Star* has followed with an even brasher and more vulgar concentration on sex. An exemplary story about Paula Radcliffe and the problems which may beset any security who may need to accompany her throughout the marathon in the Athens Olympics is headed:

> Who'll watch racy Paula?
>
> (*Daily Star*, 3 May)

The piece links the security protection to her renowned speed and stamina but implicitly, the opening question, instead of emphasizing these attributes, relies on the double entendre around 'racy' which is what commands our attention and determines the newsworthiness of the story. It is also worth noting the use of the first name which is much more prevalent in the tabloids when referring to women from all walks of life.

The *Daily Mail*, a newspaper which from its founding in 1896 has always had the construction of a national female readership very much to the fore, has been categorized as 'a humourless and slightly prudish *Sun*' (Wykes and Gunter, 2005: 78). It demonstrates another way of addressing this readership from within its own more demure approach to sexuality, when introducing women to the agenda in its *Femail* magazine. Here, the protagonist 'opens her diary' in a variation on tabloid interactivity to let *Daily Mail* readers decide for themselves whether she deserves sympathy or not.

Diary of a Mistress

She shamelessly slept with a married man, lived in a flat he paid for ...

(*Daily Mail*, 6 May)

In the following example of a soap celebrity who has announced she is pregnant we can see the combination of puns, gratuitous compliments, use of the diminutive 'girl' and categorization of female celebrity, all condensed into a few lines which demonstrate in microcosm a tabloid view of women in Britain today:

Maternity Tess

Gorgeous telly girl Tess Daly has revealed why she was such a happy sud at the British Soap Awards – she's pregnant. EXCLUSIVE

(*Sun*, 10 May)

Women stars can cross media as well as performative boundaries in the tabloids because their celebrity matches the intense interest in elites which are such an important part of their news values (Wykes and Gunter, 2005: 105). In the long running saga of Leslie Ash and her stormy relationship with Lee Chapman we see a celebrity couple as the focus for a sensationalized account of marital violence in the *Sun* (10 May). The phrase 'brute hubby' tends to deflate through its use of the diminutive at the same time as it sensationalizes, combining opprobrium with abbreviation, leading to a potential trivialization of the matter in hand (Clark, 1998). This is picked up once again when Chapman is referred to as a 'womanizing brute'. The witness to other attacks is referred to, again in abbreviated form, as Ash's 'sis' who is included in the story largely on account of the fact that she is an 'ex-Hot Gossip dancer'. The celebrity of the protagonists matters to the tabloid news agenda even in a case of wife-beating. The issue is probably safer when associated with the otherwise detached, glossy lifestyles of celebrities rather than with the more commonplace realities of everyday domestic violence. Celebrity domestic violence is at least in the public eye and can be addressed, which is not the case with more routine incidents. However, it does seem that the issue here of violence is overshadowed by the celebrity status of the protagonists and also by the side-show of the hostility between the siblings as they trade insults and accusations of lying. Leslie Ash is reported to have accused her sister of 'lying to make money' in a variation on the phenomenon of blaming victims explored by Clark (1998).

The investigative potential of the tabloids is all too often limited to an exclusive concentration on digging the dirt on celebrities or in this case women who enter their sphere alleging that they were raped by football stars. Here the investigation referred to had been published in the Sunday paper, the *News of the World*. It portrays the women as temptresses, based on a stereotype of their luring innocent males abroad into dangerous territory. The language is a strange combination of the luridly explicit and euphemisms around sex from a 'weekend of action' to 'lesbian show'.

Rape case stars' joy as hookers exposed

... yesterday's News of the World told how they had offered its undercover reporter a wild night of sex after he tracked them down to a German hotel.

Lourenco demanded £700 for a single night of vice with her, Wanjiro and Wilbert. She later agreed to £10,000 for a weekend of action, including a lesbian show. ...

The women's credibility as witnesses has now been blown apart by their repeated lies and financial greed.

(*Sun*, 10 May)

A few days later we see the language used to refer to the women degenerate further from 'Hooker' to 'Tart'.

DNA PROVES LEICESTER ACES DIDN'T RAPE TART

(*Sun*, 19 May)

Football also provides the context for another deployment of hostile vocabulary aimed at a woman, identified by Fowler (1991: 96). This time the term is reported as spoken by a woman, David Beckham's wife, Victoria, who is reported to have said:

Keep that Loos bitch away from my David

(*Daily Star*, 22 May)

A similar routine representation of women as leading celebrity men astray is implicit in the story of Chelsea footballer, Adrian Mutu, where he is represented as the innocent party, entrapped by the predatory wiles of an opportunistic woman. The fact that on this occasion they did have sex does not seem to shift the locus of blame in the account away from the woman. 'Bonk', hump', 'blonde porn star', 'Penthouse centre-fold', 'romps' are all drawn from the common tabloid lexicon of sex for the British reader. So nationally distinctive is this language that, for her American readers, Taylor (1992) felt compelled for the sake of comprehension to add a glossary of such terms with Standard English equivalents in her book *Shock! Horror! The Tabloids in Action*.

MUTU DUPED INTO BONK ON CAMERA

... and now he's got the hump

CHELSEA'S Adrian Mutu was fuming last night after being lured into a sex trap by a blonde porn star.

The £17 million striker was secretly filmed enjoying three romps with Penthouse centre-fold Laura Andresan, 27, at a flat in his native Romania.

(*Sun*, 18 May)

The daily narratives concerning women conform to a worldview dictated on men's terms. This is as true of how women are represented as conforming to stereotypes as when they depart from them. The repetition of these myths serves to endorse 'systems of belief that sustain the power of the powerful' (Macdonald, 1995: 3). As if to confirm the role of women as forced to conform to the demands of a male-orientated tabloid press in order to become newsworthy, the *Daily Star* on 14 May takes strong exception to the opinions of the partner of the England football manager, who seems to have doubly transgressed by rating her own looks highly and by being found out underestimating her age – 'big-headed', 'arrogant' and 'outrageous' are some of the adjectives used to describe her:

MARKS OUT OF 10? NANCY GETS AN 11 …

From herself!

Lexical mapping of women – typography and visuals

We have seen a brief sample of when women break into the highly gendered set of news values in the tabloids. We now turn our attention to *how* they are written about, what sort of language is routinely used to depict women. Women in the tabloids are usually young, conventionally attractive, hetero-sexual, white and slim. On occasions when they deviate from those narrow norms they are either ignored as 'news' or used as a target for denigration or humour (Butcher, 1981). Physical appearance and sexual appetite, whether real or implied, are two of the most common features of the language used to portray women in the news. Women are routinely included in stories if they can match the tabloid set of lexical indicators for newsworthiness in women, among which are the following random selection: 'busty blonde', 'Royal stunner', 'basque-clad society beauty', 'blonde bombshell', 'blonde babe', 'gorgeous star', 'sexy, swashbuckling British babe', 'beautiful babes', 'pretty tasty'.

In a strange variation of the Page 3 tradition of ogling, the *Sun* produces a series of pictures of various parts of three women's bodies. The task is to make an ideal woman from the composite pictures. This demonstrates quite literally a butcher's cut version of the female form in a graphic illustration of the objectification of women in the tabloids, 'served up as body "parts" ' (Wykes and Gunter, 2005: 95), but one which is presented in characteristically jovial fashion:

Trio create fantasy girl

3 BECOME 1

Here's the ultimate Page 3 girl – made up from the breast bits of three of our most gorgeous models.

From our identittykit photo above you'll see she has Nikkala's face, Nicola T's boobs and Anna's bum.

More than 45,000 glamour fans voted on our Page.3.com website to make up their fantasy girl choosing parts from eight Page 3 lovelies.

(*Sun*, 4 May)

In a call to women readers who are more real than those cut up and put back together in the *Sun*'s 'game', the *Daily Star* provides an entry form for a competition to become a 'High Street Honey' in a piece which echoes most of the lexical clichés of the tabloids regarding women.

Who'll scoop the honey pot?

CALLING all local lovelies – fancy strutting your stuff as a High Street Honey?

... nation's biggest babe-hunt is back in gear ... top totty ... gorgeous girls ... mouthwatering. ...

Entry form

(*Daily Star*, 14 May)

The viewpoint constructed within this story (Simpson, 1993) is one which seems to offer an attractive vantage point, at least for young women readers. Such ideologies of gender must also operate from below, from within the readership, inscribed in the rhetoric of these newspapers illustrating Teo's point that:

> The relationship between discourse and society is a dialectical one: it is not only a 'top-down' relation of dominance but also a 'bottom-up' relation of compliance, acceptance and reproduction. What this means is that the media is not merely a mouthpiece of the social structure or what Habermas calls 'social formation' but is itself, because of its unique social and political interfacing ... an amplifier spreading and reproducing the existing unequal power relations in society.
>
> (Teo, 2000: 43–4)

Women readers are appealed to as part of a discourse of fun and fashion, confirming the continuing accuracy of what Holland wrote a generation previously concerning the ways in which this reformulation of women's sexuality through popular culture was attractive to certain women because it made being young and female seem an enjoyable prospect (Holland, 1983: 94). This process is not effected simply through the pictorial display of the tabloids but more significantly through their language and the normalization of perspectives on female sexuality through the accretions of the clichés used. The patterning of vocabulary regarding women and sexuality adds powerfully to the lexical cohesion of the tabloids as the clichés enable the ideological persuasion of metaphor (Lakoff, 1987) to bring the reader closer to the worldview inscribed in this language.

To develop strategies of cohesion over this discourse on women's bodies, particular well-known characters are included within the longer narrative of the tabloids' version of female aspirations and behaviour. The newspapers can call upon the explicit support of some of these characters, as in the following story where one *Sun* model disputes the award of the Rear of the Year to another celebrity familiar to readers of the paper.

SORRY TO BUTT IN …

But I'VE got the Best bum

PAGE 3 girl Anna Taverner butts in yesterday as Alex Best wins Rear of the Year …

G-string clad

(*Sun*, 20 May)

The language which is used to relate women and sexual activity is a very significant part of the tabloids' lexical mapping of women. Sexual activity is framed and overlaps with the lexis of everyday life and readers' aspirations. This is echoed through the coverage of women celebrities acting either as role-models or represented as a part of cautionary tales through a language which is replete with moral indignation. As usual there is little room for alternatives to the binary model in the world of tabloid Britain. As above, it is probably its combination of the saucy innuendo with the explicitly sexual which enables the language to appeal to a post-feminist readership which is encouraged to approach such coverage with humour and a sense of irony. At the same time, men are reassured as the language the tabloids draws on in their depiction of women conforms to age-old stereotypes and does nothing to challenge male dominance.

Typical of the post-feminist good-time girl is Zara Philipps, represented here as liking:

Polo, rugby … anything with balls

ZARA'S 2 HUNKS

… shows she is a game girl as she has a ball with TWO sporty fellas … rugby star … polo-playing chum …

(*Sun*, 3 May)

She is represented as the ultimate male fantasy, a 'game girl' who likes sport and the men who play it and the innuendo is laboured on the 'anything with balls'. Such smutty stuff draws on traditions of the material of the seaside postcards of a previous era.

Then there are times when there is a more explicit engagement with sex, albeit in this example via the hackneyed and humorous reference to it in tabloid slang as a 'bonk'. The attraction to the tabloids in this media-related story is that the film which it covers (unusually from the high-brow Cannes Film Festival, not a routine topic for the *Sun*) is *9 Songs*, which purports to include a fair number of scenes of real action sex. It is presented as a 'Brit' film to heighten the interest within a national framework and is made more attractive as a potential source of titillation by the fact that, in the advertising cliché, it is coming to a 'cinema near you'. Through the merging of a vernacular of sexual activity, made common currency by the tabloids with the language of everyday life, the piece highlights the attraction of such representations of sex. The tabloids make them blend with the lexis of popular speech and make them seem both attainable and humorous.

REAL-LIFE BONK COMING TO A CINEMA NEAR YOU

Brit film sexiest ever

(*Sun*, 18 May)

Self-parody is a very explicit part of the appeal of the *Sun* to its readership. It presents itself to male and female readers of the nation as being the first to bring them a complete guide to the female orgasm in a new take on the exclusive:

The Ultimate female orgasm

… But your ever-thoughtful Sun has beaten them to it and tomorrow Britain's favourite paper proudly presents every woman's guide to the ultimate orgasm.

So if you need help putting the 'oo' back into your bedroom, read tomorrow's Sun.

A MUST FOR EVERY WOMAN … AND EVERY MAN!

(*Sun*, 18 May)

The 'world's greatest minds', 'Scientists' and 'boffins' are all cited as combining to give the women of Britain the guide to the ultimate orgasm. It is significant that the *Sun* presents itself as a contributor to what is presented with knowing irony as a high-minded, scientific pursuit. The repetition of the possessive adjective in relation to the paper, 'your' *Sun* implies that the readers own the paper, emotionally rather than economically. The explicit end of the spectrum is indicated in a piece concerning the pleasures of shopping. Women are referred to as both 'girls' and 'babes' and are claimed to be more interested in being 'shopaholics' rather than 'sexaholics', reworking both male fantasies of sex-mad women as well as the tabloid binary agenda. Either sex maniacs or shopping crazy, the choice for 'modern day' women of the nation seems narrow indeed. The humorous intent of the piece is reinforced by its punning headline.

TILLS GIVE GIRLS THRILLS

Shoppin' as good as sex

... Modern-day babes prefer being shopaholics to sexaholics, according to a survey ...

(Daily Star, 19 May)

When lexis and typographical tricks combine in a story like the one below, with its combination of the grotesque, word play and bedroom farce producing a vision of the sexual antics of B-list celebrities as a form of Chaucerian extravaganza, the humour is what makes such language difficult to be too puritanical or judgemental about. Fowler has written of the paradoxical attraction of this language in the *Sun* but his observations can be validated in all the tabloids today, demonstrating how influential a template for contemporary Britain the Sun has become:

> Interestingly, the Sun indulges in 'poetic' structures in places where it is being at its most outrageous about politics or sex. Cues are foregrounded to the point of self-parody. Deplorable values are openly displayed, pointedly highlighted; even a critical reader can be disarmed by pleasure in the awfulness of the discourse.
>
> (Fowler, 1991: 45)

It fits into an older tradition of sexual mockery as part and parcel of a male-dominated version of popular culture which stretches from the print culture of the late Middle Ages to the present day.

VANESSA THE UNDRESSER GOES LIKE A RACING CAR

... and I should know, says the British champ who bedded her

A RACING driver told yesterday how he bedded sex-mad Big Brother beauty Vanessa Nimmo – within TWO HOURS of meeting her.

... stunning blonde ... sizzling photos

BLONDE BEAUTY BROKE MY BED

A MALE model told last night how blonde bombshell Vanessa Nimmo BROKE the headboard on his bed during a passionate farewell romp ... bedded the stunner ...

(Sun, 31 May)

Nevertheless, there is a patterning to the language of these displays of sexual excess which is far from liberationary and, in fact, feeds back into the rather restricted moral codes of the tabloids on this issue and many others. The woman is a 'babe', a 'blonde bombshell', a 'blonde beauty', a 'beauty', a 'stunner', 'sex-mad'; in a few short paragraphs we have practically exhausted the tabloid repertoire, reinforcing the fact that women are over-lexicalized in the tabloids (Fowler, 1991: 96). This means that there is literally an oversupply of words describing women together with an oversupply of words used which draw references to female body parts and attributes. This is particularly evident where women are involved in sexual activities. This may be a feature of popular speech in general but it is nevertheless one which is emphasized in the tabloids. She is nicknamed 'Vanessa the Undresser' and she is a 'fast' woman', so much so that she is described as going 'like a race car' and her male conqueror can vouch for this because by a wonderful tabloid coincidence he just happens to be a racing driver. The man is a 'male model', a 'racing driver' and he has 'bedded' the woman. It is also significant to see the use of tabloid typographics to highlight the important issues of the story outside the headline – 'RACING … TWO HOURS … MALE … BROKE'.

Sexuality and morality

Although it is common across the tabloids, it is with the *Daily Mail* that we start to explore the rather more traditional and moralistic agenda which the tabloids often relegate behind their raucous celebration of a certain style of superficial sexual escapade which fits with their other sensationalizing and celebrity-led preferences for news. As soon as sex threatens to become real, however, the atmosphere changes very swiftly and the language used to describe it returns to the more puritanical end of the tabloid spectrum reserved for activities and people they disapprove of. Despite the representation of women as sexually available and the marginalization within their pages of women other than celebrities in the public eye, the tabloids do manage to combine this agenda with another which is redolent of conservative sexual values. To an extent it is not surprising that this features predominantly in the *Daily Mail*, which has a less prurient agenda on sex than the other tabloids.

> Family values
>
> What is it with our liberal sex gurus that they continue to ignore the evidence before their eyes?
>
> Britain has the highest rate of teenage pregnancies in Europe and the level of sexually transmitted diseases in this age group is up two thirds in five years.
>
> Yet the 'experts' persist in treating these as technical problems. They reject any attempt to reintroduce the moral dimension and parental guidance that have been so effective in the past.
>
> (*Daily Mail*, 3 May)

This piece contrasts the implied reader and their 'family values' with a range of 'liberal sex gurus', 'experts' and people who 'ignore the evidence before their eyes'. A commonsense empiricism is weighed against the 'gurus' and 'experts' who are accused of rejecting the 'moral dimension' which comes from 'parental guidance'. The 'past', which the *Daily Mail* cites as a time when the parents' moral guidance held sway, is indeed a political location and deployed regularly in this paper as a scourge of the inadequacies of the present. This constructed past is a time when common sense prevails and the piece flatters the reader that they too belong to a community which prefers the proclaimed morality of this past to the intervention of expertise in the present. It fits with a longer narrative of the past often deployed by the tabloids as a time when the world was a simpler and more moral place in an implicit invitation to take on more conservative or even backward-looking social policies and attitudes.

The rejection of attempts to deal with the issue of teenage sexuality is echoed in a different way by the shock expressed in the *Daily Star* at attempts to introduce more easily available contraception in schools.

HORROR AT CONDOMS IN SCHOOL TUCK SHOP

... caused uproar yesterday ...

SHOULD CONDOMS BE SOLD IN TUCK SHOPS?

(*Daily Star*, 6 May)

The use of standard tabloid terms such as 'horror' and 'uproar', combined with the opportunity to phone and text responses to the story both seek to reinforce the sense of a national community of readers here around the issue of sex. This provides a variant on the moral agenda of the *Daily Mail* from the other end of the tabloid spectrum. There is also an alternative agenda to the reporting of the antics and infidelities of the rich and famous, such a staple of the tabloids, when it touches upon the reality of divorce settlements which appear to challenge the patriarchal status quo. The case of a real-life story of a footballer's wife is used to elicit views of the responsibilities and rights within contemporary marriage. In the case of footballer Ray Parlour's divorce the question is posed of readers and dealt with within the restrictions of tabloid binarism:

Should she get half his money?

... Greed or justice?

(*Daily Mail*, 12 May)

The moral agenda on sex is particularly to the fore when the affair of a teenager who has been given an abortion without her parents' consent hits the tabloids. It is interesting to note that the newspapers never link the story to the sexualizing of teenage culture in which they are complicit or with the outrage at attempts to educate children better or provide better access to contraception through, for instance, condoms in the tuckshop. The story presents a typographically and lexically structured version of events which castigates the school and health workers at the same time as it presents the mother and daughter as isolated individuals outside social and healthcare trends. The mother is 'stunned', 'furious', 'outraged', 'distraught'. The school is 'blasted' or 'slammed' and the *Daily Mail* highlights the fact that the adviser was 'a girl of 21', 'barely out of her teens', indicating how women are routinely juvenilized in this discourse, while in the *Sun* and the *Daily Mirror*, the mother is reduced to the cosy and familiar 'mum'. The *Daily Mail* also connects the story to longer narratives of its own which go beyond issues of sexuality and into the area of the state's intervention in the lives of individuals, as it presents the story as part of the 'remorseless process by which the state and its agents are stripping parents of rights over their children'.

SCHOOL FIXES ABORTION FOR GIRL OF JUST 14 ... and they didn't tell mum

A SCHOOL arranged for a girl of 14 to have an abortion WITHOUT telling her parents ... stunned mother blasted the school. ... When she protested the school and health chiefs insisted she had NO right to know without Melissa's consent.

(*Sun*, 13 May)

MUM'S FURY AS SCHOOL HELPS GIRL'S ABORTION

Teachers didn't tell family

A MOTHER yesterday slammed a school which helped her 14-year-old daughter have an abortion in secret.

(*Daily Mirror*, 13 May)

ABORTION ADVICE FROM GIRL OF 21

THE scandalous truth about Melissa Smith's secret abortion emerged last night ... inexperienced 'outreach worker' aged just 21 ... barely out of her teens ...

(*Daily Mail*, 14 May)

The tabloids line up their opinion brokers to discuss the issue in time-honoured binary fashion:

YES/NO Agony Aunt and Columnist present the case.

(*Sun*, 14 May)

GMTV's FIONA PHILLIPS

Mum has the right to know

(*Daily Mirror*, 15 May)

The coverage of the abortion issue is linked to the results of a poll of *Daily Star* readers demonstrating that the paper is on the same side as its readers.

- More than 80% of Daily Star readers believe parents should be told if their daughter wants an abortion.

(*Daily Star*, 15 May)

There is then a pragmatic shift in both the *Sun*'s and the *Daily Mail*'s usually hostile line on everything to do with Europe as they report that the European Court may be a possible way to get compensation for the family:

I'LL SUE Euro court showdown

(*Sun*, 15 May)

Melissa's case heading for Europe

(*Daily Mail*, 15 May)

As if to show that the issue is not going to be allowed to fade away or the issues to be dealt with in any less sensational or personalized way the *Sun* begins to drum up interest in other cases to build a portfolio of human tragedy while continuing to ignore the social or psychological complexities of the cases.

AN outraged mum has revealed how her teenage daughter had a secret abortion too.

... decided to speak out after hearing about the case of 14-year-old Melissa Smith.

- **HAS** your underage daughter been given an abortion you found out about later? Call or email

(*Sun*, 17 May)

Meanwhile, the *Daily Mail* reveals a possibly subliminal agenda in the form of an innocent question and the coverage of a group of middle class women who, in promoting an American abstinence movement, seem to mirror its own idealized perspective on the issue.

WILL CHASTITY CATCH ON HERE?

(*Daily Mail*, 13 May)

Melodrama and sex

The representation of sexual deviancy as something located outside the community of readers yet included for their perusal and condemned when it appears within the coterie of stars and celebrities who make up the *dramatis personae* of the tabloids is enhanced by the use of melodramatic storylines to cover such events complete with alliterative flourish. The following is a very modern melodrama (Ang, 1985; Gripsrud, 1992) where the villain is unveiled as a 'tormentor', 'perverted sadist', 'evil', 'sordid', while masquerading as 'devout Christian', 'member of Ripon Choral Society and of a local gliding club', 'pillar of the community', and his victim in true melodramatic fashion is helpless as 'his plaything', 'kept as a sex slave'.

> I was kept as a sex slave
>
> Clutching her baby son to her chest, recovering heroin addict Tracey Birkett shot a tearful glance at her tormentor and then fled into the night.
>
> She had finally seen the middle-aged psychotherapist for what he was – not a Good Samaritan who was nursing her back to health, but a perverted sadist who was using her as his plaything.
>
> (*Daily Mirror*, 4 May)

Cross-media comment

The coverage of the sexual antics of celebrities (Turner, 2004) combines the newsworthiness of sex with that of celebrity but with a demonstrable moral agenda as if to indicate that being a celebrity comes with moral responsibilities to readers of the tabloids (Connell, 1992). A recent example of moral outrage, combined with the lure of titillation, comes in the coverage of a soap star who had been caught indulging in acts of what the newspaper considers sexual depravity. It is commented on with due irony in the words of the Page 3 model of the day in the 'News in Briefs' section:

> Zoe is stunned by new revelations of Leslie Grantham's sordid internet sex chats. She says:
>
> 'I cannot believe he could get involved in something so seedy. It's clearly not a one-off – he seems addicted. It's disgusting. Leslie's a big star on Eastenders and has a responsibility to his young fans. The BBC should sack him.'
>
> (*Sun*, 5 May)

When actor Leslie Grantham is revealed to have been involved in some sordid on-line sexual antics, the language of the tabloids is directed at him in its usual combination of moral outrage and punning innuendo, all couched in the overarching framework and familiar language of celebrity/sensationalist agendas. The transitivity of the verbs expresses short, sharp and brutal retribution for celebrities who fall from grace – 'gets the chopper', 'gets the boot', 'faces the axe', 'facing the sack', 'sacked', 'chopped' – and the star who has ironically made his name as 'Dirty Den' finds his real life notoriety matching his fictional reputation. He is immediately aligned with the categorization of sexual outsiders in the tabloids, 'perv', 'net perv', 'Dirty Old Den', 'Panto perv'. This parallelism is an important part of the pattern of coherence across tabloid narratives.

Page 3 tales

Yet on one day of this blanket coverage of the vicarious sexual activity of a soap star, readers are asked to behave in a similar sort of way, with a 'Build your very own Page 3 girl' on the same page as Grantham is castigated. Within the norms of the tabloids' representation of women it is no surprise that lexicalization is matched by the regular pictorial representation of women on display for a male gaze. This is often taken to deliberately and provocatively playful extremes. The innuendo present in 'you can play around with your very own ideal Page 3 girl for hours on end' seems merely an invitation to a low-tech version of what Leslie Grantham seems to stand accused of in his own interactive online way. Male readers are being exhorted to play with the body parts of Page 3 'stunners', presumably not simply as a general knowledge quiz.

> Page 3 Miss-Fits-Quiz
>
> CAN YOU MATCH UP THE SUN STUNNERS?
>
> Here's a chance to test your knowledge of The Sun's Page 3 beauties. ...
>
> Just cut out the squares and you can play around with your very own ideal Page 3 girl for hours on end.
>
> (*Sun*, 5 May)

The *Daily Mirror* is not above the sexualization of its readers, explicitly featuring a front page showing a couple in an erotic pose with the caption:

> TAKE OUR SEX TEST
>
> HOW DO YOU MEASURE UP? SEE PAGES 23, 24 AND 25
> (*Daily Mirror*, 11 May)

Traditionally, the *Daily Mirror* is not as lurid in its representation of sex but this is definitely tabloid territory and is a familiar field of engagement to various degrees across the range. Even the *Daily Mail*, which has an oblique and reactive engagement with sex, can be seen to be heavily involved in the representation of sexuality, even in its puritanical stance. Yet it too can veer close to the language of its down-market neighbours as when it publishes a picture of Rachel Hunter, the estranged wife of Rod Stewart, in a low-cut dress for an award ceremony complete with caption:

> **Looking just swell**
>
> (*Daily Mail*, 11 May)

The display of female bodies can be linked with a whole range of other features of the tabloids' agenda, reinforcing the sexualization of the entire popular tabloid spectrum in Britain. It is one of their continuing patterns of cohesion. On one occasion two models pictured in St. George's flag bikinis are depicted on the front page and as a centre page poster. Readers are instructed to take out the poster and display it in windows as a sign of support for the England football team in Euro 2004. They are connected lexically to the patriotic support for British troops in 'Our Boys', a common reference point for all the tabloids, and they are referred to by their first names only in a signifier of familiarity common in relation to women in such stories.

LUCY and MICHELLE

WE BACK OUR BOYS

(Daily Star, 13 May)

The discourse of Page 3 models can also be matched with an aspect of popular memory and advertising history. In this case, the tabloids can also make grand claims for the epoch-changing nature of a particular brand of bra and demonstrate how an advertising campaign fits in with the broader sexual agenda of their coverage of women. Both the *Sun* and the *Daily Star* feature a double page spread on the tenth anniversary of the Wonderbra.

BRA-VO! WE CELEBRATE A DECADE OF THE WORLD'S MOST FAMOUS BUST-ENHANCER

HERE'S a swell birthday party to lift our spirits – the wonderbra is ten years old!

… nifty little female friend … bonus for the fellas as top-class totty was brought in to push Wonderbra's products …

(Daily Star, 14 May)

10 YEARS AFTER HELLO BOYS – WE SALUTE THE BEST CLEAVAGES EVER

VALLEYS OF THE DOLLS

TEN years ago there was an uplifting event which changed the way women looked at the world and the way men looked at women. … To celebrate Wonderbra's outstanding contribution to the female form, we take a look back at some of the fabulous fronts to be captured on camera.

(Sun, 14 May)

This is complete with a selection of famous models who illustrate the main themes of the celebration. It is endorsed by the use of the tabloid celebration, 'We Salute …'.

Stock sex stories

Sex is neatly divided in tabloid fashion between wholesome and entertaining activity which is what their national readership is implicitly involved in and the opposite pole of the perverted, sadistic and wholly alien practices which the tabloids are drawn to partly in sensationalist mode but also as part of their moralistic agenda. Sexual outsiders are depicted very much as outsiders to the wholesome sexual community of the tabloids regulars. They are frequently written about in bestial terms for instance:

> Hunt for sex fiend
>
> *(Daily Mirror*, 6 May)

There is nothing better than being able to pin some outrageous sexual behaviour on one person, such as Lynndie England. This can detract attention from the responsibilities of an institution like the US Army. Her behaviour is described here in terms of 'orgies', not, interestingly enough, in the more fun-orientated term of 'romps', and she is significantly referred to by her first name, as in trivial cases regarding Page 3 girls and also in the stories concerning Maxine Carr, as we have already seen. This reduced lexicon of first names acts further to reduce the range of female roles on display for the British tabloid reader.

LYNNDIE'S JAIL ORGIES

Filmed having sex with soldiers in front of Iraqis
> *(Daily Mirror*, 14 May)

The most attractive stories for the tabloid sex agenda are stock stories which have passed the test of time, such as the 'dirty vicar' stories which high-light hypocrisy. They have a long tradition within printed popular forms which can be traced back in English literature to the Chaucerian comic reflex of the mighty fallen, and they allow the perpetrator and the victim to be cast in simple melodramatic terms suitable to the style of tabloid narratives:

> PASTOR'S SEX SHAME
>
> A millionaire TV evangelist was found guilty yesterday of sex offences against two women members of his flock.
>
> *(Daily Star*, 7 May)

In the above headline, there is an example of a compressed noun phrase which effectively reduces the protagonist and the story to the simplicities of sensationalized narrative and fits in with the stereotypical script of the sexual abuse of power. In the following example the contradiction is flagged explicitly in the headline and then the choice of vocabulary reinforces his contradictory behaviour, 'Father of four', 'charismatic pastor', 'evangelist'. He is portrayed in contrast as 'Sex-Mad' and as preying, again in bestial metaphor, on his 'flock'.

SEX ATTACK PASTOR WHO ACTED LIKE GOD

'£3M loss' probe as he faces jail

A Sex-Mad pastor who preyed on young women while acting like God faced jail last night.

Father of four Douglas Goodman, 46, ...

The charismatic pastor left the Old Bailey smiling, surrounded by supporters who started singing hymns. ...

But the evangelist who preached morality to his flock had feet of clay.

Goodman befriended four women, showering them with gifts and taking them on shopping trips to Harrods.

There is a characteristic set of pictures as mnemonic, designed to help readers to grasp the story, and the bold headlines:

HIS LIFE OF LUXURY

THE HOUSE

THE CARS

(*Daily Mirror*, 7 May)

The use of pictures is a familiar device in the tabloids which reinforces the excess of the accusations. You can read all about it but it is better to force home the point of the story by showing a picture!

Deviant sexual activities are often reduced to the ubiquitous charge of 'groping' and the accused is immediately placed in the linguistic category of 'perv', all the better for it matching 'rev' to make the headline more eye-catching, and once again the word 'preyed', a metaphor drawn from the animal world, comes up in the coverage of a second newspaper to indicate just how much common linguistic currency there is in such stock tales. 'Perv' has become an all-encompassing term representing a contemporary moral panic and folk devil (Cohen, 1980; Critcher, 2003) and acts to distance sexual deviance from the wholesome tabloid reader as something 'extra-societal' (Clark, 1998: 197).

PERV REV GUILTY OF GROPING

Teachers and medics are other groups of workers who are particularly favoured in stock tales of sex and depravity.

RE SIR IS JAILED FOR SEX WITH GIRL OF 14

(*Daily Star*, 14 May)

SURGEON 'GROPED PATIENT ON WARD'

(*Sun*, 18 May)

Despite the general reliance on stock tales of sexuality which map the contours of tabloid Britain's attitudes, there is always room for news which breaks out of the norm and can be drawn upon in ways which reinforce the punning sense of humour of the tabloids and amplify a particular script. In this case, one newspaper seizes on a court judgement to suggest that there may be a 'flood' of applications from transsexuals to join the police force. The hyperbole of 'flood' is one familiar to readers of the tabloids and is a key part of their narrative and ideological cohesion. It is predicated on the notion of a symbolic nation under threat from geographical or moral outsiders and metaphorically implies that the host nation will be lost beneath the waves. It features wherever it can be attached intertextually as a short-hand reference to any issue which the tabloid wishes to flag as an area of concern and to draw the range of accumulated negativity into a different area. This metaphorical device can then be paraded as evidence that the tabloid is patrolling the boundaries of decency and political prudence on behalf of its readers and wants to present the story in terms which are recognizable and unambiguous. It is used to provoke, for instance, when used in conjunction with asylum seekers or on the expansion of the EU. On both of these issues the tabloids have raised the spectre of a 'flood'. This indicates the political implications of the language selected in various examples in the tabloids.

POLICE LOSE BATTLE ON NO-CHOPPER COPPER

Transsexual can be a WPC

Cops yesterday LOST their last-ditch fight to refuse a transsexual a job as a woman police constable. ...

Experts believe the decision could now herald a flood of similar applications by transsexuals wanting to join the police as women.

(*Sun*, 7 May)

The *Daily Mail* is also attracted to tales of the bizarre to break the monotony of routine stories of sexual misconduct. Here we have a fine example of the updating of revenge for marital infidelity for a technological age. Yet it is still the revenge of the aggrieved husband!

For sale on ebay: A collection of my cheating wife's knickers

IN days gone by, unfaithful wives might be shackled in the stocks to be punished for their sins.

In the hi-tech age, jilted husbands have a more ruthless weapon at their disposal ...

(*Daily Mail*, 19 May)

Women suffering

One category of British women represented in the most glowing of terms is that of the suffering mother. Across the tabloids, mothers who suffer are accorded an heroic status and this is accentuated through many characteristic tabloid rhetorical strategies. The story of the mother of three autistic sons is told as a eulogy to a mother's determination, and the paradox is crowned with the capitalization at the end of the story of the message of the piece.

> Two of Charlotte's three sons are autistic. The strain of caring for them has destroyed her marriage and taken over her life. But, far from being a sad story, her determination and courage are inspirational.

> A VERY SPECIAL MOTHER
>
> (*Daily Mail*, 5 May)

In the *Sun* over the month of May 2004 we can see a competition, cross-sponsored by washing powder firm Daz and supermarket chain Asda, in effect locating the stereotype of mothers for the twenty-first century as it was for the previous one, where the very term 'soap opera' was coined to describe the interrelation between daytime radio addressed to the assumed audience of women at their domestic chores and advertising for soap flakes (Geraghty, 1990). It features a list of women with stories of caring, coping, disease and bereavement – women's lot is apparently not a happy one. Last year's winner cycled 1,000 miles round New Zealand with her 18-month-old son to raise money for a charity supporting the cancer that killed her husband. Readers are involved and asked to vote for one of six finalists who are featured. The lucky woman is referred to as 'SUN MUM'. When the winner is finally announced, the news is commented on in the *Sun*'s leader column with all the pomp associated with its own highest accolade of praise familiar to tabloid readers, what might be termed 'the tabloid salute', and given national pride of place in its leading article of the day:

> **Wonder Mums of Britain – that's all of you – we salute you.**
>
> (*Sun*, 21 May)

Maternity and social class

Another debate on maternity is launched from a different perspective but also one which seeks to enlist the support of the target readership. It is mediated through the seemingly unsurprising news that actress Gwynneth Paltrow is to take some time out of her career to bring up the baby she is expecting. The story breaks with a dreadful pun, 'Gwynneth Bumpgrow', and the characteristic set of categorizations: 'Movie mum-to-be', 'tot'.

I'LL QUIT MOVIES TO BRING UP TOT

Movie mum-to-be Gwynneth Paltrow proudly shows off her bump –
after telling how she will put her career on hold to raise her child.

(Sun, 5 May)

It is at this point that the story draws in a class perspective, surprising at first,
in the *Daily Mail*. It starts by declaring on its front page in a way which
exploits the mechanics of transitivity to articulate powerful criticism of
working mothers from the perspective of a very wealthy celebrity:

Gwynneth blast at working mothers

Star bares her bump and airs her views on parenting

I can't understand mothers who put their career before their children,
says Gwynneth

(who just happens to be a millionairess)

(Daily Mail, 5 May)

This has got to be appreciated more broadly as part of an extended preferred
agenda for this newspaper, as we can see from its traditionalist perspectives on
families and motherhood in a different part of the paper that same day. Here
the *Daily Mail* takes delight in interpreting a scientific paper as proof that
'curvy hips make a woman a born mother'. The paper on the relationship
between fertility and body shape published in *Proceedings of the Royal Society of
London, Series B,* is given a distinctly socio-sexual slant by the newspaper:

Science defines the female shape that's best for fertility

… But voluptuously endowed ladies really are designed by Nature for
motherhood, research has revealed.

(Daily Mail, 5 May)

A day later in the part of the paper designed specifically for women readers,
Femail, the joys of the extended family are extolled:

Happy (big) families

Yes, three generations CAN thrive under one roof

(Daily Mail, 6 May)

The next day the *Sun* moves onto the territory of outraged working class
women, drawn into the identifiably blue collar imagined community of that
paper, by using three Gwynneths from its readers to give their selected views
on Gwynneth Paltrow. The *Sun* parades itself as the working mother's champion. Three working class women are interviewed and they stress the financial

necessities of their situation. The principle of keeping a career going through the early years of a child's life is not mentioned but the selection of indicators of social status is of note and of direct relevance to the idealized readership. Their age, salary and the size of their houses are detailed with pictures, together with details of the sort of work they do, as an implied contrast to the actress and implicitly inviting readers to become involved in comparisons. The wording of the opening to the interviews is as strong as it is 'damning' of Paltrow, who is referred to as 'pampered' and told what to do in vulgar punning language.

> Put a sock Gwyn it
>
> (*Sun*, 6 May)

The *Daily Mail* broadens out this class-based response in its women's section *Femail* by calling on seven prime middle class professional respondents, including an author, a radio presenter, a journalist and a chief executive, who all stress career fulfilment while neglecting to mention salaries, mortgage repayments or rents. The headline trades on an echo from the Gulf War:

> THE MOTHER OF ALL INSULTS
>
> (*Daily Mail*, 6 May)

There is also a class perspective to the plight of the lower class mothers featured patronisingly in the following piece with all of the scripted prejudices against these outsiders to the *Daily Mail*'s idealized version of respectable Britain. Taking its headline from a popular film, the report highlights the assertion which it maps onto their behaviour, 'The state will always be there to provide.' It refers in hyperbolic and metaphorical language to the 'galloping teenage pregnancy problem' and patronisingly coins the descriptor 'chip shop lover'. It fits well with the language of the stereotypical 'scrounger' so often castigated by the tabloids in one of their recurrent scripts, removed from all social and psychological context or motivation. It is fine to be a working mother if you fit the template of motherhood expected by the readers of the *Daily Mail* targeted by the language of this piece.

> SISTER ACT
>
> Charlene was 16 when she got pregnant. Her sister Miranda was 14. But did they learn from their mistakes? It seems not. Now they have both had a second child with different fathers. But don't worry. ... The state will always be there to provide support.
>
> ... symbols of Britain's galloping teenage pregnancy problem ... Charlene did briefly manage to hold down a job, in a chip shop – but gave it up after she had unprotected sex with one of the customers and became pregnant again.

Needless to say, her chip shop lover, Mike, already had a child by another woman, and soon deserted her for someone new. Now ... longs to go out every night ... Miranda ... does not know who the father is.

(*Daily Mail*, 10 May)

Implications of tabloid triviality

Given the prejudicial language so often afforded to women, which includes representations of women as victims of circumstance, it may not be surprising to see how they are featured in a routine story already analyzed, of a tabloid villain who is accused of infecting several women with the HIV virus. He is represented as having 'sneaked', and as 'seducing'. He is variously condemned as having 'infected women', infected '4 girls' and 'condemned four women to death'.

The triviality of the language implicit in the use of the abbreviation 'Hol' in the following extract is complemented by the reference to the suspects as either 'illegal immigrants' or 'believed to be Algerians'. The trivialization serves to reduce the seriousness of the alleged rape as well as casually downplaying the racist undertones of the piece. As with the case above, it is as much the crime as the perpetrator's ethnic details which are flagged up to the reader as both significant and worthy of disapproval.

Hol rape of girl, 19

A teenage Briton was in a Costa del Sol hospital last night after she was raped on holiday by two illegal immigrants.

(*Sun*, 3 May)

Briton dragged on to Spanish beach and raped

... believed to be Algerians

(*Daily Mail*, 3 May)

The next extract is complemented by pictures of the man, his wife, the 2ft knife and part of the text message.

WIFE'S LAST TXT: HUBBY IS GOING TO MURDER ME

(*Sun*, 7 May)

In addition to the trivialization implicit in the language of these stories we can see the relish with which the tabloids indulge in the linking of sexual crime against women and ethnicity. In the '*Sun*' Woman' section, the paper literally 'talking to women, too' (Holland, 1983), we see a familiar linguistic patterning in the reports which combine marriage, sex and ethnicity. The 'bogus brides' and 'sham marriage' are short-hand mnemonics which play a political role in creating associations in the reader's mind with other similar stories, thus assisting in the narrative and thematic cohesion of the newspaper and enabling it to maintain a steady editorial perspective for its readers, albeit in abbreviated but highly effective form. The readership is invited to 'Decide for yourself' on the basis of the information provided by the *Sun*, raising both the spectre of the familiar 'bogus bride' alarm as well as the threat that readers might have been targeted by such schemes themselves. The role of the estimates in the report, despite the vague sources for the statistics, serve as cross-references to other stories where numbers of immigrants are exaggerated and the metaphor of 'flooding' is once again used. The sexual details of the second case are coarse, trivial and linked with an interactive response service for readers to air their views to complete once again the familiar circuit of the tabloid community's conversation with itself, one which seems to become more assertive with each repetition of the narrative strategy.

A SHOCK REPORT SAYS 1 IN 5 CIVIL WEDDINGS ARE A SHAM

New figures reveal one in 29 UK civil marriages are bogus and up to ONE IN FIVE in the Home Counties are a sham.

Officials say that each year there could be up to 15,000 bogus brides from Turkey and Africa – saying 'I do' just to get into Britain.

But can you be duped into a sham marriage without knowing it?. ... Decide for yourself ...

(*Sun*, 5 May)

In the accompanying feature we can read the details of one such arrangement and readers are asked to e-mail their reactions: 'We had to speak with hand signals', 'Algerian toyboy', 'He was a virgin. In bed it was a case of in, out, shake it all about' (*Sun*, 5 May).

Body shape

Linguistic flagging of female body shape in the tabloids is one of the primary ways in which they act to define norms of the female body for readers. The ways in which the mass media affect the conventions of socially acceptable body image has long been a topic for discussion, not least within the media themselves. Wykes and Gunter point out that 'the slender-is-slim norm would only be "saleable" if it fitted into wider concepts of gender and identity' (2005: 67) and demonstrate how the wider scope of the narratives around body image in the newspapers and particularly the tabloids contributes to news values which complement their overall worldview. The tabloids are particularly keen to air their views, particularly on the most desirable body shape for women. Men, as in most other trivial news categories, are most often absent. The images can be contradictory and confusing and are only occasionally linked with health-based commentary. The *Daily Mail* piece below starts by focusing on image alone and uses the tabloid strategy of visual complements to the story, with before and after scans and photos of the women as they now appear, but it then moves on to bring the report into line with government warnings.

THE CAMERA THAT NEVER LIES (Heather, Maja, Wendy)

How the incredible 3D images of a new scanner showed these women their true shape and shocked them into changing

A stark Government report recently found that three-quarters of women are risking obesity and early death by not exercising for the recommended 30 minutes, five days a week.

(*Daily Mail*, 10 May)

Another favourite lead-in to a story about weight loss is again connected to image and implicit comparison with the lives of celebrities. Wykes and Gunter quote columnist Julie Burchill condemning the influence of the *Daily Mail* on women's perceptions of body image in the flow of intertextual media reference as it 'keeps up a non-stop commentary on the weight gain of famous women and links it to their sexual orientation and career success' (Julie Birchell, *Guardian*, 8 July 2000). One cross-media perspective on a former soap star focuses in populist fashion on the dress size she has attained, as if to stress that this is to do with image rather than health:

Lean Janine

EXCLUSIVE: HOW I LOST ONE AND A HALF STONE … AND DROPPED TWO DRESS SIZES

EVERYONE knows she's in for a long diet of porridge – but it seems the lean times have already started for EastEnders star Charlie Brooks

The 23-year-old actress has shed pounds as her superbitch character Janine Butcher is about to exit the show after being jailed for murder.

(*Daily Mirror*, 11 May)

An athlete, but only when she is female, can have her figure scrutinized, in this case after the birth of a child, and then the woman in question is represented in a 'skimpy bikini', implying that the main news interest is not her 'form' but her fashionable 'six-pack':

Back on track

Two years after having a baby, Denise has regained her form (and her six-pack)

SPRINTING across the sand in skimpy bikini, Denise Lewis demonstrates why she has high hopes of winning gold again for Britain at this summer's Olympics.

(*Daily Mail*, 14 May)

DENISE IS FIT FOR FUN 'N GAMES

(Daily Star, 14 May)

The following stories highlight an extreme of male-orientated body preference. They bemoan the loss of weight of a previously famous model with the assertion that thin women are neurotic. All the tabloids from the *Daily Mail* to the *Daily Mirror* cover the story and all use a recognizably narrow range of familiar language. To capture such a refined representation of all that is most negative and repressive about the image of the female body in the tabloids, the *Sun* even imports a 'lad-mag' editor to write his opinion. Twice here we read that 'we' want her to revert to her former larger self, emphasizing the collective voice with which the tabloid nation wishes to speak.

SUPERMODEL IS A SHADOW OF HER OLD SELF

Is some

THIN

WRONG, Sophie?

[with a photo caption from 1997] Fine form ... the supermodel at her voluptuous peak

... **shocking shadow of her former self** ... once-shapely blonde appeared gaunt and emaciated ... scrawny neck ... far cry from the voluptuous sex-siren ... fabulous curves. ... She helped big women feel better about their bodies. ...

But it is clear to us Sophie has lost a lot more than puppy fat – and we beg her to bring back her beautiful curves.

(Sun, 20 May)

Fading away, model whose curves first made her name

So slim, Sophie

... championed the cause of the fuller-figured woman ... buxom size 16 ... curvy Sophie

(Daily Mail, 20 May)

SOPH THIN

What's happened to the champion of the fuller figure?

... new skinny ... voluptuous figure ...

But while she is as skinny as this she is going to have to get used to the gossip.

(Daily Mirror, 20 May)

A guest writer, imported as part of the 'male chorus' alluded to by Holland (1983: 96), *Loaded* editor, Martin Daubney, writes:

AS SOPHIE LOSES MORE WEIGHT ... WE ASK WHAT BLOKES REALLY LIKE

SLIMLASS OR HOURGLASS

FELLAS WANT LURVE CURVE

LET'S get this straight: Most men like girls who have a bit of meat on them.

Pigeon chests, pencil-thin ankles, tin ribs – turn-offs, one and all. Big bums and heaving breasts send us into meltdown but heroin chic gives us cold turkey. ...

So while droves of neurotic women think we all want starved catwalk clotheshorses, the opposite tends to be true ... Sophie Dahl ... all curved up, looking like a real woman ...

(*Sun*, 21 May)

Cliché and sex roles

This chapter started by considering when women routinely become news. We will finish the chapter by considering how women can become news not only by fitting to outmoded stereotypes but on occasion by virtue of the fact that they don't fit a stereotype. It seems the tabloids will base the newsworthiness of a piece even on an unreliable stereotype.

SO WHO SAYS WOMEN ARE BAD DRIVERS?

... Daily Mirror Women's Editor Clair Raymon writes:

If men could just stop treating every trip to the supermarket like a Grand Prix, our roads would be a whole lot safer. They are just like little boys.

It makes sense that women drivers are safest. If we drove any faster how would we get to gawp at the shoe shop window? We like looking in mirrors, we enjoy flirting at traffic lights and we accept from bitter experience that we won't always come first.

(*Daily Mirror*, 12 May)

The proof that women are the safer drivers

(But they still can't park properly afterwards)

... However, male drivers do have one statistic on their side which may explain their high percentage of offences – they drive far more than women.

(*Daily Mail*, 12 May)

WOMEN ARE THE BEST DRIVERS – OFFICIAL

… But they are better at parking than men. And women are more likely to crash in a car park, drive into a stationary car, or even reverse into one.

(*Daily Star*, 12 May)

Perhaps in a chapter on sex roles and women it is best to let the Beckhams have the last word, as the *Daily Mail* uses them to reinforce a script, reassuring to its conservative readership, that in times of crisis their footballing heroes and most importantly their wives can be relied upon to return to type if not to stereotype – 'a partial return to solid, working-class values of the East End of London'.

NOW WHO'S WEARING THE TROUSERS?

… East End boy finally realises he must see the task through

… If Victoria Beckham is prepared to lie back and think of England in such trying circumstances, then the nation is in her debt too.

(*Daily Mail*, 21 May)

In this final example the link between the representation of women and the language of the tabloids is made explicit. Women are articulated sometimes implicitly but often overtly as part of a national community. They fit into the patterns of dominant masculine discourse which by and large construct national identities at the same time as matching the highly gendered institution of the national press. This relationship between representation and institution demonstrates that:

> While real, embodied – if invisible – women continue to have only minimal roles in the shaping of our popular media, the men who produce the pages will continue to build their power on the decorative excess of the women who are pictured in them.
>
> (Holland, 1998: 32)

Conclusion

The tabloids include women in ways which conform to broader patterns of popular representation – sexualized, as victims, or playing traditional roles within traditional relationships – and these representations fit the broader discourse of national identity which acts as a cohesive factor throughout their pages. Women are however present in contrast to the routine exclusion of women from much of the elite press because of news values which can only be interpreted as androcentric (Tuchman, 1981). The popular tabloids therefore provide a significant amount of the public representation of women.

Although demonstrably trivializing in their language about women and sexuality, the tabloids are certainly not trivial when it comes to the ideologies inscribed within them. Writing about the genre of the soap opera, which has many crossovers with the coverage of the tabloids, one commentator has identified the reasons why popular forms are important to issues of social representation:

> Media forms and representations constitute major sites for conflict and negotiation, a central goal of which is the definition of what is to be taken as 'real', and the struggle to name and win support for certain kinds of cultural value and identity over others.
>
> (Gledhill, 1997: 348)

This chapter has attempted to demonstrate the continuities in the strategies of the tabloids in using their familiar rhetoric to include the representation of women into a version of the imaginary popular nation. These newspapers play an important role in the public performance of a very restricted range of female roles for the readers of these newspapers but they are consistent with popular views which claim to have an appeal to both male and female readers. Furthermore, they belong within the broader discourses of a national community drawn together from the common perceptions of women inscribed explicitly and implicitly amongst other features of that national community. Exploring language as a form of discourse which not only represents women in the tabloids but also fits them into the wider cohesiveness of their overall popular rhetoric enables us to see how this representation fits into the imagined daily space of the nation.

7   Popular politics in a national context

The tabloids do not routinely deal with much in the way of explicit party politics. They concentrate on a few headlining issues of the day while leaving the mechanics of the daily grind of political reporting to mainstream television and the elite press. What this means is that politics – and this almost always means national politics in the tabloids – is dealt with in a way which matches the coverage in the rest of the newspaper. Politics is portrayed as sensationalized and personalized, and the main protagonists draw a similar style of coverage to the celebrities and sports stars who feature elsewhere in their pages. This is structured in the language in which politics and political debate is framed. The implications of such language for political coverage are that there is a strong emphasis on what Patricia Hollis has called the rhetoric of 'old corruption' (Hollis, 1970). Such attitudes to politicians and the political processes lead not to an analysis of the shortcomings of political decisions but to an approach which can be characterized as populist (McGuigan, 1993), aligning with sceptical attitudes towards politicians which may be widely held among ordinary people but certainly do not represent a political perspective which will enable them to bring about political change. The language of this populism assists in maintaining a more generalized attack on the personalities of the politicians and their motives, highlighting wherever possible corruption and self-serving motivation. In turn, this does nothing to encourage a general engagement with political debate in its complexity but tends to represent a Britain which is cynical and apathetic with regard to its politics. Again this is nothing new in popular culture but is arguably disturbing in the context of the medium of the daily newspaper, which has a tradition of engagement with politics. Some argue that we have entered a new phase, a restyling of politics which highlights the performance and personality of politicians (Corner and Pels, 2003). If this is the case then the tabloids are an interesting terrain to consider given their traditional style and rhetoric.

Focus on individuals

Tabloid coverage of politics tends very much to focus on individuals. It is an approach more often than not detached from broader political histories or party contexts. The immediacy of their language does little to enable a reader-ship to build up a complex grasp of politics, more a series of political snapshots which match their broader entertainment agenda. Having once built up an image of a particular politician so that it fits this tabloid pattern, the coverage can then be exploited for the related entertainment factor it can provide.

The *Daily Mail* places its own response to an advert which had run in the *Times*. The original had featured a mocking CV of Tory leader Michael Howard. In this sort of coverage, one could argue that the tabloids are not entirely to blame and that they are in populist fashion merely following the lead of politicians' tactics. Yet it is the way that the tabloids map their language onto the games of the politicians which adds to the impression of parallelism between tabloids and politicians, both chasing populist positions, which reinforces at least a level of suspicion towards political culture which suits the general approach of these newspapers. The *Daily Mail* produces a replica CV for Blair with the headline:

Two can play that game

As both Labour and Tories attack Blair's sneers at Michael Howard, the Mail offers the PM a taste of his own medicine
(*Daily Mail*, 11 May)

This is significant in that it presents the tactic first literally as a game and then as a corrective, balancing up the political scales by offering Blair 'a taste of his own medicine'. One could, however, easily counter that the tabloid focus on individ-uals involved in politics is a strategy which suits an era where even the politicians concentrate on the personal and couch attacks in the format of a CV. This is part of a more generalized trend which has been observed by Blumler and Gurevitch (1995) and which they see as feeding a general cynicism about politics in Britain generated by the news media in general which forms part of British cultural and political experience. Yet Corner and Pels argue that this rejection might just as easily be explained as, 'a rejection of traditional political divisions and of the arro-gance of distanced, self-absorbed political professionals' (2003: 2).

The *Sun* has dubbed Gordon Brown 'Gord', and this abbreviated familiarity is a feature which runs through all the tabloids' political coverage, bringing with it at least the illusion of familiarity with the protagonists and placing them very much in the vernacular world of the readers, at least rhetorically. There is a corresponding simplification of political factions and the dynamics of political life itself which, far from making politics more accessible, reduces it to a tabloid rough house of winners and losers, goodies and baddies.

GORD U-TURN ON JOBS CUTS
(*Sun*, 13 May)

The enemies of the *Sun* readers are those dismissed condescendingly as 'penpushers' and 'pointless Whitehall bureaucrats' and the mechanics of political decision making are reduced to a populist gamble which posits the rationale for a 'U-Turn' on a 'poll backlash' which has led to the plan being 'watered down'. The implicit role of the electorate and within it the powerful lobby which the *Sun* claims to be able to mobilize is important in these putative dynamics. The personalization of politics is extended to the motives of Gordon Brown's economic decision making. Much political coverage is couched in terms of fears of what the people, implicitly the readers of tabloids, will do by way of reaction or protest. It is a style of primitive populist rhetoric. Here we read that it is Brown personally who is gaining and the hyperbole of the language – 'he's raking it in', 'tax hike' – is counterpoised to the 'angry motorists'. The only possible loser in the *Sun's* scenario is the Treasury, which would be the beneficiary of the hyperbolic 'flooding' of extra revenue, represented in popular terms as 'cash'. Once again it is appropriate to point out the cumulative repetition of the concept of 'flooding' as an amorphous threat which can be conjured up to offer a community an outside danger against which to define itself. The extended use of this metaphor across the tabloids thereby adds to its intertextual cohesion.

BROWN SCRAPS FUEL TAX RISE★

★He can afford it … higher prices mean he's raking it in anyway

GORDON Brown is to scrap plans for a 10p-a-gallon tax hike on petrol.

The decision comes amid fears of protests by angry motorists.

The Chancellor is able to abandon the 2p-a-litre rise as higher oil prices are flooding the Treasury with extra cash.

(*Sun*, 15 May)

Familiarity with certain aspects of the caricatured personalities of politicians featured in the tabloids is linked with nicknames to form recognizable scripts which act to amplify the concentration on personality rather than policy. 'Grumpy', 'Prezza' and 'Two jags' – the latter a reference to the Deputy Prime Minister's ownership of two rather uneconomical cars while representing a political party which has claims to being environmentally responsible – are all nicknames piled onto John Prescott. The short extract even includes a cross-over reference to the wording of a popular series of adverts for a brand of lager.

GOLDEN GRUMP

IF John Prescott did not exist, it would be necessary to invent him. Old Grumpy reaches the parts of public life that other politicians fear to explore.

So when Prezza blurts out that Blair is too close to George Dubya Bush, I believe that is what he really thinks. … Two jags. … Long may his lip remain unbuttoned.

(*Daily Mirror*, 21 May)

This familiar address is reinforced in another newspaper. It has the effect of deploying the original nickname as a background against which further attacks on his lifestyle can be launched. When echoing 'two jags', Prescott is referred to in the context of his notoriety at making publicly embarrassing mistakes. Instead of 'two jags' he has become 'two gaffes', and the *Daily Mail* enumerates them for its readers.

Two gaffes

Prescott blunders stir up new speculation over Blair's future

Gaffe Number One …

Gaffe Number Two …

(*Daily Mail*, 27 May)

The use of a surname can also denote a rhetorical position of authority *vis-à-vis* a powerful politician, as well as a mimicry of a speech act, ordering a politician to do something very specific and in language which echoes aspects of familiar and colloquial speech. This provides at least the verbal illusion that the newspaper wields power over the actions of politicians, on behalf of its associated national community of readers. Blunkett is told to 'sort it' and is asked in an expression familiar to a vernacular audience whether he has 'got a grip'. This colloquial pattern is complemented by the condensation of a myriad of complex issues into the single category of 'illegals'. Bold type adds a variety to the tone and emphasis of the piece, as found in the speech patterns that it mimics.

Sort it, Blunkett

David Blunkett says he's yet to convince us he's 'got a grip' on asylum.

You're right there, David! …

The Tories want Mr Blunkett to estimate how many illegals are in the country.

It's thought the number could be in excess of 500,000.

Mr Blunkett has said he doesn't have a clue what the figure is.

But he won't gain the public's trust until he finds out.

(*Daily Star*, 26 May)

Simple devices can also be used to reinforce a political point and to link it with the personalization characteristic of the tabloids. Below we see mnemonics and politics combined in a populist call to reckoning – 'we' are still counting – both readers and the newspaper. This is of central importance in national rhetoric as it has been observed that, 'The use of the personal pronoun appears to be of utmost importance in the discourses about nations and national identities' (De Cillia *et al.*, 1999: 163). The personal pronoun is used to reinforce the collective rhetoric of community. The capitalization of 'ARE' accentuates the deliberate speech act of counting and the fact that it is very much an act which is continuing in the present.

WMD–OMETER

(Yes, we ARE still counting, Tony)

383

(*Daily Mirror*, 17 May)

Populist and personal

The tabloids can deploy language subtly as well as emphatically to endorse the populism of their position on many fronts. Language can be used from the perspective of what Halliday calls its interpersonal function (Halliday, 1985), which sets up language as a medium through which interactional meaning so important to the ideological pact between reader and newspaper (such as attitudes, judgements and feelings) is expressed (Teo, 2000: 24). This function provides the textual link between newspaper and a constructed community of readers. In the following brief extract from an editorial in the *Sun*, there is a fascinating juxtaposition of pronouns and possessive adjectives emphasizing elegantly and succinctly the implicit responsibilities between leaders and people as one community:

Sun Says 4 May

As well as being vigilant at all times, there is something else we must do.

Give our leaders our total support in their war on terror.

The expression of the dissatisfactions of a community can also be conjured up by the introduction of a personal note to the language of public complaint. Here, a humorous variation on a familiar script of many weary train passengers can be drawn upon. The announcer of late-running train services is introduced to readers in the following terms:

I'M RAILLY SORRY

Phil is misery who announces train delays to millions

BRITAIN'S most apologetic person – the man who says 'sorry' to millions of rail passengers – has been unmasked.

(*Sun*, 14 May)

As we have seen in the previous chapter, the tabloids in general have taken a position on contemporary language use which can be described as hostile to the systematic investigation of the implications of language which may offend minorities or politically and socially marginalized groups. It is in the way that they present this hostility, directed at what they see as liberal interference or in more conspiratorial mode the work of the 'PC lobby', that we witness their attempts to claim the task of policing the vernacular for themselves. The deployment of 'politically correct' within reports as an explanation for a decision is a reduction of complex debates around language to a populist position which postulates satisfaction with the status quo. It goes beyond a mere rhetorical gesture and suggests that there exists an organized group of people, institutionally scouring the language for what it sees as unacceptable linguistic use. Critics such as Cameron (1995) and Woehrling (1996) have pointed out that it is the constant news media assertion which has created the impression that something tangible exists. An interesting case comes in the report on the publication of a new handbook with guidelines on language use for the judiciary:

'Black is banned' by judge supreme

... a politically correct legal handbook. ...

The PC instructions ...

(*Sun*, 13 May)

This is taken up in similar fashion in the *Daily Mail* with the impression being given that the battle had been won by the proponents of 'political correctness' through its use of the word 'surrendered':

The unmentionables

... Our courts surrendered to political correctness yesterday as judges were ordered to stop using everyday words and phrases such as 'immigrant', 'Asian', 'postman' and 'man and wife'.

It provides a tabloid list of terms which are included in the guide:

THE A TO Z OF POLITICAL CORRECTNESS

(*Daily Mail*, 13 May)

Yet when a former BBC presenter is referred to, his politically insensitive and ignorant remarks about Islamic culture are gently sidelined as 'controversial'. Very muted criticism of Kilroy-Silk's xenophobic outburst in the *Sunday Express* is contrasted with his favourable status as a 'poll star'. Energetic criticism of 'verbal hygiene' (Cameron, 1995) can be seen as one way of maintaining a *laissez-faire* approach to language in which insults directed towards sections of society are seen as nothing to worry about, inscribing the balance of racist inequalities within language to the advantage of the insider group (Van Dijk, 1991) or in such a way as to ensure that the powerful in society are not offended. This debate shows the tabloids at their most supportive of the status quo and yet paradoxically they are at their most populist and persuasive in taking this position. It is the rhetoric of their populism and the way in which they mesh it with a whole gamut of linguistic strategies across the newspaper which enables them to be so successful in maintaining a sense of cohesion.

Poll star Kilroy's war on Europe

... His bid to become a Brussels MEP follows his axing by the Beeb for controversial comments about Arab states in his Sunday Express column.

(Daily Star, 13 May)

Campaigns are ideal strategies for tabloids to combine rhetoric with layout. 'Stop the Highway Robbery' has been one such campaign. It is set up to criticize speed camera penalties which, it claims, are not a road safety strategy, merely a means of raising additional revenue for the government. It uses the *Sun* logo combined within the slogan and draws on its well-known sympathy with groups it has adopted as victims. In populist fashion, it does not choose a true minority but car drivers, whom it heralds as modern day heroes. 'Drivers finally had something to cheer about' signals the victory for the *Sun's* favoured victims on this occasion. It quickly moves to point out the significance in the timing of the 'U-Turn' to correspond to the 'Sun's influential campaign'. This rhetoric is underscored by the typography and the pronominal condensation of drivers, readers and the *Sun* in the final sentence emphasizing 'US'. The article prominently features ' "Stop the highway robbery campaign" from the *Sun*' within its logo.

DRIVERS finally had something to cheer about yesterday after the Government said some speed camera penalties will be cut.

... move follows The Sun's influential campaign against sneaky Gatsos.

The Government's U-turn comes after growing public protests against the huge increase in the cameras which rake in millions of pounds each year.

IT DROVE US CRAZY

(Sun, 17 May)

Although the *Sun* might have led the campaign, other tabloids responded to the news in a very similar and equally populist fashion, amplifying the popular discourse, in the case of the *Daily Star*, by the use of a footballing metaphor:

DRIVERS WIN SPEED WAR ... ON PENALTIES

They face just a two-point rap

MOTORISTS claimed a victory in the war against speed cameras last night.

(Daily Star, 17 May)

MINISTERS caved in to motorists last night and relaxed the speeding penalty system.

(Daily Mail, 17 May)

Populist politics are often expressed in personal terms, as in the asylum debate and the way in which judges and European human rights' legislation can be posited against the elected interests of the British people on this matter. This is expressed in the language of a powerful demotic:

Who rules?

... Blunkett's plans to deter bogus asylum seekers and 'economic migrants' has fallen foul of judges quoting European human rights laws.

So who exactly runs the country?

Is it the MPs whom we elect to make laws on our behalf?

Or the unelected judges who put their soft liberal prejudices before the will of Parliament?

(Sun, 22 May)

The process is stripped to its most simplistic binaries and the piece promises to get the reader to the core of the relationship between the politicians and the judiciary. 'Who rules?', 'who ... runs the country?' Questions of this sort are a perennial strategic device for the tabloids as they gesture towards a demotic position of open debate within the confines of their pages and their imagined community of readers. The judges are accountable at least in populist terms, referred to as they are as 'Our judges', which seems to make their colloquial 'slap in the face' for David Blunkett even more insulting. The judges' main fault seems to have been to have taken notice of the 'European human rights laws', and they are implicitly criticized as 'unelected' and as having 'soft liberal prejudices'.

The logic within the tabloids' language is to draw readers as a community with them into populist positions and campaigns. So issues such as the rise in petrol are channelled into how they will hit holiday makers, implicitly all of their readers involved in the usual annual routine, or the range of everyday folk who are drawn into illustrating how the inefficiencies of the Royal Mail have an effect on the whole of society.

HOLS HORROR

Fares hike as oil prices soar

HOLIDAYMAKERS will be hit with hefty rises in air fares this summer as oil prices soar ...

(Daily Star, 12 May)

TALES OF MAIL MISERY FLOOD IN AFTER SUN PROBE

... WE ASK BOSS TO SORT OUT THE VITAL QUESTIONS

... Many of your sorting staff barely speak English, let alone read it, because they are new arrivals to the UK.

(Sun, 11 May)

The list of angry respondents includes a mini-cross section of readers in the *vox pop* style of popular tabloids on the campaign trail: pensioner, Spurs fan, a furious mail victim. This story also seeks to capitalize on a previous *Sun* report. In it we see a moment of bridging xenophobic innuendo and complaints about the unreliability of a public service in the final point (Van Dijk, 1991; Hall, 1981).

Populist politics and politicians

Tabloids often summarize their own long-held political perspectives to remind a readership of where they stand on a particular topic and to refresh it in explicit terms around a contemporary issue. On the topic of the so-called NHS privatization initiatives revolution, the *Sun* is keen to express its populist credentials and once again to stress its own putative role in the political process:

To its credit the Government has listened to what the Sun has said for years.

That the biggest factor in driving major change in any public service is this: Letting the market put power in the hands of the people who use it.

(Sun, 10 May)

Politics is represented as a simplified process, contrasting binary distinctions between right and wrong, which coincide always with the opinions of the tabloid in question and its opponents, and as dependent on the familiar narratives which are woven as scripts through the language of the news they select as politically significant. Simple language is the springboard for this effective version of political engagement and it is a language very much directed towards the ear of a popular market with its resonances of popular speech. In the following example, it is reported that money ear-marked for school sports facilities is still untouched after three years:

Get set, go!

The old saying "healthy body, healthy mind" is especially true of children.

That's why Tony Blair launched a campaign to get children fit.

How strange then that £570 million of Lotto cash earmarked for school sports facilities has been untouched for three years ...

The PM should tell his Sports Minister to get his skates on.

(Sun, 4 May)

In the *Daily Mirror* we can read an account of the fears of mounting fuel costs but it is the way that the theme is dealt with which shows the combination of sensationalist, even alarmist exclamation and the jogging of readers' memories in relation to previous popular protests against increases in charges on fuel. It meshes with a characteristically tabloid attempt to present the debate in a simplified question and answer format. This device was an innovation at the end of the nineteenth century, exploited by George Newnes' *Tit-Bits* and Alfred Harmsworth's *Answers to Readers' Questions* to create an identity to appeal to the first mass market popular press (Jackson, 2000). It is a device still employed by popular papers but with even more sophistication as it draws in contemporary political themes to its rhetorical orbit. The 'Questions and Answers' respond to: 'Why?', 'Will it rise again?' and 'Will there be a recession?' The language is structured around anxiety and danger: 'crisis', 'Flammable', 'sparks', 'fears'.

FLAMMABLE

21-year high oil price sparks new protest fears

FEARS of a new fuel crisis were mounting yesterday as oil prices rose to their highest level in 21 years.

(Daily Mirror, 15 May)

In the following two examples we have two expressions, 'U-turn' and 'cave-in' which contribute to a rhetoric of simplified politics, aligned strategically with the threat of 'a public revolt':

U-turn as minister fears a revolt on the school buses

... the Education Secretary appears to have come to the conclusion that this could spark a damaging public revolt ... further stealth tax ...

(Daily Mail, 15 May)

Pensions cave-in

Chancellor Gordon Brown caved in last night and ordered a £400,000 safety net for workers whose pension funds have gone bust.

(Sun, 15 May)

Hyperbole is never far from the set of strategies employed by the tabloids in their dealings with politics and even when they do cover the reasons for industrial action, the sensationalist headline is the first thing which attracts a reader's attention:

NEXT STOP: RAIL CHAOS

Causing chaos for millions of passengers ... angry workers ... pensions, pay and travel perks ...

(*Daily Mirror*, 21 May)

The tabloids are ever eager to identify themselves on the side of the individual against the power bloc in a gesture of what Fiske (1992) sees as the attractiveness of popular cultural forms to the consumer. It is appropriate here to recall what Holland observed of the style of appeal to working people in the pages of the *Sun*.

> The *Sun* addresses a working class defined by its modes of consumption rather than its place in production. It unifies and organises its readers in terms of their forms of entertainment, by cultural attitudes rather than by class solidarity. ... The *Sun's* values are those which organise a working class – not the working class of labour histories, a class defined by self-help and hard work, but a working class which takes its pleasures when it can because they're only too fleeting.
>
> (Holland, 1983: 101–2)

It is an analysis which has become more applicable if anything in the intervening years and of broader relevance to all the tabloids in their pursuit of readers. Such a style of appeal based on the reader as consumer has become the dominant tabloid paradigm. In this model the 'power bloc' is represented as the institutional and faceless forces which are represented as grinding down ordinary people. It is ironic that the national British tabloid press is able to present itself as being on the side of these excluded ordinary people while remaining part of powerful global economic forces itself. This demonstrates, among other things, the power of their representational rhetoric. Thus it is inevitable that amorphous institutions such as 'quangos' come in for particularly harsh treatment. Here we see the implicit threat of what the *Daily Mail* threatens could be a 'superquango', a one-word judgement in the *Daily Mail's* language as it represents the antithesis of the empowered individual in control of decisions in life which is the preferred mode of identification for its reader-ideal, despite its occasional flirtation with the anarchic existentialism of the lower end of the market tabloids. This threat is made even worse through the use of a tabloid rhetorical pattern, opening 'floodgates to a tidal wave of litigation'.

Superquango

Human rights watchdog will get a £50m budget and open floodgates to litigation

(*Daily Mail*, 13 May)

Quangos are clearly institutions with few tabloid friends. Witness the *Daily Mirror*, punning on the theme of a successful advertising campaign for a soft drink as an illustration of the extended cultural referencing of popular journalism (Dahlgren, 1995). It also takes a populist position, alerting us in support of the Labour minister that:

YOU'VE BEEN QUANGOED

Reid axe to fall on NHS bureaucrats

JOHN Reid yesterday declared war on quangos ...

Half would be axed or merged ..assault on health service bureaucracy...

(Daily Mirror, 21 May)

There is possibly no more contentious issue to reduce to the simplified binaries of the tabloids than one such as asylum. Nevertheless, we can observe in the following two examples a simplification of a complex process and the reduction of criticism to the tabloid transitivity of 'slammed' and 'blasted'. Both the *Sun* and the *Daily Star* use the tabloid gambit of placing contentious claims in inverted commas and the latter manages to ask readers a question which their report has already given them an answer to, using an echoing strategy to close down identification around an issue it feels confident on with its readers.

ASYLUM 'CON' BLASTED

MINISTERS were slammed yesterday for putting out "misleading" figures about asylum.

(Sun, 26 May)

ASYLUM IS 'No.1 ISSUE'

VOTERS think the Government has lost control of immigration ... YouGov poll ...

HAS THE GOVT LOST CONTROL OF IMMIGRATION?

YES/NO

(Daily Star, 27 May)

This use of the yes/no tactic to elicit a response from readers illustrates the provocative potential of populist positions expressed in such demotic language, since the results will be used in turn to claim that it is representing its readers with such statistics. It can then claim a justification in continuing in such simplistic and provocative terms on both the issue of asylum and on the politicians charged with taking decisions and formulating policy on such sensitive matters.

On rare occasions, the tabloids can represent a genuine sense of dialogue between their readers and a politician, as in the following explicit appeal to a real community of readers by a politician. The paper applauds the fact that the

Home Secretary recognizes that many *Daily Star* readers live in streets and on estates where 'yobs run riot'. This unusual direct and populist intervention by a politician is enhanced by the realism of the newspaper's reference to its readers as being more likely to come from Britain's most disadvantaged social groups.

David Blunkett talks exclusively to Daily Star

HELP STAMP OUT DRUNKEN THUGS

DAVID Blunkett wants to recruit Daily Star readers in a massive crackdown on yobs.

(Daily Star, 27 May)

The politics of the fringes of right-wing activism are relegated to part of the same process of criticism towards mainstream politicians and their policies. The UK Independence Party (UKIP) is represented in both the *Daily Star* and the *Daily Mail* as merely a logical if regrettable response to the government. They blame the relative success of the party on 'Blair's open-door immigration policy', an accusation which is as inflammatory as it is hyperbolic and juxtapose this to his 'somersaults over the EU constitution', and can only explain the rise of this 'collection of oddballs, xenophobes and even racists' by a government which has tried to 'bamboozle' the British. The UKIP is therefore the manifestation of the 'British people's fury'! Both newspapers blame the inefficiency, even dishonesty of the government, for the rise of the UKIP and their complementary coverage meshes the accusations back into their own populist themes with language to match.

Cry of despair

It speaks volumes about the British people's fury with the European policies of the political establishment that support for the UK Independence Party is at record levels …

(Daily Mail, 25 May)

Daily Star Says

… how come the UKIP's fortunes are rising?

It's surely because voters want to protest at Tony Blair's open-door immigration policy and his somersaults over the EU constitution.

He has put the UKIP on the map.

(Daily Star, 25 May)

Duping the public

Politicians are represented almost exclusively in language which represents them as involved in an extended game of duping the public while implying that the popular tabloids themselves are doing their best to rectify this in favour of their readers. Yet these same politicians can quickly be elevated to heroic status if they happen to touch upon a favoured theme, as when Gordon Brown is credited with a characteristically tabloid imperative, telling the EU in the language of the street to 'butt out' and sending them a militaristic 'warning salvo' which the *Sun* clearly approves of.

BROWN'S WARNING SALVO TO EU

BUTT OUT BRUSSELS

CHANCELLOR Gordon Brown last night claimed he was fighting for the whole European Union by demanding changes to the new EU constitution.

(Sun, 12 May)

Similar language can be played with, as in the example below, where a more powerful expletive is knowingly replaced by 'truck up' in the *Sun* of 11 May, punning on the pictures of the trucks involved in the fake photos published by their rival the *Daily Mirror*. This ludic element is an important method of constructing a distance which enables a humorous aspect to be maintained across many news reports.

WHAT A TRUCK-UP

SHAMEFUL photographs showing British troops abusing Iraqi prisoners ARE fake, the Government confirmed yesterday.

Lorry used in photos was NEVER sent to Iraq

In the following, we see the abbreviated script technique which condenses the politicians into a usurious cabal, using pejorative terms such as 'cam con', 'milking drivers' and 'money-grabbing politicians' to drive its case home while questions and answers are bandied to and fro between the newspaper and its imagined community.

The Sun Says

The cam con

IT'S 10 years since speed cameras first appeared in Britain.

But are our roads any safer or do drivers go any slower?

No, says the leader of the Police Federation …

If the police oppose speed cameras … why do we have so many?

Because they're a simple way of milking drivers.

Don't blame the police – blame the money-grabbing politicians.

(Sun, 14 May)

The *Daily Mirror* is seen to be standing up for the people of Britain against 'cynicism and contempt' as a whole range of mixed metaphors and popular language indicates that, in the view of this tabloid, the days of the Prime Minister are numbered. Even the recurrent hyperbole of the bookies having 'slashed' their odds is in keeping with a populist rhetoric, connecting the interests of the ordinary people in political terms with what the newspaper considers the pastimes of its core readership.

The knives are out for you, Tony

… Now Mr Blair is on the ropes. … **The British people are treated with cynicism and contempt.**

(*Daily Mirror*, 17 May)

PM FACES KICKING IN THE POLLS

… Bookies have slashed the odds on Mr Blair being PM at the next election …

(*Daily Mirror*, 17 May)

In addition to the popular cultural references connecting bookies with the world of high politics, we have further linguistic markers in the *Daily Star* of the flattening of political debate (Blumler and Gurevitch, 1995). Blair is twice referred to by his first name and there are popular vernacular resonances in the comparisons with non-stick agent, Teflon, and, comic character 'Billy No Mates'. The range of metaphors adds to the personalization – 'knives out', 'vultures circling' – but most of all the image of Gordon Brown 'licking his lips with glee' completes the representation of a comic book environment.

Daily Star Says

Tony's Iraq downfall

YOU wouldn't want to trade places with Tony Blair right now.

… The man once dubbed Teflon Tony has become more like Billy No Mates these days. …

Bookies yesterday slashed the odds of him going before the next General Election for the fourth day running.

Gordon Brown must be licking his lips with glee.

The knives are definitely out for poor Tony and the vultures are beginning to circle.

(*Daily Star*, 17 May)

Hyperbole is the common currency of political debate across the tabloids. Politics is represented as always on the precipice of some drama which enables it to be best fitted to the extreme and sensationalized language of the rest of their coverage.

EXIT IRAQ OR EXIT No 10

… stark ultimatum … desperate battle to shore up his premiership. … Speculation over Mr Blair's future will rage. … Mr Blair's moral case in tatters … pilloried … fallout from the war … making him a liability. … Fevered speculation … stoked up by Deputy Prime Minister John Prescott … mounting desperation in Labour circles. … If Labour hits meltdown at the polls … hell bent on hanging on …

(Daily Mirror, 17 May)

The *Daily Mail* reports on signs that Labour will increase taxes to find a replacement for the Council Tax, and chooses language which blends hyperbole with a distinctive sort of transitivity in which Labour is depicted as hammering the middle classes – a useful reinforcement of a familiar Conservative slogan:

THE clearest signal yet that Labour will hammer the middle-classes with a local income tax came from John Prescott yesterday.
(Daily Mail, 27 May)

In keeping with the recurrent image of Blair and his party getting a 'kicking' in the polls, we can see the extension of this metaphorical violence in the report on Jack Straw's reception in Brussels.

FOREIGN secretary Jack Straw was ambushed by Germany and France last night in a stand-up row over Britain's referendum.

… read the riot act … tense showdown. … Mr Fischer believes the move is aimed at sinking the treaty … roughed up … bust-up … slammed for 'salami tactics' … first day of a month-long battle … crunch summit in Brussels.

(Sun, 18 May)

The public are appealed to explicitly in terms of resistance to being fooled by politicians, reinforcing the impression that for tabloid readers, politics is merely a process of systematic deception which the tabloid newspapers themselves enable their readers to see through.

'Blunkett's Bobbies' could replace us, say constables

PLANS to expand the role of civilian patrol officers in tackling crime could see them replacing the traditional constable, police leaders warned yesterday. …

The proposals are causing widespread alarm among rank-and-file officers, who fear police numbers could be cut in half while the public are duped into thinking the streets are safer by the presence of more 'yellow jackets' – dubbed 'Blunkett's Bobbies'.

(*Daily Mail*, 18 May)

Yet once again there is extreme ambivalence on positions towards the police in the tabloids in general; one minute they are heroes, the next they are the victims of a brand of straight-talking tabloid tirade, parallel to the language of the rest of the paper, calling their morale and competence into question as well as accusing them of scapegoating motorists as easy targets rather than serious criminals, and backing the position of an extremely populist politician through the use of a vernacular speech act:

Jump to it, PC Plod

DAVID Blunkett today faces one of Britain's most hostile crowds – rank-and-file policemen. ...

Mr Blunkett should tell his audience: 'Stop the moaning and raise your game.'

(*Daily Star*, 19 May)

The following piece contains an expression which appears to sum up the tabloids' preferred approach to Britain's political world: 'stripped of all the waffle'. There is a desire implicit here for a politically simple world, articulated in straightforward language. It is a world which reflects the image of the halcyon past which, as we have seen, plays an important part in constructing views of popular history in the tabloids. This world fits neatly into the binary divisions and the sensationalization of their campaigns, couched as they often are in simplistic personalized terms and the brief attention span of their news agendas.

CHANCELLOR'S FAINT PRAISE FOR PM

Stripped of all the waffle it amounts to this: 'I've worked with him for 21 years' ...

(*Sun*, 18 May)

A good example of this binary political world is reflected in the punning humour of the choice which Blair is presented as having:

BLAIR BETWEEN IRAQ AND A HARD PLACE

(*Sun*, 26 May)

Exceptions – linking personal to global

Very occasionally, a tabloid will move out of the closed and parochial set of cross-media references and a restricted British parochialism to provide a more developed view and even analysis of the ways in which events in this country connect to those abroad. Such prose is extremely persuasive and even if one disagrees with the analysis itself, one cannot deny its analytical dimension. It indicates that there is nothing incompatible between the plain English of the tabloids and political debate on a sophisticated level. The effective use of such language to put complex debate in plain terms for a general audience is demonstration that just because the tabloids for the most part do not engage in it, does not mean that it is because the language that they use or the readers that they target are incapable of this level of understanding of the broader political connections in the world. At its most powerful this language attempts to link the personalized 'Osama' with the assumed direct experience of tabloid readers to provide a level of analysis of international politics. Award-winning political editor Trevor Kavanagh writes:

OSAMA'S OIL THREAT TO WEST

BRACE yourselves for the £5 gallon – and the chance that one day we might consider that cheap.

Oil experts fear that the leap in fuel prices is here to stay. And if ruthless terror leader Osama Bin Laden has his way, it's only a start.

Al-Quaeda is determined to sabotage oil supplies to the hated West.

Its forces were probably involved in pipeline sabotage which slashed Iraqi exports by a third.

The next target is Saudi Arabia. ...

The world is neatly poised for one of the most benign combinations of economic circumstances in history. ...

All that is at risk unless the world wakes up – and rallies behind the Coalition in the struggle to bring order to Iraq.

(*Sun*, 15 May)

Despite this potential, coverage of overseas news is restricted to the most sensational occurrences, which means that the popular tabloids are even less able to deal with the underlying processes and causes of world events than the elite press. This leads to a practice of reporting occasional overseas news which fits with the overall tabloid agenda but represents still further a world in which tragic events erupt almost out of nowhere and have relevance only in terms of the narrowest of human empathy or horror.

10 children die as Israel halts march

CARNAGE

... crowd of marching protesters was cut down by Israeli tanks shells and helicopter fire ...

(*Daily Mirror*, 20 May)

Burlesque politics

On occasion, if politics cannot be represented simplistically then it can be taken to the extreme of baroque exaggeration. The following story from Brussels allows such an opportunity for the tabloids to indulge in the language of high farce, particularly suited to their attitude to the procedures of the maligned European Union. Foreign Secretary Jack Straw had complained that there were certain countries within the EU which alone were singled out for criticism in the same way as some individuals are singled out to be bitten by mosquitoes. The *Sun* ran the story with a collage of Straw with a can of bug spray.

EU SUCKERS

Straw's mozzie attack on rivals

(*Sun*, 19 May)

It is the *Daily Mail* which takes this the furthest, providing cartoons of various politicians as insects complete with descriptions of their habitats and diets and photos superimposed on insect bodies under the general heading of:

BLAIR'S BEASTIES

TONY BLAIR

PURPLE EMPEROR BUTTERFLY

Caesar dejectus

BRIGHTLY coloured, a prize specimen, the embodiment of vanity and ephemeral glory. Loves to travel and perch in the sun, but shies from difficulties on its home patch. Feeds off rotting fruit and backbench carrion. On the verge of extinction, so currently hiding in densely wooded areas where its movements are hard to discern.

GORDON BROWN

BUMBLE BEE

Growlingus gordius

ALASTAIR CAMPBELL

SPIDER

Doctus deceptivus

(*Daily Mail*, 20 May)

Politicians are particularly ripe for such treatment in the tabloids, as in the following story which chooses to highlight the weight of the two men selected to deal with the problem of obesity. The language is developed into an extended series of puns and metaphors which disguise the serious issue at heart as they appeal humorously to the ridiculing of the politicians themselves.

FAT'S RICH

… CABINET heavies John Prescott and Charles Clarke are throwing their considerable weight behind a campaign to tackle obesity.

(*Daily Mirror*, 11 May)

Again, when trade unionist leaders from railway union ASLEF are on one occasion involved in a violent encounter, the tabloid treatment sees them pictured in a photo-montage as prize fighters and they are given names to ridicule their public display of aggressive behaviour at the same time as the political differences which have led to the falling out are ignored. The report, complete with pictures of them in a boxing ring, is highlighted in the following terms:

UNION BASHERS

WEIGHING IN:

'BRAWLER' BRADY, 'BREAK!' BLACKBURN, 'SLAMMIN' SAMWAYS

… Aslef's three senior officials are suspended after bust-up at BBQ

(*Daily Mirror*, 26 May)

An excellent example of the binaries of tabloid political coverage woven with the principles of the 'old corruption' comes in the report of an assault on the Prime Minister in the House of Commons by representatives of 'Fathers 4 Justice' in the *Daily Mirror*. Westminster is represented as old-fashioned and out of date and in language which howls of the hostility towards undeserved deference towards the upper and privileged classes. The attackers are described in vernacular insults which ostracizes them as outsiders to the community of right-thinking readers of the *Daily Mirror*. The piece also stresses that Westminister should be treated simply as a place of work which, like any other place of work, should provide a healthy and safe environment for its employees. This is very in keeping with the broadly pro-trade union agenda of the newspaper.

PM POWDER ATTACK

Dads' army defeats duds' army

Fathers 4 Justice beat 'the men in tights'

… Westminster is a security shambles … it is run by a music hall regiment of military officers not fit to hold a p★★s-up in a brewery

… No more faffing about with fancy dress. No more doffing the cap to retired military types.

MPs should take control of the place where they work …

… madmen … nutters … male nutters … nutters … weirdo home-grown terrorists … make Parliament work for the people – not for the toffs …

(*Daily Mirror*, 20 May)

The *Daily Mail* takes a very different view but one which mingles references to popular Hollywood heroism with traditional British stiff upper lip. It also takes the opportunity to contrast the relaxed attitude of the British in security matters to unnamed but foreign countries where the paraphernalia of the security state is more oppressive. What a backhanded celebration of Britishness and what an odd context given the broader views of the *Daily Mail* on both Tony Blair and the Labour Party!

How the bomber hit the bullseye

CLINT Eastwood would have been proud of our lads yesterday. … Tony Blair, one cool gringo, stayed his ground. Strike up the tune to The Good, The Bad and The Ugly! … marvellous British phlegm in the face of this scurvy assault. …

One can think of countries where, had this happened, burly security personnel with earphones and bulging holsters would within seconds have flattened the PM. Not here. Mr Blair did not scream, or jump, or hit the deck. Just stood there. Magnificent.

(*Daily Mail*, 20 May)

Letters as political support

The thematization and language of the letters' pages are an ideal site to demonstrate the coalescence of attitudes which maintain the bridge between the ideological and editorial stance of the newspaper and the putative views of the readers whose letters are edited and published (Wahl-Jorgensen, 2001). The *Sun* uses the rather trivial matter of the Eurovision Song Contest to align with its own views on the relative merits of America and the European Union on a page which makes the contest the 'Big Issue' of the day. It is a big issue for the *Sun* as it enables it to print a variety of letters which make that cross-referential point.

Eurovision only about scoring political points

THE BIG ISSUE

… A lot of the countries involved are members of the EU. If they cannot vote honestly on a song competition why would they run Europe fairly? … Put America in it – at least we'd get 12 points for once.

(*Sun*, 19 May)

The *Daily Mirror* deploys the same extended exercise when it aligns its own political stance on a more serious issue with the dominant tone of letters which are used to echo the key themes of the newspaper's take on the invasion of Iraq.

> The great debate
>
> Now pull the troops out, Tony
>
> ... our boys ... our troops ... another Vietnam ... more spin ... weapons of mass destruction ... senseless loss of life and costing billions ... fuel resentment and hatred towards the West ... unjust war.
>
> (*Daily Mirror*, 27 May)

The tabloids are deeply implicated in the contemporary renegotiation of the language of national politics as the informality and the move towards a more colloquial political language (Corner and Pels, 2003: 11) fit so well with the longer-term shifts within of popular print culture. The serious and professionalized routines of political life may not be covered with anything like adequate rigour for an active citizenship in the contemporary popular media but in the refashioned, personalized style of exchange between popular media and increasingly populist politicians the tabloids are well placed to act as political conduits.

Radical popular

One key question in discussions of the version of Britain presented to us in the language of the tabloids is whether there is scope for any form of radical alternative within this language or is the popular press so welded to the political economy of the dominant status quo that there is no room for radical or even liberal opinion at all? Some commentators in fact see the rise of a tabloid culture as indicative of a potentially more democratic society in itself (Fiske, 1992; Hartley, 1996).

The tabloid press itself is, at least rhetorically, on the side of the indigenous, idealized ordinary people (Conboy, 2002) whether they are articulated as taxpayers, the public or even the nation. All attempt to capture a particular variant of that vernacular appeal and must adapt it to politics which can be identified as having a range of this national grouping as its target. In this process, language is once again of paramount importance.

In addressing a popular readership, can the language of the tabloids which can be identified by its binarism and simplistic sensationalizing, actually present alternatives to the ideas of the ruling elite? Does it merely represent the ideas of that elite in a vernacular form, a sort of ventriloquism of class distortion, or is it limited to a perpetual sniping at the ruling elite from within the 'existing structures of society' (Sparks, 1992: 28) because of the limitations of simplistic language itself? These questions on the relationship between complexity of language and social status are similar to a version of the restricted/elaborated code of Basil Bernstein from the 1970s which seemed to suggest that children from different social classes moved within linguistically distinct registers which enabled or disabled them from participating in the language activities of the dominant social and economic class, particularly in their schooling.

It might be observed that because of their concentration on celebrity and sensation, the tabloids do not have enough space to develop the sort of consistency of coverage which might add up to a radical take on the world. There is simply not enough physical room within the news agenda within which they work. One might add to this the lack of any concerted attempt to extract their analysis from a personalized political world. Most of the time the tabloids use a language which exploits the sentiments of a British underclass, those excluded from the power bloc either in blue collar populist terms or in terms of a disenfranchised petty bourgeoisie in the case of the *Daily Mail*. On occasion, however, they do demonstrate that there is nothing intrinsic in the tabloid format to prevent it being used for radical interventions in public debate. This might lead us to conclude that it is restricted pragmatically to a liberal role at best but it can on occasion show us that it can use the language which we recognize as characteristic of tabloid Britain to challenge the status quo for altruistic reasons or in an attempt to change the country in a way which genuinely benefits the socially disadvantaged and excluded. The language of the tabloids has at least a potential to articulate a view of Britain which, if not consistently radical, at least stands in a tradition of engaged liberalism. The characteristic irreverence of the tabloids can also be used to ironic effect as in the case of the exposé of the lack of security at Buckingham Palace unveiled by an undercover *Daily Mirror* journalist who had been able to get a job there with little screening. This story does nothing to challenge the power of the British monarchy but confines itself instead to chipping away at public deference. In its 'sensational exposé' the paper crows about its contribution to public service in bringing such a dreadful state of affairs to the attention of the Queen and graciously signs off its gesture as a form of ironic public service with an echo of the sort of unthinking deference associated with encounters with the royal family and which the series of articles has served to undermine: 'Glad to be of service, Ma'am' (*Daily Mirror*, 7 May).

Race – extending the tabloid range

One way in which newspapers may engage with a more thoughtful approach to the news is by providing context and even an historical dimension. For once, the *Daily Mirror* was able to contextualize a recent story with a more in-depth look at the state of English football. It came after the Ron Atkinson affair and all the implications it had for racism in football. The large capital letters of its headline held an immediate message for readers as they were printed white on black to underline typographically the answer to the implicit question being posed. It is a double page spread and gains in its intended impact by its being printed on a Saturday, the biggest sports day of the week in the press. The article reveals that despite the fracas over Atkinson's outburst and the reaction of all concerned in the media who ostracized him for his language, the structure of the game is as institutionally racist as ever with only 2 per cent of the top names in management and refereeing being black, despite the preponderance of black players in the game.

TRUE COLOUR OF FOOTBALL

WHEN ITV pundit Ron Atkinson called Chelsea defender Marcel Desailly a f***ing lazy n****r, the nation reacted with horror.

Fans concluded that Big Ron was stuck in a time warp, was at odds with society and his prejudice was a one-off.

But a Daily Mirror investigation today lifts the lid on racism at the heart of the beautiful game. We reveal that it isn't just Ron who's trapped in the past – it's the whole of football. Our research has discovered that racism is *still* endemic at the top level of the game.

The article ends with a quotation of anti-racist intent from Piara Powar of Kick It Out which might serve as a motto for popular newspapers in Britain in general terms:

'Change will need to be driven forward, it is not inevitable.'
(*Daily Mirror*, 8 May)

A further example of the way in which the strategies of the tabloids can be put to progressive use came earlier in the same month. A *Daily Mirror* undercover reporter had been placed at Yarl's Wood detention centre for asylum seekers in an attempt to secure accurate information concerning allegations of racial abuse there. The undercover strategy can be used to entertain, to flag alarmist fears or to bring the viciousness of institutional racism home to readers. There is nothing which restricts the undercover investigative genre in the tabloids to the merely sensationalist. It is more the ends to which the sensationalism is directed which determine its political potency. The story, with its graphic descriptions of abuse and prejudice from staff, broke in the paper in December 2002 and prompted a full enquiry. Its front page had then read:

Mirror reporter lands job as security guard at asylum centre … and discovers a culture of abuse, racism and violence that SHOULD appal us all.
(*Daily Mirror*, 8 December 2002)

The paper uses the implied community of readership to assume a benchmark of human decency and highlights the modality of its assumption by putting the word 'should' in characteristic capital letters to emphasize its outrage on the readers' behalf. This is a clear example of tabloid language and strategies being deployed in pursuit of a provocative and progressive cause and is at odds with much tabloid coverage which uses these patterns of language to stoke prejudice, as discussed in chapter 5. When it comes to the verdict of the enquiry, the *Daily Mirror* is equally unequivocal in its view, particularly in the way that it finds that racist practices do not equate to individual acts of racism. It used a single word in its response as a headline before going on to create a virtuous community of spokespersons from Liberty, the Immigration Minister and the *Daily Mirror* readers referred to twice by the same minister, Des Browne.

UNACCEPTABLE

… Barry Hugil, of Liberty, said: 'I find these conclusions staggering. The Mirror showed there is a culture of racism.'

Des Browne Immigration Minister on why racism will not be tolerated in our asylum centres

I know Mirror readers will rightly have been shocked when they read about comments made by some staff at Yarl's Wood – I certainly was.

The Mirror uncovered some appalling attitudes. …

We have a duty to treat detainees with humanity and I hope Mirror readers trust we will take a tough line on anyone who doesn't fulfil this.

(*Daily Mirror*, 1 May)

On this occasion the editorial 'Voice of the *Daily Mirror*' can congratulate itself on progressive work well done. It is interesting to note that the language of the tabloid does not break stride in this investigation nor in its reporting, indicating that the tabloids do have the potential to put their linguistic resources behind liberal causes on the occasions when it suits them and they are not distracted by the commercial imperative of more trivial matters.

End to racism

Thanks to a Daily Mirror undercover investigation, there should be no more scandalous racism and abuse at the Yarl's Wood detention centre. …

In future those who work there must act with proper professionalism, not with prejudice and foul abuse.

(*Daily Mirror*, 1 May)

Yet despite these positive elements, the structural and institutional aspects of the story are relegated to an incidental feature beneath the triumphant and self-promotional tone of the tabloid which emphasizes the end of racism at the centre. This is ultimately a rather simplistic tale of bad practice and a good campaigning newspaper with the latter winning out on behalf of its decent community of readers. More endemic issues are glossed over.

News from Africa

Occasionally there is an intervention in language which fits the hyperbole of the tabloid agenda but is transposed to a more radical perspective. In this case, it is a damning critique of Robert Mugabe's Zimbabwe and the respectable, liberal English establishment's reluctance to be seen to be opposing him. On this occasion, the article deploys much that is characteristic of tabloid vulgarity and personalization to make a strong expression of political opposition to both the regime and the hypocrisy of the cricketing authorities in England. This is a moment when news about Africa goes some way to depicting the strategic reasons behind the politics which create such havoc, even though it stays within the stereotypical parameters identified by Brookes (1995) and Hall (1981) while going someway to describing the role which British institutions and media play in remaining silently complicit with such politics.

DOMINIK DIAMOND

BLOOD ON THEIR CRICKET WHITES

The England cricketers are once again preparing to bend over and lick Robert Mugabe's jacksie by going to Zimbabwe in October.

… The Government have chickened out of stopping them going for reasons I cannot understand, but ones I know they wouldn't even contemplate if Mugabe was an Arab or if George Bush wanted him kicked out of Zimbabwe.

What I don't understand is why the Government say they cannot force the ECB to pull out of one cricket tour but they're prepared to force this whole country to join the Euro and go to war with Iraq. Christ, the ECB must have some scary bastards in its ranks. … Normal everyday people in normal everyday jobs are getting murdered every day. … Assuming he ever takes a break from his systematic genocide, Mugabe must be p*ssing himself.

(Daily Star, 8 May)

Rarely do we see any consistent coverage of Africa other than characteristic anniversary pieces on the media event of the 1980s, Live Aid, pieces which attempt to paint a fuller picture of the roots of poverty and political corruption which blight the continent. This following extract by the original architect of that event, Bob Geldof, is accompanied with graphic statistics on poverty, the decline in aid and disease facing the continent.

NEARLY 20 YEARS AFTER LIVE AID …

Why is Africa STILL dying?

But as the West gives with one hand, it takes away with the other – through crippling debt repayments and unfair trade laws. …

Africa must be the architect of its own survival. But for it to succeed, Tony Blair and George Bush must be as dedicated to the War on Poverty as they are on the War on Terror.

(*Daily Mirror*, 5 May)

However, most of the time, the tabloids restrict their coverage to isolated glimpses, in between the main diet of celebrity, sensation and personality. In fairness we could also ask, with Connell (1992), what the broadsheets contribute in the way of consistent political analysis outside the confines of their own political economies? The contrast between the daily diet of the tabloids and their occasional forays into highly ethical positions can sometimes be quite arresting. Given the tabloids' graduated but common interest, if not in pornography then certainly in the sex lives of the stars, it seems odd to find the following introduction to a review of a popular book by Jessica Williams, *50 Facts That Should Change the World*:

WHEN AS MUCH IS SPENT ON PORN AS ON AID

50 facts that make you want to change the world

(*Daily Mirror*, 6 May)

This brief selection of examples demonstrates that it is not the language, format or even propensity to sensationalize which prevents a more consistently challenging line from the British tabloid press. It has within its linguistic armoury the potential to harness a vernacular language with the concerns of ordinary people in a more positively democratic way. Popular newspapers from the nineteenth century through to the *Daily Mirror* in the post-war period of the twentieth century show how this language can be used to campaign on behalf of the interests of society's outsiders and make a profit at the same time. What has changed is not the potential of its language but a political economy which appears to demand an increasingly undemanding agenda for blue collar and lower middle class readers. This culminates in a less than challenging view of Britain and the world for many millions of readers.

Positions on Iraq

In its well-publicized opposition to the invasion of Iraq, the *Daily Mirror* has consistently attempted to present an alternative to the patriotic support for the Blair–Bush hegemony of the *Daily Star* and the *Sun*. It draws enthusiastically on outside sources such as Amnesty International and American broadsheet newspapers to endorse its own position with regard to its own readers:

DANGER TO THE WORLD

PRESIDENT Bush was accused yesterday of making the world a more dangerous place.

Amnesty International attacked the American-led war on terror, claiming it had led to the worst human rights abuses in 50 years ... one of its hardest-hitting annual reports ...

(Daily Mirror, 27 May)

The New York Times **CORRECTIONS AND CLARIFICATIONS**

Sorry. We were completely wrong about WMD and Iraq

THE New York Times apologised to its readers yesterday for misleading them about Iraq's weapons of mass destruction.

The paper, widely considered to be the most influential in America, confessed that the US Government urged it to carry unfounded claims to justify the war ... 'not as rigorous as it should have been' ...

(Daily Mirror, 27 May)

In addition, it employs the well-known radical journalist John Pilger to do that rare thing and provide an historical context to the news as part of the process of opposition. This is rare enough even in the elite press. He roots his analysis in British imperial history and American neo-imperialism and shows how demotic radicalism is not out of keeping with the brevity and directness of tabloid style.

Torture's not new but now it's news

John Pilger

Much of this modern imperial racism was invented in Britain. Listen to its subtle expressions, as British spokesmen find their weasel words in refusing to acknowledge the numbers of Iraqis killed or maimed by cluster bombs, whose actual effects are no different from the effects of suicide bombers; they are weapons of terrorism. ...

At the very least, we must demand that those responsible for this epic crime get out of Iraq now and that we have an opportunity to prosecute and judge them and to make amends to the Iraqi people. Anything less disqualifies 'us' as uncivilised.

(Daily Mirror, 7 May)

In mocking the justifications for war of the British and American governments who claimed that Saddam Hussein was hiding weapons of mass destruction, the *Daily Mirror* uses a characteristic tabloid ploy by depicting in visual form the number of days which have passed since the weapons have failed to materialize. It is called the 'WMD-OMETER' and makes a daily addition to pieces on Iraq in the paper, as a witty and striking image of the unreliability of official information on this matter. In a desperate rearguard action to deflect mounting criticism over the injudicious publication of pictures of British troops mistreating Iraqis which have been shown to be fakes, the *Daily Mirror* uses all the tabloid linguistic strategies of vicarious involvement with its readership to justify its stance on the war and call for an apology from those in power:

> Since the drums first beat for war in Iraq the Mirror has led the way in reflecting the public's unease. We questioned every facet of the desire for war.
>
> Our stance reflected an unprecedented outpouring of opposition around the world. ...
>
> In August 2002, 91 per cent of Mirror readers opposed the war plans in one of our biggest ever phone polls. ...
>
> In Britain the spectre of a Labour government backing right-wing Republicans in the White House was an outrage to many. ...
>
> Many believe the Government should come clean over sending troops into battle on the false pretext that Iraq had WMD. ...
>
> Now the Daily Mirror has apologised, how long will it take before others own up to their mistakes? We will continue to question and probe. Our readers would accept nothing less.
>
> (*Daily Mirror*, 15 May)

To justify its stance the *Daily Mirror* refers rhetorically to 'outpouring of opposition around the world', 'reflecting public unease' and 'Our readers', as well as a concrete poll of 'Mirror readers'. It masks mere repetition of its own opposition by an oblique reference to the 'many' who are outraged by the 'spectre' of Labour backing 'right wing Republicans'. The paper's stance on Iraq is represented here and throughout as a cornerstone of its relationship with a radical popular readership. The words 'we' and 'our' are repeated and reinforced by the assertions of the mass of its readership being in support '91 per cent', and 'many' is repeated. Here the tabloid rhetoric of community with its readers is enlisted to challenge pro-war positions.

On the release of the latest Michael Moore film, the *Daily Mirror* makes connections to other popular media as is the pattern in the tabloids, but on this occasion it is to stress political opposition to Bush in the run-up to the Presidential elections, not simply as a tie-in plugging the film for commercial reasons.

10 REASONS WHY BUSH WANTS TO BAN MOORE FILM

... like it could lose him the next election

(*Daily Mirror*, 20 May)

It comes as no real surprise then to read once again from a different perspective in the *Daily Mirror* a few days later of the costs of the war in Iraq, broken down into a characteristic tabloid list:

THE REAL COST OF THE IRAQ WAR

Your bill so far is 2.75bn, that could have paid for. …

IT COULD have paid for over three million heart bypass operations, trained over 70,000 nurses or built 280 badly-needed schools.

(*Daily Mirror*, 19 May)

The same strategy is employed in the *Daily Mail*, as it is clearly more hostile to Tony Blair and the Labour government than it is concerned about the alleged menace posed to the West by Saddam Hussein. Its own list of alternative expenditure includes flippantly 400 David Beckhams, twelve and a half Millennium Domes and a 3p cut in income tax, and in a populist gesture cites the nation's pensioners as being financially penalized because of the expenditure on the war and its increasingly bloody aftermath.

£10bn

… THE war in Iraq has cost the Government £10 billion in 18 months – as much as it has spent on boosting pensions during seven years in power, a pensioners' leader said yesterday.

The claim will infuriate Britain's 11 million pensioners, many of whom have slipped into poverty after a lifetime of hard work.

(*Daily Mail*, 19 May)

Overt racism

Both the *Daily Mirror* and the *Sun* deploy similar linguistic strategies to confront what is presented as the unacceptable face of overt racism in the coverage of a National Health Service story and the equally unambiguous response to the alleged racist outburst from Princess Michael. The *Daily Mirror* picks out an appropriately contemporary headline for its exclusive report. This is accompanied by a photo of 'OUR INTERNATIONAL HEALTH SERVICE' with a wide range of ethnic and national groups on a typical shift at a London hospital to reinforce the message with illustration. It also takes the opportunity to point out the fallacious nature of the language of the 'political correctness' argument, stressing instead the enlightened self-interest of drawing on the full potential of the widest range of people in order to provide the best service possible.

ZERO INTOLERANCE

… after a Mirror report on the shameful treatment of a black nurse.

... Dr Reid said: 'Let me make it absolutely clear to Daily Mirror readers that we take this problem very seriously. There's no place for racism or discrimination in the NHS.'

On the same day in its leading article, the paper praises Reid:

His reaction was immediate. He has pledged that there will be zero tolerance for racist patients or staff.

That excellent reaction isn't just being politically correct. It is the only way to make the health service work effectively.

(*Daily Mirror*, 19 May)

The *Sun* stresses the 'SHAMED' nature of the outburst of Princess Michael of Kent and uses particularly blunt and demotic language to put the Royal in her place. There is no sign of deference either in its exposure of her ambition 'to launch a lucrative new career', which it stresses has now been 'torpedoed'.

PUSH OFF, PUSHY

SHAMED Princess Michael of Kent's bid to launch a lucrative new career in the US was torpedoed last night after her racist outburst in a restaurant.

(*Sun*, 28 May)

Morality and public idiom

Two brief examples from the *Daily Mail* can indicate the ways in which the language of the tabloids can be used to propose a radical stance on certain issues of the day in a paper usually identified with socially and politically conservative positions; both have a recurrent place within the agenda of this particular paper: genetically modified food, dubbed 'Frankenstein Food' in sensationalist scripted fashion by the *Daily Mail* and the decline of respect in society. Both are presented in ways which appeal beyond the text of the paper to a wider community of identification with campaigns to protect the way things are, or used to be, and which are such an important part of the idiom of the paper. The first piece is part of an explicit *Daily Mail* campaign: 'FRANKENSTEIN FOOD WATCH':

Health fears as GM corn is let into the EU

A SIX-YEAR European moratorium on new genetically modified foods ended yesterday after bureaucrats in Brussels approved imports of a GM sweetcorn despite health worries.

Opponents of so-called 'Frankenstein foods' attacked the decision for failing to protect the health of consumers.

(*Daily Mail*, 20 May)

It can also use its dominant discourse to provide the sort of radical conservative campaigning which is also part of the tabloid spectrum and one which can claim an authenticity as the voice of a frustrated lower middle class sensibility which in its way is as characteristic of contemporary Britain as the more raucous end of the popular market.

HOW RESPECT BECAME A DIRTY WORD (Melanie Phillips)

... The root of the problem is the widespread breakdown of the very notion of authority. ... Values have become privatised ... loss of moral nerve ... despite Mr Blunkett's very real concerns, government policies have greatly contributed to this disastrous loss of respect and galloping culture of selfishness. For government ministers have an urgent electoral need to be thought 'nice'.

(*Daily Mail*, 21 May)

In the following two examples from the *Daily Mirror* there is a contrasting demonstration of how the public idiom of the newspaper can be aligned with a particular expression of morality very much in keeping with its historical traditions. We can see the language and sentiments which underscore much of William Cobbett's 'old corruption' analysis almost 200 years previously. This really is a social analysis restricted to the perspective of 'the rich man in his castle, the poor man at his gate', where class difference is merely posited in terms of financial envy:

FIRE CHIEF IN £70K JAG FURY

FAT CAT 1

A FIRE chief has sparked fury by accepting a brand new £70,000 Jaguar – while his staff wait for a pay rise that is six months overdue. ...

£100 THE STAFF XMAS BONUS AXED BY SAINSBURY'S

£1.4M THE FREE SHARES GIVEN OUT TO ITS BOSS YESTERDAY

FAT CAT 2

SAINSBURY'S yesterday gave new boss Justin King £1.4 million in shares – as it confirmed it was axing workers' £100 Christmas bonus.

(*Daily Mirror*, 22 May)

The second example has an even stronger resonance with Cobbett in its echoes of his frequent criticisms of the British Army's treatment of the lower ranks during the Napoleonic War some 200 years earlier, and is also shot through with suspicions of class exploitation and the cynical undermining of patriotic spirit which the *Daily Mirror* attempts to expose. Furthermore, in terms of the traditions of the *Daily Mirror* itself, it is reminiscent to a large degree of the sort of language used by Cassandra among others in exposing the reckless disregard of the ordinary soldier by certain ignorant and arrogant officers in World War II at the start of the newspaper's rise to its zenith of influence. At both moments in the newspaper's history we can see the language of radical dissent but with little more than a liberal, humanitarian politics as its goal.

BETRAYED

Sick soldiers slung on the scrapheap with no Army pension

EXCLUSIVE

HUNDREDS of sick soldiers are being booted out of the Army without pensions.

… backdoor dismissal … loophole to terminate their contracts … axed … scandal revealed by Lib Dem MP Paul Keetch …

(Daily Mirror, 25 May)

The language of the tabloids is available for radical deployment despite its simplicity and direct appeal. It is restricted more by its location within a particular political economy and the news agenda which that supports. This constrains the opportunities for a more consistent radical critique and seems designed to remind a potentially oppositional readership of that potential, but little more.

8   Celebrity and national community

Much has been written about the trend towards the inclusion of more celebrity-based news in our media in general. In fact, this is one of the trends which Harcup and O'Neill (2001) identify as most significant in redefining the taxonomy of news values for the twenty-first century, and Golding (1999) has also claimed that this move towards the inclusion of more and more celebrity-driven news is one of the core characteristics of what has been called 'tabloidization'. The tabloids are leading this trend in many ways in their representation of Britain as a community of interrelated media celebrities and compounding it with a style of language which matches that culture. Much analysis and even anecdote regarding celebrity culture in the news tends to concentrate on the personalities themselves or the often dubious hard news elements of such stories. In this chapter, we will persevere in our effort to keep the language of these stories very much in the foreground and to explore the extent to which this language is directed towards a specifically British community. Various commentators believe that it is a mistake to view the tabloids' representation of celebrity-based news out of the wider context or 'cultural discourse' (Dahlgren, 1988) of such journalism. Such views are reinforced by the evidence in this book that the intertextual network of meanings generated by the language of the tabloids in a specifically national setting, while only having limited relevance to agendas of traditional news, nevertheless contributes to a wider sense of everyday mediated reality. These meanings form part of a 'semiosphere' (Hartley, 1996) of understanding which reflects the multi-faceted environment from which we increasingly make sense of our world, whether it be in a banal or a profound way. Celebrity has always formed an important part of the news but it has 'expanded and multiplied in recent years' (Turner, 2004: 4). In doing so as part of the formation of mediated social identity it has begun to play an even fuller part in the construction of an imaginary Britain for a national audience. The tabloids have been particularly astute in harnessing and even directing this trend:

> The British tabloids have almost categorically redefined what qualifies for them as news, so that tabloid news is now utterly personalised and dominated by the actions of well-known people – politicians, public officials,

sportsmen and women, celebrities, soon-to-be celebrities and wanna-be celebrities.

(Turner, 2004: 75)

For all its superficial triviality, celebrity news has become what Marshall has identified as one of the key places where cultural meanings are negotiated and organised (1997: 72–3) and this has an important influence on the contemporary patterning of the imaginary popular nation. Rojek sees this contemporary phase of celebrity culture as a significant factor in the normative achievement of social integration according to the values of dominant social and political values (2001: 99). This has been demonstrated in interviews with media audiences which confirm that: 'seeing media figures as real and as part of our everyday cultural and emotional experience is part and parcel of how media texts come to have meaning' (Hermes, 1999: 71). Rodman echoes a point made earlier on ideology in general by Teo that the celebrity process is one which depends on the active involvement of readers:

> Stardom is not a purely mercantile phenomenon imposed 'from above' by profit-hungry media conglomerates as much as it is a socially based phenomenon generated 'from below' at the level of real people who make affective investments in particular media figures.
>
> (Rodman, 1996: 12)

At the same time, the popularity of celebrity-based news has become a double-edged attraction. Sales of tabloids are in overall long-term decline, despite the claims of editors that this sort of content is what the people of Britain want, and the dependency of tabloids on celebrity rather than on hard news risks making them less distinctive and therefore at risk from other news and entertainment media. The tabloids have therefore developed their own strategy for presenting celebrity news so as to maintain their grasp on their claims to remain identifiable to readers as newspapers. This strategy entails not only presenting a news agenda which is dominated by the lives and loves of celebrities but the way in which this is integrated with other broader aspects of their coverage. This means that each time a story emerges which would otherwise be relatively newsworthy but which has the added attraction of a celebrity angle with cross-over potential, the story moves up the hierarchy of newsworthiness. This can work with domestic violence, health scares, political comment, not to mention the straightforward celebrity tales of who is dating who and what they are wearing. Reading the tabloids one sees that despite the fact that celebrity culture is newsworthy across the world, it is the concentration on UK-based celebrities which reinforces an impression that these newspapers are representing a particularly British sense of community. Celebrities and the language which enables them to cross between different areas of the tabloids' news are an important part of understanding the tabloid version of Britain in 2004 and demonstrate throughout how the network of cultural communication which supports that community manages to remain coherent.

Banality and tragedy

Celebrity lives are often represented as two-dimensional rollercoaster rides between elation and depression, which certainly fits neatly with the overall binary nature of tabloid news structures. In the *Daily Mail* of 3 May, we read of the 'good news' for Paul Merton, host of *Have I Got News For You*, who 'lost his wife to cancer' and has now 'found love again' all in the brief and trite nutshell of a self-enclosed celebrity universe where stars move from tragedy to normality with a minimum of fuss.

> Merton's good news
>
> Star who lost wife to cancer finds love with comedienne
>
> Paul Merton has found love again after his wife died of cancer.
>
> The star of TV's Have I Got News For You is planning to set up home with fellow comedian Sukie Webster.
>
> (*Daily Mail*, 3 May)

In fact, celebrity is one of the semiotic hooks which can be used to report on the general topic of disease. It allows the mundane facts of illness and death a newsworthiness which gives readers an opportunity to read about issues which would not otherwise be covered in the paper unless associated with a well-known celebrity face and the language associated with the world of the stars. Elaine Paige is used to draw empathy from readers as the personal story of her 'battle' with cancer is appended to a brief CV which appears to endorse her newsworthy credentials. The end of the story uses a quotation to reinforce the human empathy which is invited from ordinary reader to star.

> **SINGER VOWED: I'LL BEAT THIS**
>
> ELAINE'S SECRET BREAST CANCER BATTLE …
>
> She said: 'To have had a health scare and having to face your mortality changes you …'
>
> (*Daily Mirror*, 8 May)

The next piece includes a moment of self-critique from *Coronation Street* star Suranne Jones, who comments on the shallowness of showbusiness behaviour in comparison with the reality of people whose lives are blighted by the Aids epidemic. It runs as part of Christian Aid Week to encourage an appeal for donations from readers. The celebrity connection which is used as a conduit to readers' empathy may be an attempt to humanize the problem and to relate it in terms which readers will grasp, but the same tabloid techniques and expressions end up trivializing the problem. The *Sun* may claim to have 'put the Aids holocaust at the top of the political agenda' but it may well be swamped in the rest of the interconnecting tabloid trivia. One could stretch one's generosity and say that the *Sun* is trying to broaden and popularize the campaign among its readers but it could also more plausibly be seen as simply another publicity stunt. Certainly it seems to be compromised by being fitted into the familiar tabloid language of 'Sun readers', 'dying mums', juxtaposed with 'Corrie star' and 'TV Suranne'. In addition, it fits with a familiar self-promotional paradigm of campaigns in the tabloid which undercuts its claims to present the 'full horror' of this 'holocaust'. Despite its claims to keep the issue high on the agenda it suffers from a lack of analytical continuity like much else in the tabloids.

CORRIE STAR'S HARROWING TRIP TO CRISIS CONTINENT

Showbiz air kisses seem so silly when Aids is killing Africa

SAYS TV SURANNE AFTER SHE MEETS DYING MUMS

CORRIE star Suranne Jones has seen at first hand the full horror of the Aids disaster engulfing Africa .....

Suranne appealed last night for Sun readers to dig into their pockets to help Africa fight Aids.

The Sun has fought to put the Aids holocaust at the top of the political agenda...

(Sun, 10 May)

The newspaper also uses Suranne Jones in an appeal in its leading article. This integration of celebrity into the editorial opinion of the paper demonstrates the potential for an alternative agenda within the tabloid format and rhetoric, using a popular personality to support a humanitarian appeal and using a formulaic vernacular to address a wider world mission. It is the rarity of this breadth of ambition that is the restriction on the tabloids and the world they present to a British audience, and not necessarily the strategies or the language themselves. Celebrity-based news can begin to cross into challenging political areas and in terms which begin in populist terms from the point of view of contemporary consumers.

When criminals become famous, they quickly acquire certain of the semantic features of celebrity. In reports on Maxine Carr, the woman who is so vilified in other parts of the tabloid press, she is referred to by her first name. The only explanation for this, given the vitriol of the language usually reserved for her and others associated with child murders, is that she has been drawn into the generic language of celebrity coverage. She is referred to in the language of familiarity despite her notoriety because of her location in the everyday consciousness of the tabloid readers.

MAXINE WASTES AWAY

(*Daily Mirror*, 28 April)

Celebrities' private lives are shared with the imagined community of readers in ways which draw that community into the details of confession and gossip. First names and familiar nicknames are used to reinforce the confidential tone of the reports. Following on from a scoop in the *Sunday Mirror*, Colin Montgomery is invited to share more of his innermost thoughts, combined with his appreciation of the 'support of the crowd', a populist sentiment in keeping with the overall tone of the *Daily Mirror* itself.

I'M DEVASTATED

Monty tells of heartbreak over wife's secret affair

And the top golfer revealed he would not have been able to make it through his final round at the British Masters yesterday without the 'superb' support of the crowd.

(*Daily Mirror*, 10 May)

Two Georges make an appearance, albeit for different reasons. George Clooney, reduced to 'film hunk' is reported with a blend of vulgarity and punning metaphor while ex-football star, George Best, one of the tabloids' favourite running stories, is drawn into a report on his son which conforms to the pattern of his father's 'destructive legacy' of 'drugs, booze, women'.

GEORGE SNOGS EX LOVER LISA

FILM hunk George Clooney has been reunited with old flame Lisa Snowden – and is making up for lust time

(*Sun*, 10 May)

LIKE FATHER LIKE SON

Drugs, booze women ... already they are beginning to consume Calum Best. So can he escape the destructive legacy of his troubled father George?

(*Daily Mail*, 15 May)

Family values, morality and patriotism

Celebrity comes as a contemporary prism through which the standards of Britain are paraded and judged. It also fits well with a popular history of celebrities dead and gone who can be revived within an agenda of anniversaries. This is all the better when the celebrity in question can be revived through the words of a surviving family member or friend. In the case of Diana Dors, a sex icon of the 1960s, the link in the historical chain prompted by the twentieth anniversary of her death is her son. The piece by Lynda

Lee-Potter takes a very moral line on how the years of high living took their toll on the famous actress, a line which is familiar across the tabloids when it comes to exploring the downside of fame and celebrity.

DIANA'S DEMONS

Orgies, drugs, booze-fuelled rows. On the 20 anniversary of Diana Dors' death her son reveals the terrible toll her self-destructive excesses have taken on him ...

(*Daily Mail*, 1 May)

Celebrity news, however, is not a one-way street of prurient gossip, sensation and revelation. It can also be used to drive an alternative and highly moralistic agenda (Connell, 1992). Here it is used in the case of the Beckhams to reinforce traditional notions of the family and even the centrality of the mother in family life, long a central feature of the newspaper's own set of traditional values.

England captain decides to put his marriage before his career

Posh gets her way as Beckham tells Real: I must go back to England

... In what can be seen as the ultimate sacrifice for his wife, Victoria ...

(*Daily Mail*, 1 May)

Some weeks later, the *Daily Star* applauds what it sees as a victory for traditional male-dominated family values:

Becks: my family are joining me in Madrid

DAVID Beckham has won the big battle with his wife over who wears the trousers in their house.

... Posh, 30, devotes more time to being a wife and a mother ...

(*Daily Star*, 21 May)

The *Daily Mail* poses the question of the cost of media celebrity, in this case placing it firmly within a gender-orientated perspective and suggesting that the level of success that Gaby Logan desired was beyond the bounds of normality, categorizing it as a 'lust for fame'. The newspaper is acting here to monitor the acceptable boundaries of celebrity behaviour as well as the reach of female celebrities' ambition, demonstrating what can go wrong if, Icarus-like, one flies too high.

Her chat show was axed, her stage debut flopped and this week her marriage fell apart. Is this the price of GABY'S LUST FOR FAME?

(*Daily Mail*, 22 May)

Garry Whannel (2002) argues that sports celebrities are most often explicitly linked with definitions of nationality and even ethnicity, despite the more complex connections between the global and the local within which the national now operates. David Beckham is a prime example of this; a global star but one whose significance for Englishness is inscribed in most everything written about him or his family in the British tabloids and that is before we even consider what is written about him when he plays football! Whannel's book examines how within a cycle of 'celebration, transgression, punishment and redemption', contemporary social anxieties within the imaginary frame of the nation are explored through the conduct of sports celebrities. Beyond sporting achievement, one of the inevitable prices for the sort of global fame which David Beckham has acquired is the interest of the people of Britain in his every action or utterance in the context of the tabloids. His decision to have a new tattoo on the back of his neck led to a range of outrage which touched upon taste, deference to the Queen, comparisons with English football hooligans and his overall level of intelligence as one man's fashion statement became a barometer of national debate on all of these issues. This particular celebrity story became a one-man national identity crisis when represented in the language of the national tabloid press. The *Sun* chose a number of popular voices to respond:

> An onlooker at his Real Madrid training ground said: 'It's horrible – the worst yet. He looks like a yob.' ...
>
> *In Manchester, student Brook Fenton, 22, said: 'It's just getting ridiculous.'*
>
> 'What's he going to do at formal occasions representing England? It will be embarrassing standing before the Queen with that sticking out of his collar.'
>
> (*Sun*, 22 May)

The same paper even used its fashion editor to condemn the fashion choice of the footballer:

> **DAVID, THAT REALLY IS A LOAD OF OLD TAT**
>
> **... With one stroke of the tattooist's needle, you have well and truly fallen from your fashion pedestal.**
>
> (*Sun*, 22 May)

The *Daily Mirror* was more concerned with the similarity between the England captain and a football hooligan:

> **LOOKING more like a soccer thug than the England captain, David Beckham shows off his latest tattoo yesterday. ...**
>
> With his cross and shaven head, the 29-year-old would probably not even be allowed on the plane for Portugal if he was a fan.
>
> **STAR'S HARDMAN TATTOO**
>
> (*Daily Mirror*, 22 May)

This paper's Woman's Editor also draws the tattoo into abbreviated discussions about the latest turmoil in the life of the Beckham family, before challenging his intelligence in the most vulgar terms:

> A father spreading his protective wings around his family, perhaps? An unfaithful husband turning to God for forgiveness, maybe?
>
> Or a right plonker with too much money and time on his hands?
>
> (*Daily Mirror*, 22 May)

Beckham is throughout the pages represented as a cross between a fashion icon and a moral victim of his own narcissism. He is very much a representative of the 'other news' of Langer but he is described and criticized as emblematic of much broader debates about masculinity, male violence and the fashion for tattoos, which can be drawn together within the semantic space of 'David Beckham' to provide an outlet for something which, given the vociferous condemnation across the tabloids, has clearly touched a raw nerve with the newspapers and the public which they seek to address.

Celebrities can be enlisted within the tabloids to contribute to the particular newspaper's version of a low-key form of patriotism (Billig, 1995). In the following story there is the implied criticism of the alleged shallowness of US celebrities. The British star in question is from the East End of London, an area with a special mythical resonance in terms of working class spirit of patriotism, largely founded on its resilience in the bombing raids of World War II and also on its association with a certain core working class Englishness. It forms part of a popular historical reference point in a particularly tabloid variation on how Barthes considers that narratives of the past function to remove material processes and related politics and leave mythical representations which can be moulded to suit the contingencies of contemporary political requirements (1974). It is therefore no surprise that the former star of *EastEnders* is endowed with an almost Churchillian 'fighting spirit' in the face of hostility from her critics:

EAST END STAR SHOWS HER FIGHTING SPIRIT

MARTINE McCUTCHEON has just lived through another week of being slated by her critics.

This time they claim the actress got tipsy and trod on Hollywood toes at an industry party – scuppering her best chance of hitting the big time.

... Hollywood liars are trying to destroy me

Her home-grown, rags-to-riches, vernacular appeal is contrasted to a list drawn up to condemn the contrasting values of the Hollywood culture which is presented as so very different to the Britain inhabited by idealized ex-soap stars.

LAWS OF LA-LA LAND

1. **Be painfully thin**
2. **Never be seen eating or drinking at ANY showbiz event**
3. **Be humble**
4. **Hook up with a star**
5. **Join an obscure religion**

(*Sun*, 8 May)

Nevertheless, it is interesting that the anti-American agenda stops at anti-Hollywood and does not stretch to anti-Washington, and that the *Sun's* disapproval of the hypocrisy of the acting community does not ever extend to the failings of the dominant political grouping in the USA under George W. Bush, of whom it will brook no criticism at all.

Celebrity news as tabloid news

The tabloids do not only report on the lives of celebrities, they use this information to enhance as many stories as they can with a plethora of intertextual references to them. This enables the newspapers to make other news stories fit this agenda and supplement their value by their inclusion of celebrities. It may limit the reach of the news agenda and further restrict the people who register as 'elite persons' (Galtung and Ruge, 1973), but the tabloids in their defence maintain that it is what their readers buy the papers for. Celebrating an increase in circulation of 6.17 per cent month on month, the *Daily Star* claims:

> This success story goes on and on because we give YOU – our growing army of readers – exactly what you want.
>
> Our brilliant mix of news, pictures, sport, glamour, pop and showbiz is simply unmissable.

(*Daily Star*, 15 May)

The complexity of the relationship between readers and the tabloid newspaper is reduced to a simple equation of 'we give YOU – what you want'. The 'brilliant mix' referred to is in many ways the formula which enables tabloids in general to use celebrity connections across the paper to ensure that news fits that agenda as consistently as possible. This is constructed to a large degree by the language they use. If there is a celebrity connection which will enable the tabloid to deploy its armoury of characteristic rhetoric then it stands a very good chance of becoming news.

The *Daily Mirror* uses a throwaway comment by the media-omnipresent chef Gordon Ramsay that he hasn't attended the birth of any of his four children on the grounds it would have ruined his sex life, to launch a debate on sexism today, structured around the convenient tabloid device of the binary list:

Gordon Ramsey

SO IS GORDON A MALE CHAUVINIST?

YES   MAYBE

Women's editor   Writer

Clare Raymond   Bill Borrows

(*Daily Mirror*, 28 May)

Ramsay is also used in a different context in the *Daily Mail* of 22 May, illustrating by his own personal experience the tribulations of having a drug addict in the family.

Celebrity connections can present an opportunity to turn a brief and otherwise inconsequential story into something which can be used to make a joke and lighten the mood:

KIDDY KAT

Eastender Jessie is 12 weeks pregnant

Delighted mum-to-be Jessie Wallace kisses her fiance yesterday as she leaves hospital clutching a scan of their baby

(*Daily Mirror*, 28 May)

Fans go Rooney loo-ney

Trophy hunters have pinched Wayne Rooney's old toilet seat from a skip outside the council house where he grew up

(*Daily Mirror*, 28 May)

At the opposite end of the spectrum, the threat of violence in the Middle East, which does not regularly feature in the tabloids can suddenly become front page news if it is related to a celebrity, in this case Madonna:

MADONNA has axed three gigs in Israel – after terrorists threatened to kill her and her kids.

The singer, *below*, was terrified by a blitz of poison-pen letters ... source said ... symbolises the West ...

(*Sun*, 24 May)

Aids can become news because of a scare on the set of the popular hospital soap *Holby City*, and economic migrants because of the remarks of Prince Charles on the role they play on his farm:

HOLBY AIDS SCARE OVER NEEDLE NUT

He 'stabs' two extras

… Crew member (unnamed) jabbed, scratched, pricked … bosses believe the worker scratched the two women by mistake.

(Sun, 29 May)

CHARLES: WE NEED MIGRANT WORKERS

(Daily Mirror, 4 May)

There are celebrity values sunk in many other tabloid stories. The common occurrence of infection in hospitals is personalized in the story of Leslie Ash, who has contracted MRSA while in hospital being treated for injuries sustained during an encounter with her partner which had been the subject of extensive coverage by the tabloids.

Secrets of the superbug that laid Leslie low

(Daily Mail, 4 May)

Debate about racist language and changing linguistic tolerance in a popular television show is engaged in the following extract, partly because the programme in question is still one of the most watched programmes on British television and partly because this celebrity hook can also fit with the broad tabloid objection to sensitivity towards language which can be categorized as what Cameron calls 'verbal hygiene' (1995).

Del Boy episode is 'racist'

BBC bosses are chopping the word 'P★★★' from future screenings of a 1981 show.

(Sun, 11 May)

Ramblers, not usually a group to attract tabloid headlines, can become news from the *Daily Mail* to the *Daily Mirror* when the report is linked to an inquiry into whether Madonna and her husband, Guy Ritchie, are to be allowed to keep the public off their land. The *Daily Mail* refers to Madonna playing 'the human rights card' and presents it as a game, whereas the *Daily Mirror* takes a more forceful opposition as the starting point in their report:

Madonna v Ramblers

Star plays the human rights card in battle to keep the public off her estate (and save £1m)

(Daily Mail, 6 May)

MADGE: TAKE A HIKE

(Daily Mirror, 6 May)

It is not only in areas which are infrequently covered that we can observe celebrity involvement increasing the news potential of an item. The ability of soaps to generate melodramatic and moralistic storylines can be drawn upon as popular reference points for a British readership in the financial pages in an attempt to popularize and personalize financial issues such as debt and the relative merits of renting or buying a house. On the financial pages of the *Daily Mirror* there is a photograph from soap opera *EastEnders* of Alfie Moon paying off a loan to local villain Andy, with Alfie's wife Kat Slater hidden behind the door. Kat had already slept with Andy to pay off the loan, unknown to Alfie. The paper turns the name of the actor into part of the story and continues the punning on the double entendre of 'shafted' in the punchline as it begins to give advice on how to avoid getting in to difficulties with debt by planning for financial emergencies.

Don't get caught in a loan Katastrophe

... Kat Slater sleeps with thug Andy to pay off the £7,000 that husband Alfie owes him. ... Clearly in the real world you wouldn't have to make such a sacrifice if you pay off loans ahead of time. But that's not to say that you won't be shafted.

(*Daily Mirror*, 19 May)

The *Daily Star* addressing the broadest audience implied in the word 'YOU', advertises its 'Cashpoint' section as:

THE MONEY PAGES YOU CAN'T AFFORD TO MISS

Here we see a story advising young people to buy property rather than rent, and using the example of the Ferreira family, also in *EastEnders*. It couches the advice to readers as advice to the scriptwriters in terms of the best financial option to the fictional family.

Their home loan has been put in jeopardy because they're behind with the payments – and to try to cover the amount outstanding, son Ash put their remaining money on a horse.

Typically, the horse lost and now the family is desperate.

But if the soap's scriptwriters choose the best way forward for the family, the Ferreiras won't end up renting.

That's because it's cheaper to pay a mortgage than to rent.

(*Daily Star*, 25 May)

On both occasions the papers can be seen to be offering financial advice not in the usual abstract terms of the broadsheets but through a popularized voice which draws explicitly on storylines with which it assumes its readers will be more familiar.

The celebrity agenda is even more welcome when it can be used commercially to draw upon a well known face to directly endorse the paper. In the following case it can gain additional spice by playing on the notoriety of the controversial Manchester United player, Rio Ferdinand, who is sitting out the season having been banned by the FA for failing to report for a routine drug test. His name is deliberately misspelt and with the letters 'AD' in the red of the *Sun* emphasizing his presence in an advertising campaign for the newspaper reminiscent of the television campaigns which signalled the arrival of the newly relaunched *Sun* in the years immediately after Rupert Murdoch's acquisition of the title in 1969.

RIO FERDINAD

WATCH MAN U STAR IN HILARIOUS SUN TV ADVERT

Hilarious TV ad for Britain's best-selling paper

(*Sun*, 2 May)

Yet it need not only be self-promotion that draws celebrities into the pages of the tabloids for advertising purposes. Male soap stars are used in the *Daily Mirror* to increase awareness among young men of the dangers of testicular cancer by posing naked, in a discreet fashion, every day of the week. The campaign has further intertextual media links. First, it is part of a money-raising effort by the testicular charity Everyman, and second, it is part of a series of photographs which will also feature in parallel with centrefolds in women's magazine *Cosmopolitan*. The pictures are prefaced by an assertion that the woman who works in the launderette, Pauline Fowler in *EastEnders*, would be shocked that this was being staged in her launderette in Albert Square, the location humorously referred to as 'Albert Bare' in the headlines:

Albert Bare

SOAP STARS IN CHARITY STRIP

PAULINE Fowler would get in a right lather if she could see this pair baring all in Albert Square's launderette.

EastEnders stars Mohammed George, 21, and Joe Swash are two of the celebrity hunks to have stripped off to raise money for testicular cancer charity Everyman.

And the Daily Mirror is bringing you a revealing new picture each day this week.

(*Daily Mirror*, 10 May)

When a soap star, practically a national institution, already regaling in the nickname of 'Dirty Den' is revealed in the tabloids to have been involved in sordid sexual antics away from the fictional arena, the language used draws upon the full range of smutty innuendo, popular reference and bawdy humour. Dolly Parton's song is alluded to in a caption accompanying Leslie Grantham leaving his wife for a day at work:

STAND BY YOUR DEN

(*Daily Mirror*, 4 May)

References to sexual arousal and euphemisms for the male member abound in headlines and throughout the coverage as the story makes the front page in all of the popular tabloids:

Keep your pecker up!

(*Daily Mirror*, 4 May)

Bye dear, another hard day at the office ...

(*Sun*, 4 May)

Eastenders

STARS GIVE DEN A HARD TIME

(*Daily Star*, 4 May)

Tabloid language does enable a wonderfully compact expression of the actor's problems when the *Daily Star* of 7 May refers to 'his addiction to seedy cyber-sex'. Another national treasure of the soap opera world, Barbara Windsor, is called upon for her comments and complains that her dressing room has been 'contaminated' by Grantham's behaviour. This is fed into the general hilarity through the punning headline:

DIRTY DEN'S MADE MY TV 'DEN' DIRTY

(*Daily Star*, 8 May)

The *Sun* provides a compendium of terms of reference for such stories, complete with the notion that he is addicted to sex and needs therapy, which fits in with certain of the *Sun*'s own editorial fantasies around sex. There is also the celebrity cross-over to Hollywood actor Michael Douglas:

... sex antics ... shamed actor ... sordid sex-cam chats ... a blonde stranger ... explicit online sessions ... married dad of two ... – just like Hollywood star Michael Douglas who admitted he was a sex addict ... pleasured himself ... depraved sexual fantasies ... flashed his manhood ... pervy antics ...

(*Sun*, 15 May)

Blurring the lines

Despite claims (Modleski, 1982; Gledhill, 1997) that identification with the narratives and characters of soap operas has a positive social potential for people which enables them to empathize vicariously with situations both inside and outside their everyday experience, there are times when the tabloids portray the fictional storylines in such a strong way that they erode the boundaries between reality and televisual fiction. This can devalue any sort of true empathy since the storyline is represented and reported as real. 'Cancer shock' is part of a standard pattern for dealing with the reality of the onset of sudden illness in the tabloid lexicon. The reductive noun phrase 'Corrie Dev' also depends on an intimate knowledge among readers of the television character referred to. It is only when we move our eyes to the report which follows as an exclusive in the *Sun*'s 'TV Biz' section that we realize that the 'storyline' of the soap opera is what is being referred to and not reality. The language of the two spheres merges completely.

CORRIE DEV IN CANCER SHOCK

Street stud's hell

… in a shocking new storyline … breaks down when he learns he may have bowel cancer. … Last month we told how EastEnders' Dot Cotton is to develop breast cancer.

(Sun, 12 May)

The *Daily Mirror* also illustrates this merging of fictional and real spheres where the storyline is first represented in terms of reality.

DEVASTATED

CORRIE EXCLUSIVE 1

Heartache as Street romeo fights cancer

CORONATION Street romeo Dev Alahan is to be hit by bowel cancer amid fears he has only months to live......

Researchers have given script teams careful background on the disease which kills 18,000 people a year.

(Daily Mirror, 12 May)

On occasion, these stories can be as harrowing as real life tragedies, since empathy with fictional characters and even their equally fictional babies is taken to melodramatic extremes, for example in a preview of the 7 June episode of *Coronation Street* in pictures with a description of the death and funeral of newborn Billy, the 'CORRIE BABY', in the *Sun* on 14 May. It leads one to wonder what impact the language of celebrity melodrama has when it is used to refer to real life issues. It may ultimately have a disempowering and trivializing effect on the readers' view of the real world.

The conflicts of rival characters in the soaps are represented with all the relish of accounts of real people involved in fights, as readers are presented with pictures from the set of the soap opera, further shifting television preview towards the style of news reporting of reality. The illustration of the storylines by pictures enhances the similarity to the reporting of the real world in the rest of the news media.

Streetfight

HAIR-RAISER AS GAIL AND EILEEN CLASH

GAIL Platt can't keep her hair on when she finds out her pregnant daughter's fella had a gay fling … brawling … in Coronation Street's punch-up of the year.

(*Daily Mirror*, 19 May)

When celebrities' lives are really hit by shocks and violence then the real life aspects are of course reported in the same language which is used to refer to their fictional selves. This is another blurring of the distinctions between the real and the fictional.

CORONATION street stars were fuming yesterday after being trounced by EastEnders at the British Soap Awards.

(*Sun*, 10 May)

The allegations of wife-beating which have plagued Lee Chapman in the popular tabloids have migrated into wider stories of his wife's relationship with her sister and denials of her husband's culpability in a drama which seems to have been designed to fit the language and structures of a celebrity soap. The characters are reduced to short caricatures, 'bully Lee', 'Bedridden Leslie', 'Shocked Leslie', 'wife beater', 'Former Hot Gossip Dancer' and for good measure the *Sun*'s columnist Jane Moore provides a piece of instant tabloid archive work, joining the fray by reminding readers that she urged Leslie Ash to leave him back in 1997.

WHEN Lee Chapman was injuncted after viciously attacking his wife Leslie Ash in 1997, I wrote in this column that she should leave him.

(*Sun*, 12 May)

All is hyperbole in celebrity land.

JADES'S TORMENT

Hurt by 'bully' jibe

FORMER Big Brother star Jade Goody was 'shocked' at claims by ex-boyfriend Jeff Brazier that she beat him up.

Hunky telly host Jeff says they split up last week because he could no longer stand being a victim of her attacks and abuse.

But now his revelations about their private life have left Jade – who is pregnant with his baby – reeling.

(Daily Star, 10 May)

At both ends of the weighing scale, celebrity body image is something which is routinely covered in a language which sets up normative and even moral standards by which readers are invited to judge celebrities' bodies and attitudes to weight as well, perhaps, as implicit comparison with their own.

VAN HEL [illustrated with flames] OF A WEDDING

HOLLYWOOD bride Kate Beckinsale ... curvy Kate ... saucy hen night ... blow-up doll as guest of honour ... superfit star ... in perfect shape ... clean-living Kate

(Daily Star, 10 May)

OH FOR GOD'S SAKE GRAB SOME NOSH, POSH

[illustrated with photos]

... shocking stick-thin figure ... gaunt appearance ... skinny frame

(Daily Star, 14 May)

Sexy soap!

The sexual attractiveness of the soap stars draws the *Daily Star* in particular to a celebration of its commitment to covering as much as possible from this angle in a language redolent of a vernacular sexism. Suranne Jones announces that she will be leaving *Coronation Street*. The language of the story – 'Sex fest', 'Sexy Suranne', 'more totty', 'sexpot', 'busty babe', 'ravishing redhead', 'vixen' – draws an explicit picture of the presentational mode of the paper. The *Daily Star* is most prominent in the sexualization of popular television as part of its overall agenda to be the tabloid with the most television coverage, a point reinforced by the frequent placing of this news on the front page. The sexualization of television is almost exclusively driven from the perspective of an idealized male reader or even voyeur.

CORRIE SEX FEST

ANOTHER DAILY STAR TELLY EXCLUSIVE

CORONATION Street bosses are bouncing back from the shock departure of Sexy Suranne Jones by looking out for even more totty ... To make the soap the sexiest on screen.

(Daily Star, 15 May)

A few days later the same paper has Amy Nutall posing in fashion wear in a variety of barn settings, promoting both the soap star, the programme she stars in and the clothes featured:

Barn storm

SOAP siren Amy Nuttall is certainly stirring things up down on the farm.

The Emmerdale babe, who plays vixen, Chloe Atkinson, is shaping up for a sizzling summer in the top TV show ... scheming sexpot ... ravishing redhead ...

(*Daily Star*, 18 May)

The *Daily Mirror* shows that if you deal in British soap operas then you are inevitably drawn into similar sorts of areas and language to match with its story from *Coronation Street*.

BEV IS BACK ON THE PULL

Star's new Corrie deal

TARTY Liz McDonald's back in Weatherfieled doing what she knows best – pulling pints and blokes in the Rovers.

(*Daily Mirror*, 18 May)

The *Sun* deals with an issue adjacent to the plot of the actual soap opera when it reports, in trivializing fashion, of a case of sexual harassment on the set. The perpetrator is characterized as 'grope pest', 'sex pest', 'groping a woman' and 'fondling a fellow extra's bum'.

A SEX pest actor kicked off EastEnders for groping a woman has been allowed back on set, it was revealed last night.

Women on the BBC soap have protested furiously after Ulric Browne ... was told he could start filming again ... after fondling a fellow extra's bum. ...

Fury at 'bum pinch' extra

(*Sun*, 24 May)

Reality TV and celebrity

Tabloids in general, but in particular the *Daily Star*, stress their connection to the world of popular television as we have seen. The *Daily Star* is proud of this connection and does all it can to reinforce that part of its identity and to advertise it to its readers. One of its principle selling points and a reason often forwarded for its success in terms of recent rising sales is its direct appeal to a readership which wants to be first with news about television. On the occasion of a preview of a new celebrity cookery series, the news about the programme itself is matched perfectly with the language of the *Daily Star*'s salacious approach to sex. It stresses its own appeal, punning on 'switched on'. 'Boiling point', 'sizzling new reality show' and 'tasty dishes' are all full of the double entendre which links the celebrity show to a sexualization of cookery in keeping with the *Daily Star*'s popular image. This is added to by the complementary rudeness of the celebrity chef of the moment whose vulgarity of language ideally suits the bawdy vernacular of the tabloids.

YOUR SWITCHED-ON DAILY STAR

BATTLE OF HELL'S BELLES

Girls to spice up Gordon's kitchen

FIERY telly chef Gordon Ramsay is set to reach boiling point as Abi Titmuss and Jennifer Ellison cook up mischief in his kitchen.

The two blonde babes ...

... tasty dishes Jen and Abi plan to give Gordon some lip back.

(*Daily Star*, 13 May)

In its leading article of that day the *Daily Star* uses this privileged space to reinforce the innuendo:

GORDON 'F★★★★★★ Hell' Ramsay will have Kate Price, Abi Titmuss and Jennifer Ellison in his new show Hell's Kitchen.

He might have trouble keeping his hands off their buns.

(*Daily Star*, 13 May)

The *Daily Star* claims prominence as the 'Official Big Brother paper' and begins its preview on 13 May by leaking to readers the news that live sex will this time be on the schedule in language which typifies the paper's attitude to sex: 'romp', 'raunchy couple', 'dirty dozen', 'love shack'. These sort of intertextual media games help to reinforce its reputation as the paper with the most explicit stories about popular television, reinforcing in its language the bond with a particular readership.

The *Sun* leaps with enthusiasm into the Big Brother previews and is able to sensationalize the sleazy auditions with a 'GAY SNOGS' story.

BIG Brother bosses made male hopefuls SNOG each other at auditions.

(*Sun*, 25 May)

It continues a few days later with an account of how a porn star finds the new series too extreme, adding to the advance publicity and the hope of more sales, driven by the prurient nature of the writing. It also links up with another popular cultural activity, that of betting, to include odds offered by the high street betting chain Ladbrokes on there being a 'romp'.

> BB5 too filthy even for me, says porn star
>
> BIG Brother bosses have been branded too sex-mad – by a shocked ex-porn star ...
>
> **... Ladbrokes is offering 2–1 odds that contestants WILL romp in the ten-week show.**
>
> > (*Sun*, 27 May)

In an excellent illustration of where the celebrity agenda meets the hyperbole of the *Daily Star* in the global newspaper market we can read on its front page:

> WORLD EXCLUSIVE
>
> **BIG BRO'S DIRTY DOZEN**
>
> - **The Page 3 girl**
> - **The stripper**
> - **The serial stud**
> - **Er, and the one who's into sheep**
>
> > (*Daily Star*, 28 May)

Eventually, we can read literally all about it in the *Daily Star* on 31 May, '**Big Brother special: Pages 4, 5, 6, & 7**'. This sort of splash coverage through the first part of the newspaper has been a tabloid characteristic for some time with regard to disaster coverage but now, in an indication of how important the celebrity television agenda has become, particularly to the *Daily Star*, it can be applied to such media-based pseudo-news.

More celebrity coverage needs more celebrities even if this means that a lower tier of ordinary people needs to be recruited for a brief glimmer of fame in order to feed audience demand. Reality television formats have enabled the celebrity agenda to migrate down the social scale to include people whose celebrity depends exclusively on appearing on a reality television programme. These are given the same treatment and are framed in the same language as their more famous celebrity counterparts. Celebrity thereby becomes not just a metaphor through which we are invited to interpret other parts of the news but literally begins to invade the realm of the ordinary. A contestant in *Wife Swap* described as 'loud-mouth Lizzie' and her husband appear to have been claiming unemployment benefit while living on the husband's earnings.

WIFE Swap scroungers Lizzie and Mark Bardsley have escaped court over a benefits scam.

The pair stunned telly viewers after it emerged they were pocketing £37,500-a-year in benefits while Mark worked as a jobbing builder.

... SHOULD LIZZIE BE PUT IN THE DOCK? Phone/text vote

(*Daily Star*, 18 May)

The whole tenor of the piece together with the appeal to populist justice by phone or text ties in with the judgemental moral agenda and the script of the 'scrounger' which was discussed in an earlier chapter.

On another television show a trainee stylist had the chance to swap places with a glamour model. What for the tabloid merely constituted a 'boob show' was sufficient for the young woman to be thrown out of her family home by her enraged mother. The superficial attitude to public nakedness comes up against, in this case, the reality of a more traditional working class concern for decency within the family:

SEXY hairdresser Katie Wakefield was booted out of her home by her mum for going topless on ITV's new reality show Poor Little Rich Girl.

(*Daily Star*, 27 May)

The conflict between celebrity-endorsed behaviour and the expectations and morality of a normal working class family expose the difference between the triviality of the 'boob show' within the celebrity media culture and the reaction of the mother to the antics of her daughter, now dubbed in the impersonalized and objectified jargon of such reports, 'Curvy Kate'.

Conclusion

Celebrities assist in the commodification of a very British sphere which is specifically contemporary. This is to be contrasted to the other powerful axis in the construction of popular narratives of nation in the tabloids, replete with historical references. There are however moments when the two can be merged, as for instance in the cases of Bobby Moore or Diana Dors, where a celebrity from the past can be drawn upon in order to redouble their impact in the present.

We need to ask whether celebrity coverage in the tabloids is merely parasitic and replacing other news values or part of the cultural loop referred to by Dahlgren, Marshall and Hermes, which enables the discursive flow between various media which is such an important part of contemporary popular media and their intertextuality. Turner puts the debate in succinct terms when he outlines: 'The more pessimistic accounts argue that the public sphere is progressively impoverished by such a shift; the more optimistic ones argue that the media are now simply serving different purposes than they used to' (Turner, 2004: 102).

Tabloid celebrities are usually drawn in the national media formats from national media culture and its music, showbusiness and soap culture. The American global version of tabloid culture draws predominantly from Hollywood cinema culture while the British draws chiefly from the world of television soap opera or popular music. The form of intimacy generated through this concentration on the parochial between reader and tabloid is an important element in establishing and developing a resonant and authentic sense of print community in Britain. The lack of real contact between the public and celebrities may enhance the structuring of the imaginary nature of this national community. Giles (2000) and Rojek (2001) stress the importance of 'para-social' activities such as media identification in the contemporary patterns of domestic existence, where increasing numbers of people are dependent on 'second-order intimacy' to provide social recognition and belonging.

Celebrity news is a perfect conduit for the tabloids as it allows the fluid interchange between fact and fiction as well as the easy generic transfer from information to entertainment (Hill, 2005: 15) upon which their values are centred. Celebrity representation in the tabloids, whatever other impact it has on debates on the quality of public life, certainly provides further evidence that it is constructed very much within the contours of a contemporary Britain which is enlivened and most importantly made imaginable by its recourse to celebrity news and its embroidering of this news with their characteristic language.

9 'Tabloidization' – global formats, national contents

It is difficult to attend an academic conference on the media or to read a broadsheet newspaper without coming across the debate about whether the news media are suffering from a process of decline referred to as 'tabloidization'. Despite the commercial success associated with the popularization of newspapers over the course of a century and a half on both sides of the Atlantic, this chapter will examine the ways in which the tabloid phenomenon is considered to have become, from cultural and political perspectives, the defining detrimental trend within our news media. It will briefly consider the extent to which the push towards tabloid genres within the news which has been experienced globally is located within specifically national cultures.

Put in its simplest terms, 'tabloidization' is the refinement of a commercialized journalism which prioritizes the desires of advertisers to reach large audiences above all other concerns. Sparks (2000) outlines a range of print media from newspapers of record to fully tabloidized supermarket tabloids to indicate the spectrum within which aspects of the process are claimed to be at work. He claims that the breadth of anxiety connected to the phenomenon of 'tabloidization' is as significant as whether it can actually be demonstrated to be happening in any material way. He identifies three ways in which the term is used: to identify shifts in the boundaries of journalism, shifts within the priorities of journalism and shifts of tastes within media forms. Paletz has identified four trends within tabloidization which impact upon subject matter, priorities concerning content, forms of presentation, journalistic techniques or ethics (1998: 65–8). Whatever its complexities, 'tabloidization' can be said to have begun to emerge as a recognizable set of trends about 100 years ago (Esser, 1999: 291). Bourdieu has noted the increasing impact of commercialization on the other contingent areas of journalistic activity which characterize the contemporary continuation of the phenomenon. This process may have been speeded up by the widespread introduction of commercial television from the 1950s and may have been further accelerated by the fall of the Berlin Wall in 1989 and its political and economic consequences in a wave of commercially driven waves of deregulation within media markets throughout the former eastern bloc and beyond. Certainly this latter event's timing would coincide with its first recording as a phenomenon in Webster's dictionary in 1991.

Bromley (1998: 25) has observed that the 1990s saw what he considers an obsession with the decline in standards in the 'quality' press in the UK under pressure from the influence of the tabloids. He summarizes the debate thus:

> At first, the 'quality' press ignored the substantive issues of tabloid news; then decried them. These papers … subsequently began reporting and commenting on the behaviour of the tabloid press, which led to the vicarious reporting of the issues themselves. Finally, the broadsheet papers, too, carried the same news items.
>
> (1998: 31)

The sensationalism and personalization of the popular press have long been the subject of discussion and complaint on a national basis, particularly in advanced capitalist democracies. What has happened over the last fifteen years is that a combination of political, cultural and technological changes have triggered a set of ripples which have spread across national as well as media boundaries to cause a range of debates about how processes which were once confined to the lower end of the market are now perceived to have infected the whole market. As concern has spread, within the elite news media, political circles and parts of the academic community, the perception of the acceleration towards 'tabloidization' has become a moral panic in its own right (Gripsrud, 2000: 287). Yet as this panic unfolds, the perceived process of 'tabloidization' has begun to move beyond the description of a particular kind of journalism to become a portmanteau description for what is regarded as the trivialization of media content in general (Turner, 2004: 76). This tendency is exaggerated because the process is not restricted to the tabloid newspaper but is connected to a more complex set of changes, a 'dynamic structural transformation' within the whole media sector from new technology to general social changes (Sparks and Tulloch, 2000:160).

As discussion of 'tabloidization' moves across into genres other than print journalism we can see negative critiques as well as more optimistic assessments of these changes. Television journalism's contemporary developments fit easily into a catalogue of criticism attached to the perceived trend towards tabloid format, content and philosophy: 'image crowding out rational analysis' (Bird, 2000: 221). This is especially so in the relative decline of older style public service broadcasting and the rise of celebrity/docu-drama styles of factual popular television and entertainment-led news. From the other end of the spectrum, MacDonald attempts to recuperate some of this generic material for positive ends. She explores the particular implications of 'personalization' in current affairs journalism in order to argue that when it is properly integrated and when it is used to clarify otherwise abstract concepts, it can help to demystify complex and potentially arcane subjects for a broader and more democratic public appeal (MacDonald, 1995: 264–5). She quotes Norman

Fairclough as a pivotal voice in this debate, indicating how these processes of an increasing conversationalization in public affairs' discourse within the media can be read either as a concession to market forces or as an opportunity for extending democratic access (Fairclough, 1995: 10–12).

National differences

Despite the fact that the trends which have come to define the process of 'tabloidization' are identifiable on a global scale, Esser is correct in drawing our attention to the fact that the term can only be analyzed adequately with a long-term cross-national framework. He points out that the degree of 'tabloidization' in any given country depends on a complex of journalistic values, media cultures and economic and legal conditions, which are often highly specific to particular national communities (Esser, 1999: 291). He even goes so far as to claim that 'tabloidization' means 'different things in different societies' (Esser, 1999: 318). This can be considered briefly by identifying a small range of examples which indicate the range of culturally differentiated practices within news media depending on their national contexts before returning to our assertion that the language of the tabloid representation of Britain is a highly pervasive feature of a contemporary sense of national community.

In the United States where popularization within the news media has been established the longest, the main explicitly tabloid medium is the supermarket tabloid, whose most successful exponents are titles such as the *National Enquirer*, the *Globe* and the *Weekly World News*, which concentrate entirely on celebrity news, human interest stories and sensation. Despite the fact that these tabloids eschew political stories as a rule, there have been occasions when they have led with important political news, as with the O.J. Simpson case or the Clinton affair when there was a sufficient celebrity crossover. The *National Enquirer* in particular prides itself on its accuracy and this clearly limits the extent to which it could ever be fully incorporated into the publicity agenda of the major agencies (Turner, 2004: 73). Sloan (2001) stresses that for all the sensationalism and celebrity-driven nature of their content, these newspapers remain informed by many traditional journalistic standards.

Despite criticism that there are observable trends towards a 'tabloidized', market-driven journalism in the USA (Macmanus, 1994), analysts have demonstrated that there is not a clear divide between two types of newspapers (the high-brow and the populist) and readership. There, Esser claims, weekly tabloid supermarket readers are also likely to be reading a serious regional paper (Esser, 1999: 298). Peter Preston has commented: 'The Enquirer and the rest don't need to worry about mainstream news or sport. They're free to plough a narrower patch of field while the editors of 'proper' papers pretend they don't exist' (2000).

In Germany, debate has often focused on what Klein has referred to as 'tabloidized' political coverage (1998: 80). She considers the debate as chiefly concerned with the impact of the opening of the television market in Germany for private channels since the mid-1980s, which has led to a more competitive market in which the personalization and celebrity-driven agendas of tabloid culture have come to be felt in mainstream political news coverage. The presence of the dominant national tabloid *Bild* is felt to be compensated for by the survival of a thriving regional press including several qualities with national reach. German journalists are, according to the research which she summarizes, identified as less likely to upgrade soft-news on German quality newspapers. Despite this, the most popular national newspaper *Bild* captures the essential populist national community as effectively as ever, continuing to act as a sounding board for an idealized voice of the people. The way in which it directs itself to the local reader has always been through a strong articulation of the vernacular to a very specifically German audience. It has strong resemblances to the diet of print tabloid culture from a global format but deploys them to represent a strong sense of local national identity for its readers. Dieter Brumm (1980: 127–30) claims that it delivers the templates of conversation for millions of ordinary Germans and presents itself thus as the speech of the speechless. Its appeal draws upon connections to wider popular cultural concerns and always in an identifiable vernacular and with a specifically German national appeal, once again demonstrating the specificity of the local within the global patterning of the language of popular tabloid culture.

The fall of the Berlin Wall, which saw the commercialization within West Germany's media culture extend its reach further to the East, has generated influences which have spread throughout the former arena of Central Eastern Europe (Sparks and Reading, 1998; Downing, 1996; Splichal, 1994). However, this was not a uniquely contemporary moment of formation. Gulyás describes the development of the first Hungarian popular press in the first decade of the twentieth century, based, as later, on the German mass circulation newspapers indicating how the phenomenon has always been one of international, cultural exchange and economic emulation (Gulyás, 2000: 111–12). Again, in the 1990s the Hungarian popular press looked for economic and cultural models from the West to satisfy new consumer demand. In format these were copied from the West but in content they had to incorporate some local aspect to their coverage of celebrity and entertainment, although a popular Americanization acted as a brake on the development of an entirely Hungarian-dominated news agenda. Gulyás describes the similarities and differences in the following terms:

> Hungarian sensational titles have the usual characteristics of tabloids when compared to quality newspapers. They focus on 'light' news and human interest stories, and the articles are shorter. The proportions of various subjects also vary in range and detail in qualities and tabloids. However, there are some differences between tabloids in post-Communist Hungary and in Western Europe. Compared to British tabloids, for example, they differ in format, structure, and, to a certain

degree, in content as well. There are more news stories on the front pages of Hungarian tabloids, the headlines are smaller, and there are fewer advertisements in the papers. These differences are mainly due to the different market conditions, different press culture, and history.

(Gulyás, 2000: 124)

The confluence of national history and news media format is again demonstrated in the work of Hayashi, who demonstrates that the history of popular newspapers aimed at a mass market is as complex in Japan as it has been in Western Europe and the United States over the past century and a half. It has also taken a very different direction, with the mass newspapers having gained more gravitas and a broader social agenda since their beginnings in the 'little papers' of the nineteenth century, and continuing to be distinct from the more recognizably tabloid 'sports papers' (2000: 148). They have achieved this despite retaining extraordinarily high circulation figures. Yet, here too there has been a rise in softer styles of news, in keeping with more general global patterns of news production and consumption.

Hallin has demonstrated how a particular form of television tabloid culture has evolved in Mexico within the popular television journalism formats of the 1990s with the movement known as La Nota Roja. He identifies one characteristic of the rhetorical appeal of these documentaries: 'The journalists, meanwhile, increasingly present themselves as representatives of the public and often adopt an adversarial stance toward government officials legitimated by the authority they claim in that "representative" role' (Hallin, 2000: 278). At the same time he stresses that the location of this national variant of popular journalism within a commercial sphere places restrictions upon the directions it can move in while highlighting a very specific version of the contradictory play between global capital and a variety of populism entirely in keeping with local demands (Hallin, 2000: 282).

It is in the British newspaper market in particular where the stylistic convergence so characteristic of 'tabloidization' causes such concern. In Britain, where Jamie Oliver's tirade against the low nutritional value of school meals can generate hundreds of column inches across the elite press, and the political opinions of a member of Coldplay can be flagged on the front page of the *Times* (11 April 2005) in the run-up to a general election, it is clearly not only in the business of political reporting from parliament where there are concerns about the balance and quantity. Franklin has noted that: 'in both quality and tabloid press. ... Journalists' commentary on parliamentary affairs has, moreover, departed from its traditionally balanced character to become increasingly negative and disdaining' (Franklin, 1996: 305). Both the negativity and the disdain, although part of longer trends within popular print culture, are in his study demonstrably spreading across all news media. Critics of these trends which are so characteristic of political life in Britain see the shift towards sensation, emotion and scandal as a major element in what amounts to a crisis in public life: 'the negation of the kind of journalism that is essential to democracy' (Sparks, 1998: 6). Within the newspaper industry itself, there is a clear acknowledgement that the trends towards tabloid format as well as content and strategy are well advanced: 'Since the 1980s broadsheet newspapers have adopted many of the commercial, as well as editorial, practices of the tabloid press, including promotional stunts, cover price discounts and brand exploitation' (Greenslade, 1996: 17). More recently the editor of the *Guardian* has highlighted that it is the way that quality newspapers in Britain adapt to the pressures of this commercialized and tabloidized market which will define the next generation of serious newspapers in this country (Rusbridger, 2005).

Despite the narrowing of certain differences between the quality and the popular tabloids, there are many who perceive that it is in the language, or even the 'unity of tone' (Engel, 1996b) in which the difference is maintained. Sparks (1992: 37–8) argues that the forms of address, and language of the British popular press form an important part of its own distinctive news values. This language lies within the traditions of working class entertainment and is thereby more connected to everyday life and tends to relegate the serious to a secondary place and foreground the carnival and the colloquial. Bromley and Tumber argue that the superficial convergence of the two types of newspaper in Britain may mask a longer-term divergence as the orthodox bourgeois press becomes detached from the popular magazines of miscellany (Seymour-Ure, 1996: 164–5): 'the distinctiveness of the "popular" press, which we have argued has been evident since the mid-1930s, may become more transparent when it is no longer masked by the more superficial similarities of newspaper production' (Bromley and Tumber, 1998: 376).

Despite the fact that the content and influence of tabloid news media worldwide generate a great deal of hostility from elite commentators, they emerge from the complex of commercial and social exigencies which drive the whole globalized media market. Comparisons of tabloid media with idealized versions of what the news ought to be doing not only ignore the historical evidence that tabloid news and its varied predecessors in popular print culture have always sought to contest dominant bourgeois values. The tabloid press are located within, and draw on, the 'popular' traditions of entertainment and consumption, rather than attempting to provide a single, bourgeois form of rational public debate (Bromley and Tumber, 1998: 365), and are central to debates about the wider manifestations of 'tabloidization'. From a social perspective, it is because of the close association of these news media forms with the ordinary people as consumers that investigating the value of certain varieties of news media brings us into what Sparks calls 'the explosive territory of social worth' (2000: 29).

Tabloidization is too complex a phenomenon to judge as a single entity and too fraught with questions of taste and commercialism for simple judgements on its quality. It can be considered either as a lowering of the standards of idealized journalism or as a re-orientation of popular national markets within globalized competition for news within wider media markets.

According to this latter perspective, it may be considered neither a good nor a bad set of processes but simply a pragmatic approach to maintaining a market share using the familiar strategy of constructing an appeal to an 'imagined community' of nation which has traditionally structured the content of news. This may not be to the tastes of established social elites and it may not serve the political interests of the politically marginalized either, but little mainstream commercial journalism ever has.

Conclusion

The popular tabloids in Britain provide a view of a community with a strong sense of nation. They do this to a large extent through the deployment of a range of language appropriate to that sense of national belonging. This language betrays all of the political and cultural limitations of national identification but it remains a highly successful commercial strategy. Despite the fact that tabloids are a highly specific part of a national culture, they are also linked to global trends within news media conglommerates. A heightened awareness of national and ethnic differences, combined with the counter-dynamic of media fragmentation which pressurizes local audience retention, has a paradoxical appeal within the acceleration of global flows of information and transport. The tabloids have become internationalized as a media format with the ability to adapt across language and cultural barriers. One significant variation of the tabloid pattern has been the American supermarket tabloid, which is an export triumph for a globalized variation of American popular culture. While the American model highlights a particular form of global Hollywood celebrity gossip (Sloan, 2001; Bird, 1992), the British version is a more proletarian model of tabloid celebrity which focuses much more on television personalities, who are restricted to the national in the main. This is reinforced by the axiomatic consequence of the tendency in British tabloid newspapers to concentrate less on foreign news which gives an even more nationalistic slant to their content. This is true even for the American supermarket tabloids even if the status of their global stars and celebrities is more complex a manifestation of American cultural identity than it would be in a country without the global reach of the Hollywood factor.

The trends within the tabloids form part of a successful commercial exploitation of many of the long-standing traditions within popular culture which relate to dominant groups and the perceived threats of outsiders to the national group. Popular culture in its contemporary tabloid guise may not be enlightening but it may force cultural and political elites to ponder what alternatives are on offer to the nation as an imaginary community.

The narrowing of the gap between the tabloid and the broadsheet over the last fifteen years, between overt politics and entertainment, whether in liberal democracies or one-party states, has contributed to distinct national configurations even within the extent of resistance to or integration of American global influences. Tabloid culture is a global format but one filled with and structured by national expectations. What this book has illustrated, it is hoped, is the role that language, the vernacular everyday language of the ordinary people and their interests, plays in building those national structures of community. This language is harnessed within that format for profit, enjoyment and ultimately political influence. It is also to be hoped that the book has illustrated that there is a great deal of wit and skill involved as well as an ability to keep these particular newspapers in step with the wider sensibilities of a variety of British nationalism. In reflecting upon what this author considers the negative aspects of the tabloids, the situation remains the same as it was some years ago when a contributor to the *Economist* opined:

> If the tabloids echo the *vox pop*, it may be said that the tastes and mood of the British *pop* are pretty ugly. But if the tabloids do often reflect them more accurately than the posh press does that alone is a necessary if wretched service.
>
> (*Economist*, 1992: 20)

Even within a global economy, this local vernacular is an essential part of the appeal of these newspapers as conduits for a national culture with all of the commercial strengths and political weaknesses which such national cultures continue to generate. The performativity of language in the narratives of the nation (Bhabha, 1990: 3) is an essential tool in the construction and maintenance of the tabloid version of Britain today.

Bibliography

Aitkenhead, D. (1999) 'Our Brave Boys. Their Lunatics'. *Guardian*. 26 April: 15.

Alabarces, P., Tomlinson, A. and Young, C. (2001) 'Argentina versus England at the France '98 World Cup: Narratives of Nation and the Mythologizing of the Popular'. *Media, Culture and Society*. 23: 547–66.

Anderson, B. (1987) *Imagined Communities*. London: Verso.

Ang, I. (1985) *Watching Dallas: Soap Opera and the Melodramatic Imagination*. London: Methuen.

Barker, H. (1998) *Newspapers, Politics and Public Opinion*. Oxford: Oxford University Press.

Barthes, R. (1974) *Mythologies*. New York: Wang.

Bauer, O. (1996) 'The Nation', in G. Balakrishnan, *Mapping the Nation*. London: Verso.

Bauman, Z. (1997) *Postmodernity and Its Discontents*. Cambridge: Polity.

Bell, A. (1984) 'Language Style as Audience Design'. *Language in Society*. 13: 145–204.

—— (1994) *Language in the News*. Oxford. Blackwell.

Berger, P.L. and Luckman, T. (1976) *The Social Construction of Reality*. London: Penguin.

Bernstein, B. (1971) *Class, Codes and Control*. Vol. 1. London: Paladin.

Berridge, V.S. (1978) 'Popular Sunday Papers and Mid-Victorian Society', in G. Boyce, J. Curran and P. Wingate (eds) *Newspaper History From The Seventeenth Century To The Present Day*. London: Constable.

Bessie, S. (1938) *Jazz Journalism*. New York: Dutton.

Bhabha, H. (1990) 'Introduction: Narrating the Nation', in H. Bhabha (ed.) *Nation and Narration*. London: Routledge.

Billig, M. (1995) *Banal Nationalism*. London: Sage.

—— (1992) *Talking of the Royal Family*. London: Routledge.

Bird, S.E. (1992) *For Enquiring Minds: A Cultural Study of Supermarket Tabloids*. Tennessee: University of Tennessee Press.

Bird, S.E. (2000) 'Audience Demands in a Murderous Market', in J. Tulloch and C. Sparks (eds) *Tabloid Tales*. Maryland: Rowman and Littlefield.

Blumler, J. and Gurevitch, M. (1995) *The Crisis in Public Communication*. London: Routledge.

Bourdieu, P. (1998) *On Television and Journalism*. London: Pluto.

—— (1990) *The Logic of Practice*. Cambridge: Polity.

Brake, L., Jones, A. and Madden, L. (eds) (1990) *Investigating Victorian Journalism*. London: Macmillan.

Brass, P. (1991) *Ethnicity and Nationalism: Theory and Comparison*. New Delhi: Sage.

Bromley, M (1998) 'The 'Tabloiding' of Britain: 'Quality' Newspapers in the 1990s', in H. Stephenson and M. Bromley (eds) *Sex, Lies and Democracy*. Harlow: Addison Wesley Longman.

Bromley, M. and Tumber, H. (1998) 'From Fleet Street to Cyberspace: The British 'Popular' Press in the Late Twentieth Century. *European Journal of Communication Studies*. 22 (3): 365–78.

Brookes, H.J. (1995) 'Suit Tie and a Touch of Juju – The Ideological Construction of Africa: A Critical Discourse Analysis of News on Africa in the British Press'. *Discourse and Society*. 6 (4).

Brookes, R. (1999) 'Newspapers and National Identity: The BSE/CJD Crisis and the British Press'. *Media, Culture and Society*. 21 (3): 247–63.

—— (2000) 'Tabloidization, Media Panics, and Mad Cow Disease', in C. Sparks and J. Tulloch (eds) *Tabloid Tales*. Maryland: Rowman and Littlefield.

Brumm, D. (1980) 'Sprachrohr der Volksseele?', in M.W. Thomas, *Porträts der deutschen Presse*. Spiess.

Burke, P. (1978) *Popular Culture in Early Modern Europe*. London: Temple Smith.

Butcher, H. (1981) 'Images of Women in the Media', in S. Cohen and J. Young (eds) *The Manufacture of News: Deviance, Social Problems and the Mass Media*. London: Constable.

Cameron, D. (1995) *Verbal Hygiene*. London: Routledge.

—— (1996) 'Style Policy and Style Politics: A Neglected Aspect of the Language of the News'. *Media, Culture and Society*. 18: 315–33.

Cannadine, D. (1993) 'The Context, Performance and Meaning of Ritual: The British Monarchy and the 'Invention of Tradition' c. 1820–1977', in E. Hobsbawm and T. Rainger (eds) *The Invention of Tradition*. Cambridge: Cambridge University Press.

Chaney, D. (2001) 'The Mediated Monarchy', in D. Morley and K. Robins (eds) *British Cultural Studies: Geography, Nationality and Identity*. Oxford: Oxford University Press.

Chippendale, P. and Horrie, C. (1992) *Stick It Up Your Punter*. London: Mandarin.

Clark, K. (1998) 'The Linguistics of Blame', in D. Cameron (ed.) *The Feminist Critique of Language*. London: Routledge.

Cohen, S. (1980) *Folk Devils and Moral Panics. The Creation of Mods and Rockers*. 2nd edn. New York: St. Martin's Press.

Cohen, S. and Young, J. (eds) (1973) *The Manufacture of News: Deviance, Social Problems and the Mass Media*. London: Constable.

Chan, J., Ericson, R. and Baranek, P. (1987) *Visualizing Deviance: A Study of News Organization*. Toronto: University of Toronto Press.

Conboy, M. (2002) *The Press and Popular Culture*. London: Sage

—— (2004a) *Journalism: A Critical History*. London: Sage.

—— (2004b) 'Heroes and Demons as Historical Bookmarks in the English Popular Press', in R. Phillips and H. Brocklehurst (eds) *History, Nationhood and the Question of Britain*. Palgrave.

Connell, I. (1991) 'Tales From Tellyland', in P. Dahlgren and C. Sparks (eds) *Communication and Citizenship*. London: Routledge.

—— (1992) 'Personalities in the Popular Media', in P. Dahlgren and C. Sparks (eds) *Journalism and Popular Culture*. London: Sage.

Corner, J and Pels, D. (eds) (2003) *Restyling Politics*: London: Sage.

Critcher, C. (2003) *Moral Panics and the Media*. Milton Keynes: Open University Press.

Cudlipp, H. (1953) *Publish and Be Damned*. London: Andrew Dakers.

Curran, J. (1987) 'The Boomerang Effect: The Press and the Battle for London 1981–1986', in J. Curran, A. Smith and P. Wingate (eds) *Impacts and Influences: Essays on Media Power in the 20th Century.* London: Methuen.

Curran, J., Douglas, A. and Whannel, G., (1980) 'The Political Economy of the Human Interest Story', in A. Smith (ed.) *Newspapers and Democracy: International Essays on a Changing Medium.* Cambridge, MA: MIT Press.

Curran, J., Gaber, I. and Petley, J. (2004) *Culture Wars: The Media and the British Left.* Edinburgh: Edinburgh University Press.

Curran, J., Smith, A. and Wingate, P. (eds) (1987) *Impacts and Influences: Essays on Media Power in the 20th Century.* London: Methuen.

Dahlgren, P. (1988) 'What's the Meaning of This? Viewers' Plural Sense-making of TV News'. *Media, Culture and Society.* 10: 285–301.

—— (1995) *Television and the Public Sphere.* London: Sage

Dahlgren, P. and Sparks, C. (eds) (1992) *Journalism and Popular Culture.* London: Sage.

De Cillia, R., Reisigl, M. and Wodak, R. (1999) 'The Discursive Construction of National Identities'. *Discourse and Society.* 10 (2): 149–73.

Downing, J. (1996) *Internationalizing Media Theory.* London: Sage.

Economist (1992) 5 December: 20.

Edensor, T. (2002) *National Identity, Popular Culture and Everyday Life.* Oxford: Berg.

Emery, M. and Emery, E. (1992) *The Press and America: An Introspective History of the Mass Media.* Prentice Hall.

Engel, M. (1996a) *Tickle the Public: One Hundred Years of the Popular Press.* London: Gollancz.

—— (1996b) 'Papering over the cracks'. *Guardian 2.* 3 October: 2–4.

Entman, R.M. (1993) 'Framing: Toward Clarification of a Fractured Paradigm'. *Journal of Communication.* 43 (4) 51–8.

Esser, F. (1999) ' "Tabloidization" of News: A Comparative Analysis of Anglo-American and German Press Journalism'. *European Journal of Communication.* 14 (3): 291–324.

Fairclough, N. (1989) *Language and Power.* London: Longman.

—— (1995) *Media Discourse.* London: Edward Arnold.

—— (2000) *New Labour, New Language.* London: Routledge.

Fish, S. (1994) *There's No Such Thing as Free Speech and It's a Good Thing Too.* Oxford: Oxford University Press.

Fiske, J. (1992) 'Popularity and the Politics of Information', in P. Dahlgren and C. Sparks (eds) *Journalism and Popular Culture.* London: Sage.

—— (1994) *Reading the Popular.* London: Routledge.

Foucault, M. (1974) *The Archaeology of Knowledge.* Trans. A.M. Sheridan-Smith. London: Tavistock.

Fowler, R. (1986) *Linguistic Criticism.* Oxford: Oxford University Press.

—— (1991) *Language in the News.* London: Routledge.

Franklin, B. (1996) 'Keeping It "Bright, Light and Trite": Changing Newspaper Reporting of Parliament'. *Parliamentary Affairs.* 49: 299–315.

Galtung, J. and Ruge, M. (1973) 'Structuring and Selecting News', in S. Cohen and J. Young (eds) *The Manufacture of News: Social Problems, Deviance and the Mass Media.* London: Constable.

Geertz, C. (1973) *The Interpretation of Cultures.* New York: Basic Books.

Geraghty, C. (1990) *Women in Soap Opera.* Oxford: Blackwell.

Giles, D. (2000) *Illusions of Immortality: A Psychology of Fame and Celebrity.* London: Macmillan.

Gilroy, P. (1987) *There Ain't No Black in the Union Jack: The Cultural Politics of Nation.* London: Hutchinson.

Gitlin, T. (1980) *The Whole World is Watching: Mass Media in the Making and Unmaking of the New Left.* Berkeley, CA: University of California Press.

Gledhill, C. (1997) 'Genre and Gender: The Case of Soap Opera', in S. Hall (ed.) *Representation: Cultural Representations and Signifying Practices.* Milton Keynes: Open University Press.

Goatly, A. (1997) *The Language of Metaphors.* London: Routledge.

Golding, P. (1999) 'The Political and the Popular: Getting the Measure of Tabloidization', in *Moving On: Changing Cultures, Changing Times.* Proceedings of the AMCCS Conference. Sheffield Hallam University.

Greenfield, L. (1992) *Nationalism – Five Roads to Modernity.* Cambridge, MA: Harvard University Press.

Greenslade, R. (1996) 'The Telling Selling Game'. *Guardian 2.* 12 August: 17.

Gripsrud, J. (1992). ' The Aesthetics and Politics of Melodrama', in P. Dahlgren and C. Sparks (eds) *Journalism and Popular Culture.* London: Sage.

—— (2000) 'Tabloidization, Popular Journalism and Democracy', in J. Tulloch and C. Sparks (eds) *Tabloid Tales.* Maryland: Rowman and Littlefield.

Gulyás, A. (2000) 'The Development of the Tabloid Press in Hungary', in J. Tulloch and C. Sparks (eds) *Tabloid Tales.* Maryland: Rowman and Littlefield.

Habermas, J. (1992) *The Structural Transformation of the Public Sphere.* Oxford: Polity.

Halbwach, M. (1985) *Das Kollektive Gedächtnis*: Frankfurt: Fischer.

Hall, S. (1973) 'Encoding/decoding', in S. Hall, D. Hobson, A. Lowe and P. Willis (eds) *Culture, Media, Language.* London: Hutchinson.

—— (1975) 'Introduction', in A. Smith, *Paper Voices.* London: Chatto and Windus.

—— (1978) 'The Social Production of News', in S. Hall, C. Critcher, T. Jefferson, J. Clarke and B. Roberts (eds) *Policing the Crisis: Mugging, the State and Law and Order.* London: Macmillan.

—— (1981) 'The Whites of Their Eyes', in L. Bridges and R. Brunt (eds) *Silver Linings.* London: Lawrence and Wishart.

—— (1988a) *The Hard Road to Renewal: Thatcherism and the Crisis of the Left.* London: Verso.

—— (1988b) 'New Ethnicities', in *Black film/British cinema.* ICA Document 7. London.

—— (1992) 'The Question of Cultural Identity', in S. Hall, D. Held and T. McGrew (eds) *Modernity and Its Futures.* Cambridge: Polity.

Halliday, M.A.K. (1978) *Language as Social Semiotic: The Social Interpretation of Language and Meaning.* London: Arnold.

—— (1985) *Introduction to Functional Grammar.* London: Edward Arnold.

Hallin, D.C. (2000) 'La Nota Roja. Popular Journalism and the Transition to Democracy in Mexico', in J. Tulloch and C. Sparks (eds) *Tabloid Tales.* Maryland: Rowman and Littlefield.

Harcup, T. and O'Neill, D. (2001) 'Galtung and Ruge Revisited'. *Journalism Studies.* 2 (2): 261–80.

Harris, M. and Lee, A.J. (1978) *The Press in English Society from the Seventeenth to the Nineteenth Century.* London and Toronto: Associated Presses

Hartley, J. (1996) *Popular Reality.* London: Arnold.

Hayashi, K. (2000) 'The "Home and Family" Section in the Japanese Newspaper', in J. Tulloch and C. Sparks (eds) *Tabloid Tales.* Maryland: Rowman and Littlefield.

Hermes, J. (1999) 'Media Figures in Identity Construction', in P. Alasuutari (ed.) *Rethinking the Media Audience. The New Agenda.* London: Sage.

Herrstein-Smith, B. (1984) 'Narrative Versions, Narrative Theories', in W.J.T. Mitchell (ed.) *On Narrative.* Chicago: University of Chicago Press.

Hill, A. (2005) *Reality Television.* London: Routledge.

Hobsbawm, E. (1992) *Nations and Nationalism Since 1780: Programme, Myth, Reality.* 2nd edn. Cambridge: Cambridge University Press.

Hodge, R. and Kress, G. (1993) *Language as Ideology.* London: Routledge.

Holland, P. (1983) 'The Page 3 Girl Speaks to Women Too'. *Screen.* 24 (3) (May–June): 84.102.

—— (1998) 'The Politics of the Smile: "Soft New" and the Sexualization of the Popular Press', in C. Carter, G. Branston, and S. Allen (eds) *News, Gender and Power.* London: Routledge.

Hollis, P. (1970) *The Pauper Press.* Oxford: Oxford University Press.

Holmes, P. and Jermyn, D. (2004) *Understanding Reality Television.* London: Routledge.

Iwamoto, N. (1995) 'The Analysis of Wartime Reporting: Patterns of Transitivity'. *Applied Linguistics.* 6: 58–68.

Jackson, K. (2000) 'George Newnes and the 'loyal tit-bitites' – Editorial Identity and Textuual Interaction in Tit-Bits', in L. Brake, B. Bell and D. Finkelstein (eds) *Nineteenth Century Media and the Construction of Identitites.* Basingstoke: Palgrave.

Johnston, W. (1935) 'Newspaper Balladry'. *American Speech.* 10: 119–21.

Keeble, R. (1997) *Secret State, Silent Press.* Luton: University of Luton Press.

—— (1998) *The Newspapers Handbook.* London: Routledge.

Kitis, E. and Milapedes, M., (1997) 'Read It and Believe It: How Metaphor Constructs Ideology in News Discourse'. *Journal of Pragmatics.* 28 (5): 557–90.

Klein, U. (1998) 'Tabloidised Political Coverage in *Bild-Zeitung*'. *Javnost – The Public.* 5 (3).

Koss, S. (1981) *The Rise and Fall of the Political Press in Britain.* Vol. 2. Chapel Hill, NC: North Carolina Press.

Kumar, K (2003) *The Making of English National Identity.* Cambridge: Cambridge University Press.

Lakoff, R. (1987) *Women, Fire and Dangerous Things.* Chicago, IL: University of Chicago Press.

Langer, J. (1998) *Tabloid Television: Popular Journalism and the 'Other News'.* London: Routledge.

Law, A. (2001) 'Near and Far: Banal National Identity and the Press in Scotland'. *Media, Culture and Society.* 23: 299–317.

Lycan, W.G. (2000) *Philosophy of Language.* London: Routledge.

Macdonald, M. (1995) *Representing Women: Myths of Femininity in Popular Media.* London: Edward Arnold.

McDowell, P. (1998) *The Women of Grub Street.* Oxford: Oxford University Press.

McGuigan, J. (1993) *Cultural Populism.* London: Routledge.

—— (2000) 'British Identity and the "People's Princess" '. *Sociological Review.* 48 (1) (February): 1–18.

McLachlan, S. and Golding, P. (2000) 'Tabloidization in the British Press: A Quantitative Investigation into Changes in British Newspapers, 1952–1997', in C. Sparks and J. Tulloch (eds) *Tabloid Tales.* Maryland: Rowman and Littlefield.

McLuhan, M. (1995) *Understanding Media.* London: Routledge.

Macmanus, J.H. (1994) *Market-Driven Journalism. Let the Citizen Beware?* London: Sage.

McQuail, D. (2000) *McQuail's Mass Communication Theory*. London: Sage.

Mann, M. (1996) 'Has Globalization Ended the Rise and Rise of the Nation-State?', in J. Hall and I. Jarvie. (eds) *The Social Philosophy of Ernst Gellner*. Amsterdam: Rodopi.

Marshall, P.D. (1997) *Celebrity and Power: Fame in Contemporary Culutre*. Minneapolis and London: University of Minneapolis Press.

Matheson, D. (2000) 'The Birth of News Discourse: Changes in News Language in British Newspapers, 1880–1930'. *Media, Culture and Society*. 22 (5) (September).

Modleski, T. (1982) *Loving with a Vengeance: Mass Produced Fantasies for Women*. London: Methuen.

Montgomery, M. (1986) 'Language and Power: A Critical Review of *Studies in the Theory of Ideology* by John B. Thompson'. *Media, Culture and Society*. 8: 41–64.

Morley, D. and Robins, K. (1995) *Spaces of Identity*. London: Routledge.

Mott, F.L. (1961) *American Journalism: A History of Newspapers in America through 250 Years 1690–1960*. Basingstoke: Macmillan.

Munslow, A. (1997) *Deconstructing History*. London: Routledge.

Nairn, T. (1977) *The Break Up of Britain*. London: New Left Books.

O'Connor, T.P. (1889) 'The New Journalism'. *New Review*. October.

Ogden, C.K. and Richards, I.A. (1985 [1923]) *The Meaning of Meaning*. London: Ark

Ong, W. (1982) *Orality and Literacy: The Technologizing of the Word*. London: Methuen.

Paletz, D.L. (1998) *The Media in American Politics*. New York: Longman.

Philo, G. (ed.) (1996) *Media and Mental Distress*. Harlow: Addison Wesley Longman.

Preston, P. (2000) *Observer*. 20 August: 7.

—— (2004) 'Admit it we're all in the dark'. *Guardian*. 15 March.

Ram, U. (1994) 'Narration, Erziehung und Die Erfindung des jüdischen National-ismus'. *Österreichische Zeditschrift für Geschichtswissenschaft*. 5: 151–77.

Renan, E. (1990) 'What is a Nation?', in H.K. Bhabha (ed.) *Nation and Narration*. London: Routledge.

Rhoufari, M.M. (2000) 'Talking About the Tabloids: Journalists' Views', in C. Sparks and J. Tulloch (eds) *Tabloid Tales*. Maryland: Rowman and Littlefield.

Robins, K. and Morley, D. (1995) *Spaces of Identity*. London: Routledge.

Rodman, G.B. (1996) *Elvis After Elvis: The Posthumous Career of a Living Legend*. London: Routledge.

Rojek, C. (2001) *Celebrity*. London: Reaktion.

Rooney, R. (2000) 'Thirty Years of Competition in the British Tabloid Press: The *Mirror* and the *Sun* 1968–1998', in C. Sparks and J. Tulloch (eds) *Tabloid Tales*. Maryland: Rowman and Littlefield.

Rusbridger, A. (2005) The Hugo Young Lecture. University of Sheffield. 9 March.

Said, E. (1978) *Orientalism*. London: Routledge and Kegan Paul.

Samuel, R. (1989) *Patriotism: The Making and Unmaking of National Identity*. London: Routledge.

Schlesinger, P. (1991a) *Media, State and Nation: Political Violence and Collective Identities*. London: Sage

—— (1991b) 'Media, the Political Order and National Identities'. *Media, Culture and Society*. 13 (3): 297–308.

—— (1993) 'Wishful Thinking: Cultural Politics, Media and Collective Identities in Europe'. *Journal of Communication*. 43 (2): 6–17.

Schudson, M. (1978) *Discovering the News: A Social History of American Newspapers*. New York: Harper.

Searle, C. (1989) *Your Daily Dose: Racism in the Sun*. London: Campaign for Press and Broadcasting Freedom.

Seton-Watson, H. (1977) *Nations and States: An Enquiry into the Origins of Nations and the Politics of Nationalism*. Boulder, CO: Westview.

Seymour-Ure, C. (1996) *The British Press and Broadcasting Since 1945*. 2nd edn. Oxford: Blackwell.

Shepard, L. (1973) *The History of Street Literature*. London: David and Charles.

Simpson, P. (1993) *Language, Ideology and Point of View*. London: Routledge.

Sloan, B. (2001) *'I Watched a Wild Hog Eat My Baby': A Colourful History of Tabloids and Their Cultural Impact*. New York: Prometheus.

Smith, A.D. (1975) *Paper Voices*. London: Chatto and Windus.

—— (1978) 'The Long Road to Objectivity and Back Again: The Kinds of Truth We Get in Journalism', in G. Boyce, J. Curran and P. Wingate (eds) *Newspaper History from the Seventeenth Century to the Present Day*. London: Constable.

—— (1986) *The Ethnic Origins of Nations*. Oxford: Basil Blackwell.

—— (1990) 'Towards a Global Culture', in M. Featherstone (ed.) *Nationalism, Globalization and Modernity*. London: Sage.

—— (1993) 'The Nation: Invented, Imagined, Reconstructed', in M. Ringrose and A.J. Lerner (eds) *Reimagining the Nation*. Milton Keynes. Open University Press.

—— (1999a) ' "Ethno-symbolism" and the Study of Nationalism', in A.Smith (ed.) *Myths and Memories of the Nation*. Oxford: Oxford University Press.

—— (1999b) *Myths and Memories of Nation*. Oxford: Oxford University Press.

Snoddy, R. (1992) *The Good, The Bad and The Unacceptable*. London: Faber.

Sommerville, J. (1996) *The News Revolution*. Oxford: Oxford University Press.

Sparks, C. (1992) 'Popular Journalism: Theories and Practice', in P. Dahlgren and C. Sparks (eds) *Journalism and Popular Culture*. London: Sage.

—— (1998) 'Introduction: Tabloidization and the Media'. *Javnost – The Public*. 5 (3).

—— (2000) 'Introduction: The Panic over Tabloid News', in J. Tulloch and C. Sparks (eds) *Tabloid Tales*. Maryland: Rowman and Littlefield.

Sparks, C. and Reading, A. (1998) *Communism, Capitalism and the Mass Media*. London: Sage.

Sparks, C. and Tulloch, J. (eds) (2000) *Tabloid Tales*. Maryland: Rowman and Littlefield.

Spencer, P. and Wollman. H. (2002) *Nationalism: A Critical Introduction*. London: Sage.

Splichal, S. (1994) *Media Beyond Socialism: Theory and Practice in East-Central Europe*. Boulder, CO: Westview.

Stephenson, H. and Bromley, M. (eds) (1998) *Sex, Lies and Democracy*. Harlow: Addison Wesley Longman.

Taylor, S.J. (1992) *Shock! Horror! The Tabloids in Action*. London: Black Swan.

Teo, P. (2000) 'Racism in the News: A Critical Discourse Analysis of News Reporting in Two Australian Newspapers'. *Discourse and Society*. 11 (1): 7–49.

Tomlinson, J. (1997) 'And Besides the Wench is Dead: Media Scandals and the Globalization of Communication', in J. Lull and S. Hinerman (eds) *Media Scandals: Morality and Desire in the Popular Cultural Marketplace*. London: Polity.

Toolan, M.J. (1998) *Narrative: A Critical Linguistic Introduction*. London: Routledge.

Trudgill, P. (1995) *Sociolinguistics*. London: Penguin.

Tuchman, B. (1971) *Stilwell and the American Experience in China 1911–1945*. London: Macmillan.

Tuchman, G. (1978) *Making News: A Study in the Construction of Reality*. New York: Free Press.

—— (1981) 'The Symbolic Annihilation of Women by the Mass Media', in S. Cohen and J. Young (eds) *The Manufacture of News: Deviance, Social Problems and the Mass Media*. London: Constable.

Tunstall, J. (1996) *Newspaper Power*. London: Clarendon.

Turner, G. (2004) *Understanding Celebrity*. London: Sage.

Van Dijk, T.A. (1984) *Prejudice in Discourse*. Amsterdam: Benjamins.

—— (1987) *Communicating Racism*. Newbury Park, CA: Sage.

—— (1991) *Racism and the Press*. London: Routledge.

—— (1993) *Elite Discourse and Racism*. London: Sage.

Van Leeuwen, T. (1987) 'Generic strategies in Press Journalism'. *Australian Review of Applied Linguistics*. 10 (2): 199–220.

Van Zoonen, L. (1994) *Feminist Media Studies*. London: Sage.

Wahl-Jorgensen, K. (2001) 'Letters to the Editor as a Forum for Public Deliberation. Modes of Publicity and Democratic Debate'. *Critical Studies in Media Communication*. 18 (3): 303–20.

Watt, T. (1991) *Cheap Print and Popular Piety 1550–1640*. Cambridge: Cambridge University Press.

Whannel, G. (2002) *Media Sports Stars: Masculinities and Moralities*. London: Routledge.

Whitby, G. (1982) 'The Penny Press and the Origins of American Journalistic Style', in *Studies in Journalism and Mass Communication: A Review from the Texan Education Council Annual Conference*.

Whyte, H. (1984) 'The Value of Narrativity in the Representation of Reality', in W.J.T. Mitchell (ed.) *On Narrative*. Chicago: University of Chicago Press.

Wiener, J. (ed.) (1988) *Papers for the Millions: The New Journalism in Britain 1850–1914*. New York: Greenwood.

—— (1994) 'The Americanization of the British Press, 1830–1914', in M. Harris and T. O'Malley (eds) *Studies in Newspaper and Periodical History*. London: Greenwood.

Williams, J. (1995) *PC Wars*. London: Routledge.

Wodak, R. and Matouschek, B. (1993) ' "We Are Looking at People Whose Origin One Can Clearly tell Just By Looking": Critical Discourse Analysis and the Study of Neo-Racism in Contemporary Austria'. *Discourse and Society*. 4 (2): 225–48.

Woehrling, E. (1996) 'The Logocentric Assumptions Behind Political Correctness'. *Imprimatur*. 1 (1) (Spring).

Wright, P. (1985) *On Living in an Old Country*. London: Verso.

Wykes, M. (2001) *News and Crime*. London: Pluto.

Wykes, M. and Gunter, B. (2005) *The Media and Body Image*. London: Sage.

Younge, G. (2000) 'The Badness of Words'. *Guardian*. 14 February.

Index

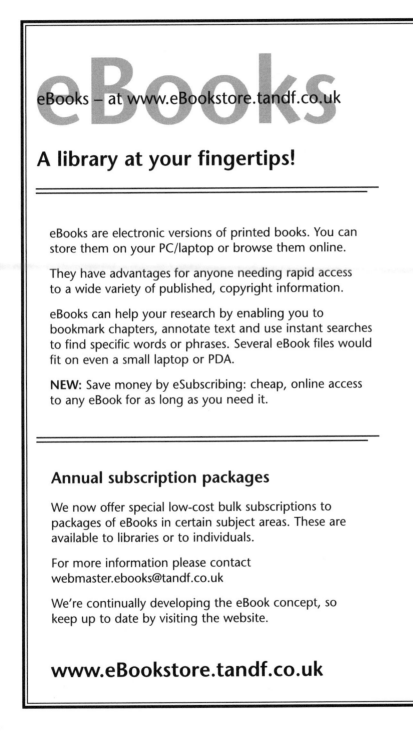